MM000104926

Welcoming the Word in Year B
Sowing the Seed

Verna A. Holyhead, S.G.S.

LITURGICAL PRESS
Collegeville, Minnesota

www.litpress.org

Cover design by Ann Blattner.

Year A: ISBN 978-0-8146-1832-5
Year B: ISBN 978-0-8146-1833-2
Year C: ISBN 978-0-8146-1834-9

1	2	3	4	5	6	7	8	9

Library of Congress Cataloging-in-Publication Data

Welcoming the word in Year C : with burning hearts.
    p. cm.
    ISBN-13: 978-0-8146-1835-6 (set)
    ISBN-13: 978-0-8146-1834-9 (alk. paper)
    ISBN-10: 0-8146-1834-0 (alk. paper)
    1. Church year meditations.   I. Holyhead, Verna.

BX2170.C55W58 2006
242'.3—dc22   2006005796

Contents

Acknowledgments

Excerpts from "Little Gidding" and "Burnt Norton" in *Four Quartets* and "Journey of the Magi" are from *The Complete Poems and Plays of T. S. Eliot* by T. S. Eliot (2004). By permission of Harcourt, Inc. for the United States, its territories and possessions, and the Philippine Republic. By permission of Faber and Faber Ltd. for world rights outside of the United States.

Excerpt from "He Wishes for the Cloths of Heaven" taken from *The Collected Poems of W. B. Yeats* by W. B. Yeats (2000). By permission of A. P. Watt, Ltd., London.

Excerpt from "Poem for Shelter" taken from *The Collected Poems of George Mackay Brown*, eds. Archie Bevan and Brian Murray (2005). By permission of John Murray Publishers.

Excerpt from "The Reed of God" taken from *The Mary Book* by Carryl Houselander (1950). By permission of Ave Maria Press.

Excerpt from "The Dream of the Rood" in *The Earliest English Poems*, trans. Michael Alexander (1966). By permission of Penguin Books, Ltd.

Introduction

In both the Old and New Testaments, the seed is a rich image of the Word of God: fertile and nourishing (Isa 55:10-11), scattered generously and inclusively (Mark 4:3-9), implanted for salvation in those who welcome it (Jas 1:21).

At every Sunday assembly the seed of the Word is scattered over us, different soils that we are. Sometimes we may be unreceptive to the Word, our bodies physically present but our hearts on the margins, trampled down by passing concerns and worries. At other times, we come with our hearts cluttered with rocks and thorns that we are too physically, emotionally, or spiritually exhausted to remove. But we still gather as God's field (1 Cor 3:9), and the Sower welcomes us.

And then there are the times when we are the good soil, when we offer to God the richness of our individual and communal lives, when we are eager to "Listen!" and allow God to break up the hardness and dryness of our hearts so that they yield thirty, sixty, a hundredfold harvest of discipleship (Mark 4:20). Then God, too, rejoices.

During his life, Vincent van Gogh produced many well-known "parables in paint" of wheat fields. There are fields under stormy skies, fields dotted with cornflowers, fields over which larks soar joyfully, or fields viciously attacked by marauding crows; sometimes his fields are crisscrossed with paths that stray out of the picture and then reappear. Sometimes the sower is present, always casting the seed with generous abandon, sometimes vigorous yet solitary, sometimes in the company of other sowers against a village background. Often a brilliant sun shines over the field, regardless of its great or small yield. When the sower is absent, it seems to suggest that the viewer is invited into the painting to cast the seed.

The Word of God longs to be welcomed no matter what the season of our lives: whether they are sunny or stormy, fruitful or parched; whether it is the harsh calls of crows or the soaring songs of larks that we hear; whether our lives seem to be following well-marked paths or ways that suddenly seem to disappear and leave us feeling lost and unsure.

In this "Year of Mark," the first evangelist is realistic about the hard sowing and difficult yield of discipleship. Those who at their first call along the Sea of Galilee left everything to follow Jesus (Mark 1:16-20) leave everything to run away from him in Gethsemane (Mark 14:50-51). It is not until he is crowned with death so that he may reign in risen life that the Markan disciples recognize and confess the meaning of suffering and Servanthood, and accept that this is the way they must follow. In our Sunday assemblies there are also people who fiddle on the edge of their seats, ready to flee for various reasons: perhaps because of the irrelevance or the negativity of the homily; perhaps because of the poor quality of the liturgy; perhaps they are divorced, remarried, angry or disillusioned by their experiences of hypocrisy, injustice, or lack of compassion in the church. But they still gather as "God's field," needing and hoping to experience the hospitality of the Sower in the words that are scattered over them by the one who is entrusted with this ministry.

To try to be true to the times we live in, true to people's struggles, true to the demands of the biblical word, and true to one's own integrity, makes great demands on the preacher. But I am convinced that it is not the smooth and polished verbal performance that is shod with self-confidence, but the honest, often stumbling effort that is welcomed by hearers of the Word who know from their own life experiences that:

> . . . all is seared with trade; bleared, smeared with toil;
> And wears man's smudge and shares man's smell; the soil
> Is bare now, nor can foot feel, being shod.[1]

And these verses are in the poem Hopkins entitled "God's Grandeur" because this is the raw material of our lives over which, as he concludes, the Holy Ghost "Broods with warm breast and with ah! bright wings."

In many places, Sunday worship in the absence of a priest means that Christ's nonordained faithful are now the ones who are entrusted with breaking open the Word and breaking open the hearts of their hearers to the work of the Spirit. I hope these reflections may be some small help for those who, reflectively and prayerfully, either alone or with others, want to prepare the soil for the sowing of the seed of God's Word on Sunday or harvest its fruits by their *lectio divina* (sacred reading) throughout the following week. Having received the Word, we are called to be generous and joyous in casting abroad this seed in our families, communities, workplaces, and places of leisure—

without being too concerned about how and if it takes root because, as Paul reminds us, it is God who gives the growth (1 Cor 3:6).

I have also been privileged to have sown in my life the words of the Rule of Benedict.[2] In his Prologue, Benedict writes that our seeking of God is always to have "the Gospel as our guide" (RB Prol 14), and in his last chapter he repeats his conviction that the Old and New Testaments are "the truest of guides for human life" (RB 73.3). The biblical word is the constant companion of Benedict's wise and humane "modest Rule" as he himself describes it (RB 73.8). Benedict's and our own times are sixteen centuries apart, yet they have much in common. Benedict, too, witnessed great changes: wars, the collapse of the Roman Empire, social and economic insecurities that widened the gap between rich and poor, turmoil and controversy in the church about faith issues. Yet he found his way through this social and ecclesial minefield to found communities that provided rich soil in which the love of God and one's brothers and sisters could flourish. As with the two former books in this series,[3] I have added for those who may be interested, and as a sixth chapter, a brief weekly reflection on the Rule of Benedict related to the Sunday lectionary. This is another small scattering of seed that can be ploughed into our lives along with the biblical word and, perhaps, increase its yield.

Verna A. Holyhead SGS
Melbourne
September 2007

Notes

1. Gerard Manley Hopkins, "God's Grandeur," *Poems and Prose of Gerard Manley Hopkins.* Selected with an introduction and notes by W. H. Gardner (Harmondsworth, Middlesex: Penguin Books Ltd., 1963) 27.

2. References to the Rule of Benedict are indicated by RB or RB Prol for the Prologue. Unless otherwise indicated, the reference is to Terrence G. Kardong, *Benedict's Rule: A Translation and Commentary* (Collegeville, MN: Liturgical Press, 1996).

3. *Welcoming the Word in Year C: With Burning Hearts* (Collegeville, MN: Liturgical Press, 2006) and *Welcoming the Word in Year A: Building On Rock* (Collegeville, MN: Liturgical Press, 2007).

1

The Season of Advent

"Coming, ready or not!" How often we heard or shouted this as children when we played hide-and-seek. The season of Advent is rather like a liturgical game of hide-and-seek. God calls to us that he is coming, whether we are ready or not, and will never give up the search, even though there are plenty of hiding places for us in our contemporary culture and commerce: in the frenetic shopping and conspicuous consumption encouraged by different shouts of "so many days to Christmas," a countdown that in many places seems to start in October; in a succession of parties where Advent is submerged in the toasts to a "Happy Christmas"; in the personal and family worries about shopping lists, greeting cards, provisions for family gatherings, the juggling of who goes where and when for the Christmas visits and meals; in the end of the civil year and the many exhausting tasks that have to be completed before the new year begins.

In Year B, God calls to us through the Advent voices of the prophet Isaiah, King David, John the Baptist, Paul, Peter, and Mary of Nazareth. They speak to us with an urgency that is both fierce and gentle. The Old Testament readings proclaim that we should hope for big things: for heavens split open by God's intervention in human history; for a world transformed, a cosmos where deserts blossom and rough places are made smooth; for the discovery of a genealogy that will make all humanity the sons and daughters of our messianic Ancestor. The second reading, from the apostolic letters, calls us to the Christian way that disciples should follow in the "in-between" time of the church as we wait for the end time.

A well-known process to help police in their search for a suspect is asking eyewitnesses to help them put together an "identikit," a composite picture of remembered features of the sought one. Our Advent search is not for a criminal, but for a Savior, and the memories and witnesses of both Testaments help us to recognize him.

The readings for the First Sunday of Advent begin by resetting our liturgical clocks, fast-forwarding them to the time that is still ahead of us, the time when Christ will return in his Second Coming, the *parousía*, to claim the world definitively for himself, and the reigning presence of God will be everything to everyone (cf. 1 Cor 15:28). In this sense, history is always a waiting for this culminating advent at the end of human and cosmic time. And these particular four weeks are not a bored queuing and waiting for Christmas; rather, they are expectant, hopeful, the yearly "pregnancy" of the church, full of possibilities as we go into labor for the birth of a better world of justice and peace that will be worthy of becoming the new heaven and the new earth. On the Second and Third Sundays, the Advent clock is turned back to the adult John the Baptist, who tells us that the Christ stands among us, often unrecognized, so preoccupied are we with other concerns. Then it is the first hour of the new age and the new transformation of our humanity so that we can now say with the poet:

> In a flash, at a trumpet crash
> I am all at once what Christ is, since he was what I am . . . [1]

An angel's annunciation of Immanuel, God-with-us, flashes from heaven, and the trumpet crash that will resound through the ages is muffled in the womb of a young and poor woman in the unimportant town of Nazareth. This is the advent of Christ in the flesh that has come once, in the past of a particular time and culture.

Our Advent clock is also an alarm that the church sets to wake us up to a continuing coming of Christ in our daily lives, to a greater awareness of the divine presence and a deeper knowledge of the divine love. Christ is still being born, not in his own human flesh but in our hearts if we offer him the hospitality of our discipleship. Ours is the dignity and challenge to accept the Son, through the power of the Holy Spirit, into the most intimate depths of our lives, and then bear him to others. This is not the season for gazing nostalgically into a crib or fearfully into the heavens. It is a time to rise from sleep, to pray, to avoid the premature celebration of Christmas, to wait with eager readiness rather than exhausted idleness for the advent of the Lord who has come, is coming, and will come again.

First Sunday of Advent

• Isa 63:16b-17, 19b; 64:2-7 • Ps 80:2-3, 15-16, 18-19 • 1 Cor 1:3-9 • Mark 13:33-37

The Advent liturgy is full of shouting—and needs to be, as the Word of God competes with the external noise of Musak jingles or blasts of pre-

Christmas bargain advertising, as well as the internal noise of our own worries about what has to be planned in family, at work, for holidays, in these weeks before Christmas. "O that you would tear open the heavens and come down!" shout the returning Babylonian exiles of the sixth century B.C.E. They were a community in crisis, a ragged group of exiles who had returned from Babylon (in present-day Iraq) to the devastation of their Jerusalem Temple and their land. They are facing opposition from the "locals," those who had not been exiled and did not welcome the return of people who might upset their settled life. Bold and audacious in their hope, familiar and abrasive in their speech, the remnant people still recognize God as their *go'el*, "redeemer" or nearest kin, charged in the Jewish tradition with the protection of the weak and needy. The returned exiles implore God to make their present sorrow and disillusionment the birth pangs of something new. Isaiah's wonderful imagery can speak to us, no matter what our present climatic season, for we recognize that we often walk in the winter of personal sinfulness; that we can be withered people blown about aimlessly like a heap of dead leaves; that although exiled by sin we can beg our redeeming God to help us return home and live. We may look back on the past year and realize that there have been times when our lack of integrity and our lethargy have piled up like dirty laundry on those frenetic days when we had neither the time nor energy to do any washing. The days of Advent call us to some vigorous "laundering," to the repentance that enables us to continue our journey of faith clothed in the fresh grace of our baptism. The responsorial Psalm 80 is insistent about the need for the Advent repentance as we pray: "Lord, make us turn to you, let us see your face and we shall be saved," even though it is a gentler repentance than that of Lent.

"And yet . . ." our God is like a potter who also gets dirty, but not because of lethargy. Just as a potter gets dirty because of willingness to engage in the messy business of shaping and reshaping the clay, our Potter God is immersed in the shaping and reshaping of our human clay. In the fullness of time, the clay of Israel's and our humanity was formed by the Potter into the body of Jesus. It is our Christian privilege to know, in faith that goes infinitely beyond even prophetic imagery and imagination, that God has heard our cry, has torn open not only the heavens but also the womb of a young and poor woman, so that Jesus might become flesh among us. What was begun in a humble, hidden way in Mary, was fired in the kiln of his passion, shattered on Calvary, and recast in risen glory—a glory beyond the vision of Isaiah.

Through the words of Isaiah, God assures the people that he is always their *go'el*, their redeemer and nearest kin, has never been absent from them, is always ready and waiting to be found, even by those who have given up seeking their God. "Here I am, here I am," God also calls to us this Advent. Meister Eckhardt, a fourteenth-century mystic, described spirituality as "waking up" to the presence of God in our lives, especially in our sisters and brothers—those elbowing, jostling, lonely, unloved, and (we might consider) unlovable people around us or distant from us to whom we are called to reach out in practical compassion, justice, and prayer.

"Keep awake!" are the first words with which Mark greets us at the beginning of this new year of the church. They are also the last words spoken by Jesus in Mark's gospel (Mark 13:37) before the vortex of violence begins to suck Jesus into the passion and death that he will conquer by his resurrection. So even as we begin Advent, we are reminded of the paschal mystery of Christ, the hub of the liturgical year. Today's gospel is part of Mark 13, the chapter that is known as his "little apocalypse." Apocalypse is sometimes called the literature of the oppressed, as it usually arises from and is addressed to people in a time of uncertainty or suffering, present or imminent. Such was the situation of the Markan church, persecuted and unsure what the next day would bring in terms of fidelity to or betrayal of their faith. In one sense, uncertainty is always the season of the church as we await the return of Jesus, the great Traveler, who has gone abroad from the home of his human presence with us, but will return at his Second Coming when human history has run its course. We are uncertain about the day or the hour *of* this, because it is known only to the Father; but we have the certainty of faith that there is an end *for* the world: a faith that Christ will come again to pour out upon the cosmos the extravagant love of God that will transform it into the new heaven and new earth. When the new impinges on our lives to threaten the established order, we often express our reaction to this in terms of cosmic collapse: "I felt as though my whole world was collapsing!" In the verses immediately before today's gospel, Jesus has spoken about the end of the old order in terms of the "passing away" of heaven and earth. The old order is the predictable, the ingrained habits, the mindless and often oppressive "business as usual." Jesus' words announce a new reality for which we must be awake and alert. Advent is our yearly reminder that, immersed in the present as we necessarily are, nonetheless we always stand on the edge of the future, secure in the words of Jesus which will not pass away but will help us journey into a new and hopeful transformation (cf. Mark 13:31-32).

> What we call the beginning is often the end
> And to make an end is to make a beginning.
> The end is where we start from.[2]

Mark describes the "Jesus journey" through the parable of a man who goes abroad and leaves his servants in charge of his household. Just as each one of the servants in the parable is given a specific work to do during his master's absence, so we, as members of God's household, are to be daily committed to our baptismal calling in our own circumstances, "evening, morning, cockcrow, dawn." Especially as "doorkeepers," we are to watch out for and open our personal and communal lives to the advent of God. Modern science speaks of the cosmos in terms of millennia of millennia, yet we know that this is not the scale of our own lifetime. The natural process of aging, perhaps the diagnosis of our own or our loved one's terminal illness, the sudden fatal accident, the ravages of natural disasters—all these are reminders of our much shorter time and our need to be prepared for that "personal parousia," Christ's advent in our death.

It may sound from the reading of the beginning of Paul's First Letter to the Corinthians that everything was going well in their church, but to read the Letter in its entirety makes it clear that the Corinthians were also experiencing crises. Disturbed by internal rival factions, deviant sexual practices, marital difficulties, disputes about liturgy and community roles, they too needed to be encouraged to use the gifts of the Spirit that they had received in baptism, and so recognize the revelation of Christ and endure in fidelity to him. Paul encourages them to put their lives under the loving reign of God until this is definitively established on earth "on the day of the Lord Jesus Christ," the second coming of Jesus. Like the Corinthians, we are still waiting for that day, are still in the "in-between-time" that stretches from Pentecost to parousia. Waiting can sap our energies unless it is pregnant with hope, compassionate for those who have no hope, vigilant for justice, and faithful to the promises of God spoken to us by Jesus.

Today in our churches or homes we light the first candle on the Advent wreath: a small flame is struck on an evergreen circle, a simple ritual and symbol of the first flicker of hope in the One who is the Light of the world, who will lead us through every darkness to eternal life with God who is without beginning or end. "Marana tha," "Come, Lord," is our persistent Advent cry.

Second Sunday of Advent

• Isa 40:1-5, 9-11 • Ps 85:9-14 • 2 Pet 3:8-14 • Mark 1:1-8

"The beginning of the good news of Jesus Christ, the Son of God . . .": these are the first words of the first Gospel to be written. When we hear these words proclaimed in the assembly, do we experience any of the excitement of other beginnings—the birth of a child, the new lease of life after radical surgery, the breaking of dawn after a dark spiritual night? Mark's proclamation is abrupt; it has none of the narrative charm of Matthew's and Luke's infancy narratives, nor the meditative poetry of John's Prologue. It plunges us urgently into the good news of God's promised salvation that comes through the anointed humanity of Jesus the Christ who, in his Sonship, is also the presence of God among us. Mark will not write of an "ending" to the good news because it continues to be proclaimed and lived by disciples of all future millennia.

The prophet Isaiah had been the spokesman for God who promised to send "my messenger" to prepare the way for the people's deliverance from the wilderness of Babylonian exile (Isa 40:3). Again, when the people become disillusioned with the priestly leadership of the fifth century B.C.E., the prophet Malachi speaks of the messenger who will come to the Temple in turbulent times to show the way to prepare for the day of the coming of the Lord (Mal 3:1). Add to these words a hint of the guiding wilderness angel (Exod 23:20), and Mark is building up an "identikit" of the one whom he then presents to us as John the Baptist.

For the next two Sundays, Mark will encourage us in our fidelity to the good news of Jesus Christ through the voice of John the Baptist, a voice that cannot be silenced. Herod Antipas tried to do just that by beheading John (Mark 6:27-29), yet here we are, two thousand years later, listening to him. The Liturgy of the Word puts the adult John before us today and next Sunday to block our view of "baby Jesus," and so remind us that the Advent–Christmas mystery is less about the child and more about the adult Coming One and the mystery of his life, death, and resurrection that he offers to us as our own mystery. We are called to make our way down to the Jordan with the hopeful and curious crowds to see this wilderness man. John had accepted the hospitality that the desert had offered him. Cruncher of the desert food of bitter locusts sweetened with wild honey, he is satisfied with the food of the poor; clad in rough camel hair, he is dressed like a new Elijah (2 Kgs 1:5-8); tempered in his spirit by solitude, John, in his turn, welcomes the crowds with a bittersweet message in sparse words that are honed to a fine cutting edge for slicing through consciences and exposing them to the truth.

Son of a priest though he may be, John does not deliver his message in the Temple or anywhere else in Jerusalem, but on the banks of the Jordan River. At this busy crossing place, so significant in the history of Israel's journey into the Promised Land (cf. Josh 3), John urges the people to cross over into God's forgiveness through the waters of a ritual baptism of repentance. The Baptist invites us, too, to honest mindfulness of the water—not of the Jordan, but of our baptism—and to examination of our consciousness about our fidelity to the Christ into whom we are baptized. Despite the crowds he draws,

John's self-evaluation has nothing of self-exaltation. At this high point of his popularity he speaks directly to the people to point them away from himself to the Stronger One who is coming, and declares that he is unworthy even to be a slave who would bend down and untie the sandals on the smelling and sweating feet of this Coming One. John resists the temptation of successful ministers: to allow our own popularity to become the main concern of our ministry. When we do this, we are proclaiming what we consider the good news of ourselves, not of Jesus.

In the Puerto Rican city of San Juan, named for John, there stands a huge stone sculpture of the precursor. It is located between the ocean and a main highway of this busy modern city. With the relentlessness of the stone from which he is carved, the Baptist stands with head bent and eyes looking down the highway. But one arm is raised high with a determined finger pointing to heaven. The statue expresses the gospel paradox of John the Baptist, the earthy man of both the wilderness and the Jordan crowds, and the heaven-directed prophet; the paradox of disengagement and engagement—and so the embodiment of the paradox of the Advent season. Day after day, as surely as the waves break on the shore, our lives must be directed to heaven, and yet we must also be involved in the rush and business of daily life. The former is almost certainly the more difficult during these weeks. But it can be done if we opt to deliberately turn off the TV or transistor, to unplug our ears from iPods or mobile phones and turn to a few moments of silent reflection about the hopes and promises of Advent; if we plug our listening into some quiet reading of Scripture (*lectio divina*)—perhaps a reread of some of the Sunday texts; if we seize a few moments of prayerful repentance or awareness of the presence of God in our traveling companions along our highways or on public transport or shopping. These are ways in which we can respond to Psalm 85 and "hear what the Lord God has to say."

In the first reading, Second Isaiah shouts to the returning exiles God's message of comfort found at the beginning of what is called "the Book of the Consolation of Israel" (Isa 40–55). God will be faithful to the people who have suffered the terror of exile, even though at times their fidelity to God has withered like dried-up grass, and their love has faded like a dead flower. With the strength of a gentle Shepherd who cares for the weakest and most vulnerable in his flock, God will carry the exhausted ones to rest once more in their own land. How like the Shepherd can we be in these Advent weeks? Will we make any personal, communal, or financial effort to carry the weak and the lonely that may be as near as our own families? In our communities or parishes will we be heralds of Good News to the exiles: the asylum seekers, the refugee families, those unvisited in aged care facilities or hospitals?

On their way to expensive boutiques, casinos, pampering health clubs, or cosmetic surgery, do those who travel past their sisters and brothers in need ever suspect that it is the affluent "beautiful people" who may themselves be the exiles in most need of human and divine consolation? If our lives and our world are to prosper according to God's plan, it is time for mercy and faithfulness to meet, for justice and peace to embrace, as we have prayed in the responsorial Psalm 85.

The Second Letter of Peter reminds us that God who is "from everlasting to everlasting" (Ps 90:2) does not measure time as we do. It may be difficult for us to keep focused on the importance of waiting during the four Advent weeks; God can outwait us, patient for the whole world to come to repentance so that it can be transformed into what God has promised: "new heavens and new earth, where righteousness is at home" (2 Pet 3:13). This will happen through the men and women who live holy, just, and peaceful lives, and so establish the reigning presence of God in themselves and others throughout human history. Such people will be ready to be "stolen" by Christ for the new creation.

Third Sunday of Advent

• Isa 61:1-2a, 10-11 • Luke 1:46-50, 53-54 • 1 Thess 5:16-24 • John 1:6-8, 19-28

Today the adult John the Baptist appears at the beginning of John's gospel, but in a very different context to last Sunday's Markan appearance. In the Fourth Gospel, the Baptist is situated right in the middle of the Prologue, the great Johannine hymn to the glory of Christ, the Word and the Light, in whose human flesh God pitched his tent among us. John is there as a lamp who will guide the feet of God's people to the true Light, announcing to them the secure way to cross from the old order to the new. The closer the lamp-carrier comes to the Light, the dimmer his own radiance becomes until, no longer needed, it disappears completely.

The interrogators have been sent by the religious authorities in Jerusalem; John has been sent by God. When questioned by the Jewish priests and Levites, John humbly gives his testimony. Quite deliberately, the evangelist contrasts John's self-effacing "I am not . . ."—not the Messiah, not Elijah, not the long-awaited prophet (cf. Deut 18:15)—with the "I AMs" that Jesus will speak. Once again the Baptist describes himself, in the words of Isaiah, as only a voice crying in the wilderness: a voice enabled by the Spirit/Breath of God that will call Jesus to baptism in the Jordan waters, and a voice that calls us today to renew our own baptismal commitment and so prepare a straight way for the Lord to enter the wilderness places of our own lives. The priests and Levites have been sent to discover the mystery of John the Baptist, but he points them away from himself to the greater mystery of the One who is coming, who already stands among them, and they do not recognize him. John seeks no status with the Jewish leaders or the crowds; he is not even worthy to be a menial sandal-slave of the Christ.

In the screenplay for Robert Bolt's *A Man for All Seasons*, there is a poignant example of someone who, because of personal ambition, was not content with any self-effacement. The young Richard Rich pesters Thomas More for patronage, begging him to use his influence at Henry VIII's court for Richard's advancement. But More, disillusioned by the corruption he sees there, tries to convince Rich that his ambition is misconceived. He offers Rich a post in a local school, urging him to become a great teacher. Rich's cynical response is to query who would know about this so-called greatness. More replies that Rich himself would know it, his pupils would know it—and God would know it. This would not be a bad audience. But it is not good enough for the ambitious Rich who has his eyes on the political summit and those whom he considers will be a more adoring audience. He eventually perjures himself and betrays More, going on his self-centered and crooked way to become the Lord Lieutenant for Wales while, like John the Baptist, Thomas More goes on to be beheaded.

In the first reading, (Third) Isaiah proclaims a jubilee, "a year of the Lord's favor," to the depressed postexilic community. It is uncertain if such a fiftieth year was ever actually celebrated in Israel, but the Jubilee nevertheless remained in the Jewish tradition as a powerful metaphor of God's blessings that establish freedom for the dispossessed and disadvantaged. As one of the oldest dreams of the traditions of Israel, the Jubilee waits to be dreamed again, not in sleep but in action. Isaiah has the tongue, the imagination, and the boldness to bring to speech and consciousness not only what has happened but also what should happen. The goodness and justice of God will bring another springtime for the winter people of Zion; their joy will be like that of a newly married couple in whose love is the promise of new life. In Luke's gospel, the adult Jesus quotes the beginning of this text to announce his mission of justice for the poor and disadvantaged (Luke 4:18-21). At the dawn of the third millennium, the United Nations General Assembly proposed eight Millennium Development Goals (MDG) in the social sphere: to eradicate poverty; achieve universal education; promote gender equality and empower women; reduce child mortality; improve maternal health; combat HIV/AIDS, malaria, and other diseases; ensure environmental sustainability; develop a global partnership for development. As W. B. Yeats wrote:

> But I, being poor, have only my dreams;
> I have spread my dreams under your feet;
> Tread softly, for you tread on my dreams.[3]

How softly or roughly do we tread as individuals, communities, nations, upon the fragile dreams of the poor? Or is our soft treading a tiptoeing away from their needs expressed by the MDGs? The response to the Isaian reading is the freedom song of Mary, who proclaims out of her poverty the richness of God's salvation whom she carries in her womb: Jesus, the Coming One, who will be liberty for the oppressed in a way that infinitely surpasses Isaiah's dreams and hope.

This Third Sunday of Advent is also known as "Laetare" (the Latin for "rejoice") Sunday because of the theme of joy in the readings and because we are more than halfway through Advent, and coming closer to Christmas. Isaiah assures the exiles that their mourning will be turned to joy; the Baptist is humbly confident in the Coming One whom he announces. Paul tells his Thessalonians to "Rejoice always!" because they now live in Christ Jesus. Filled with his Spirit, they are prophets: men and women who speak forth God's word with freedom and courage. For this, discernment is needed so that the Thessalonians hold fast to whatever is good, and avoid every evil. Joy, prayer, and gratitude are the fitting responses to the promises of our faithful God who will never fail us.

Fourth Sunday of Advent

• 2 Sam 7:1-5, 8b-12, 14a, 16 • Ps 89:2-5, 27, 29 • Rom 16:25-27 • Luke 1:26-38

The heavens have been torn open; God has come down, not with mountain quaking and fire burning, but in the gentle descent of the Spirit who broods over the womb of Mary of Nazareth. And as at the first creation life was called forth, so now the first cell of the new creation is conceived. The *shekhinah*, the cloud of the Presence of the Most High, overshadows Mary (cf. Exod 40:35), and the Son of God is at home among us. During Advent the Liturgy of the Word tells us that we bump into God in strange places: in the poor, in crowds and, strangest of all, in the obscure village of Nazareth and one of its backwater young women. Mary is a powerless female in a world ruled by males; poor, in a highly stratified society; found to be pregnant before she cohabits with her husband, and so obviously not carrying his child to validate her existence. That God should find her a "favored one" is hugely surprising, especially to Mary!

The Lukan biblical imagination has captured the imagination of artists down through the centuries. With their own prophetic insight, they have set the extraordinary faith of Mary among familiar things: a half-read book, a meal in preparation, a door open on children and animals at play, people passing by. One of the more unusual depictions is that by Henry Ossawa Tanner, an African American painter (1859–1937). In a Middle Eastern-style bedroom, Mary sits enfolded in the heavy drapes of bedclothes and her own robe, her gaze attentive. All is simplicity, not luxury, and there is no winged angel. What Mary's gaze is fixed on is a tall, thin pillar of white cloud at the end of her bed. Perhaps Tanner is remembering the presence of God, the "angel" of Exodus 14:19, described as a cloud, that led the Israelites into their future, would lead Mary into hers, and will lead us through the ordinary and familiar events and places where God is present—if we will only recognize him and respond with our own, "Here I am, the servant of the Lord; let it be with me according to your word."

The Greek Orthodox church at Nazareth is built over an ancient spring that fed the village well, and clear, fresh water can still be drawn from it. The Orthodox tradition is that the annunciation occurred at a well, for that was the place of betrothal for the Old Testament lovers such as Isaac and Rebekah, Jacob and Rachel, Moses and Zipporah, and so was a fitting place for the New Testament betrothal of the Word to humanity in the womb of Mary.

God's dream of a fitting home for his Son was very different from that divine place David proposes in the first reading. After he has "settled down" (the phrase is significant) in his house of cedar, David has the bright idea of also building a fine house in which Israel's God could dwell. David is surprised by God's response, spoken through the prophet Nathan after some prophetic second thoughts and dreams! Settling down, says Nathan, is not characteristic of Israel's God, who is not a God to be circumscribed and enthroned like the gods of their pagan neighbors. The God of Israel is a free, exodus God, who prefers to move among the people, pitching his tent where he pleases. David's God, Mary's God, our God, is a surprising God who always takes the initiative and often turns upside down the tables of our expectations. With skillful word play, the biblical author announces through Nathan that *God* will build *David* a house! This will be the genealogical house of the Davidic dynasty where God will be at home with his people in a special way. And in the future, one of David's descendants will build a house for God's name and establish a kingdom that will be everlasting.

This does not happen in the stone-and-cedar Temple built by David's son, Solomon, nor in the Second postexilic Temple. Its beginning, as the gospel proclaims, is in human flesh and blood, in the womb of Mary of Nazareth.

This is the surprising and humanly unimaginable mystery that Paul describes as kept secret for long ages but now revealed in Christ. We sing our way across the bridge between the first and second readings with the repeated refrain of the responsorial Psalm 89. "I will sing for ever of your steadfast love, O Lord." God's faithful love for David is made incarnate in Jesus Christ, and in Paul's concluding doxology to his Letter to the Romans he reminds his Gentile Romans that they, too, have inherited the promise of this love. We Gentiles, gathered as a community of praise around the tables of word and sacrament, are called to sing our praise to God—not just in the eucharistic liturgy, but with lives that are committed to "the obedience of faith."

Every Advent we are challenged to have the attentiveness of Mary to the flutter of Christ-life that stirs in the womb of our complacency. So often our world seems starved of stars; and so often we watch or participate in rituals of mourning for acts of terrorism, natural disaster, the local tragedies of road deaths, or other dark events. Usually in these rituals there are candles: small pieces of self-consuming wax and flame that say light has more right to exist in our world than darkness. This is the message, too, of our Advent wreath as we light the last of its four candles. But those candles, like all ritual candles, will burn out. It is up to us, disciples of the Light of the world, to catch fire from Christ's mystery and bring something of this fire and light into our own lives and, especially, into the lives of those for whom Christmas may not be a feast of joy but a time of darkness that stirs painful memories of those with whom they can no longer celebrate because of death, separation, divorce, family quarrels. For the friendless, the homeless, the abused, Christmas may arouse bitter comparisons and regrets. The fire we catch from Christ, our readiness to be consumed like him in the flame of loving service of our sisters and brothers, may be as simple a gift as a visit, a letter, a phone call, an invitation to a meal, a present on the parish "Giving Tree." But it will mean that, together, we will truly celebrate something of a "Happy Christmas."

Notes

[1.] Gerard Manley Hopkins, "That Nature is a Heraclitean Fire and of the comfort of the Resurrection," *Gerard Manley Hopkins: Poems and Prose*. Selected and edited by W. H. Gardner (Harmondsworth, Middlesex: Penguin Books Ltd., 1982) 66.

[2.] T. S. Eliot, "Little Gidding," in "Four Quartets," *The Complete Poems and Plays of T. S. Eliot* (London: Faber and Faber, 2004) 197.

[3.] W. B. Yeats, *The Collected Poems of W. B. Yeats* (Ware, Hertfordshire: Wordsworth Poetry Library, 2000) 59.

2

The Season of Christmas

Our waiting is over; our cry "Marana tha," "Come, Lord," has been answered with a baby's cry in a small town of Bethlehem and an angelic proclamation of God's glory to the ends of the earth, with an intimacy as familiar as human birth and a cosmic significance as large as the stars. Now it is God who waits, God who cries to us to "Come!"—come to the Child who witnesses that God is no disembodied idea, but a personal reality among us, sharing our humanity so that we may share his divinity. Born in a stable, laid in an animal's eating trough, Jesus gives us confidence to believe that he can also be born in the poverty of our hearts. Love makes him small; his silence makes him undemanding; his humanity challenges us never again to act in an inhuman way.

The Christmas season, like all the seasons of the church year, also celebrates the paschal mystery:

> The incarnation, the scandal of the eternal Word of God made flesh and thus becoming subject to all human frailties, even to death itself, reveals the paschal nature of God—the sending of Jesus is God's self-emptying that humankind might be filled with the Spirit of grace and life.[1]

The baby's cry matures into the strong adult voice that announces the kingdom and calls to repentance and discipleship; the wood of his feeding trough becomes the wood of the cross; the glory of God announced by angels on a hillside is announced over an empty tomb in a Jerusalem garden.

The mosaic of readings from the Old Testament and gospel readings during this season is pieced together to create a work of biblical and liturgical art, the "exact imprint of God's very being" (Heb 1:3), while the second readings from the apostolic writings interpret the significance of God's plan in Jesus and the response to this that is asked of all those in whom Jesus is again conceived in the Spirit and born into the world, the Child:

Who was so rich
He owned diamonds and snowflakes and fire,
The leaf and the forest,
Herring and whale and horizon—
Who had the key to the chamber beyond the stars
And the key of the grave—
Who was sower and seed and bread
Came on a black night
To a poor hovel with a star peeking through rafters
And slept among beasts
And put a sweet cold look on kings and shepherds.[2]

May this Child gaze on us and we on him during these Christmas weeks.

Christmas Day

Mass During the Day

(The readings for Christmas Day are the same in Years A, B, and C. The reflection for Midnight Mass is found in *Welcoming the Word in Year C: With Burning Hearts*, and for the Dawn Mass in *Welcoming the Word in Year A: Building on Rock.*)

• Isa 52:7-10 • Ps 98:1-6 • Heb 1:1-6 • John 1:1-18

Christmas Day is always a day of joyful singing, of voices caroling both well-known and loved and new melodies. In the first reading, the prophet Isaiah allows us to hear a chorus of voices that sings the joy so appropriate to this festival: the glad good news of peace and the arrival of a king. And yet it will take a longer journey through hundreds of years of fidelity and infidelity, exile and return after the time of Isaiah, before the definitive King will return to his people and tabernacle among us.

The first voice in Isaiah's joyful chorus is the messenger of peace whose feet are speeded by the Good News, the "Gospel" that he brings to the people left behind in a ruined Jerusalem. Almost out of breath, he blurts out the news that God is victorious over other powers, and that (as the verses immediately following this reading tell us) the people will return from exile with God as their traveling companion and guard. The ecstasy of the messenger is contagious. The sentinels on the walls of ruined Jerusalem join their voices to the runner as their imagination and their faith look to the horizon and see their God and their people no longer captives of the Babylonian Empire, but freely advancing home. Despite her fears and her ruins, the sentinels invite the city of Jerusalem to add her voice to the chorus of praise of God. In his even wider vision, Isaiah sees God baring his holy arm, showing his strength to all the nations of the world.

And today we remember this God who pitches his presence among us, not as he tented with his people in the desert or in the Jerusalem Temple, but in bared human flesh like our own. At the end of his gospel, John tells us his reason for writing: ". . . so that you may come to believe that Jesus is the Messiah, the Son of God, and that through believing you may have life in his name" (John 20:31). But the beginning of his gospel, the Prologue that is proclaimed at this Mass, asserts John's conviction that to believe in Jesus we must understand the entire journey of the Word: his beginning in eternity, his becoming flesh among us to open heaven for us, and his return to heaven, "close to the Father's heart" (John 1:18). The movement of the Prologue to John's gospel is like a pendulum swinging: from the glory of the Word in eternity who was with God and was God, arcing down into our world, and then again swinging upwards through death and resurrection into the glory of the Father, and catching us up with him.

John names Jesus as the Word. When a word is spoken it is the extension of something of the inner person into the outer environment. In this sense, God most truly speaks God into the world through the Word made flesh whose mission is that we might understand, most clearly and most humanly, the overwhelming love of God that offers us eternal life (cf. John 3:16). "In the beginning" of Genesis 1:1 there was the moment of the first creation called into existence by the word of God. The coming of the Word made flesh into the world is another beginning, a renewing creation of life and light that no darkness can overcome. Jesus the Word, although without sin, is not remote from the darkness of our world, from the human sinfulness that will raise him on a cross, but from which he will draw all people to himself and to his Father (cf. John 12:32).

As if to make sure that we do understand the mystery of the Word as grounded in time and place, John the Baptist makes what we may at first regard as a surprising appearance in the Prologue as a witness to the light. Witnessing is the way the Word is still made known by each one of us in our own worlds of family, friendship, workplace, and leisure. The Baptist comes as a voice for a time; Jesus is the Word for all eternity. The Word is the radiance of the Father's glory; the Baptist is the lamp-carrier who becomes unnecessary when the Light is among us. And John the Baptist is humbly content to be only voice and lamp. Such humble witness to the Word, and not to ourselves, is the privilege of all who accept the Word into their lives. It is not an optional extra for those who have heard the Word and seen the Light.

That the Word "became flesh and tented among us" recalls the tenting of God's presence in the portable wilderness tabernacle (Exod 40:34) and the pitching of Wisdom's tent in the midst of the people (Sir 24:8). In the Word, the glory and wisdom of God are now present in humankind to reveal God's truth. In this gospel we are given a vocabulary with which to name the mystery: Word, life, light, glory. Its effects are the actions of revealing, birthing, overcoming, living.

In the Letter to the Hebrews there is both continuity and discontinuity between the Jewish and Christian revelation. "Long ago" fades into "these last days"; "our ancestors" give way to "us." The author affirms that "in many and various ways" God spoke through the many prophets of the Old Testament, but now this chorus gives way to the single, richly textured voice of God's Son who sings the truest song of creation and redemption accomplished by God through him. With a medley of Old Testament quotations, Christ, the great Canticle Singer, is affirmed as more excellent than the angels, most truly the beloved son of David to whom God is Father (cf. Ps 2:7; 2 Sam 7:14).

We celebrate this daytime Mass in full light, and this reading shines upon us the radiance of God's glory reflected in and through Christ. It takes us beyond any romanticized story of Christ's birth, any sentimental attachment to the child in the crib into the cosmic implications of Christ's Sonship. With the responsorial Psalm 98, we praise the saving power of God revealed to the end of the earth. The first reading from Isaiah is the prophetic counterpart of this psalm, as both proclaim that "all the ends of the earth shall see the salvation of our God." This psalm was also the Old Testament text Isaac Watts used for his Christmas hymn, "Joy to the World," transforming the "new song" into the praise of the nativity of Christ.

Sunday in the Octave of Christmas

Feast of the Holy Family

• Gen 15:1-6; 21:1-3 • Ps 105:1-4, 6-9 • Heb 11:8, 11-12, 17-19 • Luke 2:22-40

On the Sunday within the Christmas Octave, or on 30 December if there is no Sunday between 25 December and 1 January, we celebrate the wonder of the Word becoming flesh in a human family. Given the situation of many families today, this most recent of the feasts in the Christmas cycle is also one of the most challenging to integrate both spiritually and practically into the season. Leo XIII established the feast of the Holy Family as an optional celebration in 1893 to be celebrated on what was then the Third Sunday after

Epiphany. It was a call to remember the sanctity of family life and morality in the face of the threats from social changes in the nineteenth century. Made a feast of the universal church by Benedict XV, it continued to wander through the liturgical calendar until the reform of the Roman Calendar following Vatican II in 1969, when it settled in its present position.

In the twenty-first century, there is little settling down for Christian families in the face of many challenges. In society, the notion of "family" is undergoing radical change. We are all aware of those who belong to separated, divorced, blended, or single-parent families. Discussion of same-sex "marriage" and civil partnerships takes place in parliaments, churches, gay and lesbian groups. In some countries the language of family is transmuting, for example, into "Progenitor 1" and "Progenitor 2"; the long tentacles of pornography and child abuse have the potential to reach into our homes, schools, church, tourism, and the Internet, to strangle family relationships and erode trust in those whom parents have long considered loving guardians of their children. Yet the home is indeed a holy place. As Daniel O'Leary writes: "Perhaps nowhere more than in the heartfelt dynamic of married life, where the human spirit stretches itself, in its trusting and letting go, to the limits of its potential, is this sacrament of incarnate love more clearly sacramentalised"[3] . . . in both joy and pain. This feast is sometimes referred to as an "idea" feast, a feast dedicated to the idea and ideal of the family as "the beginning and basis of human society"[4] and a foreshadowing of the hope that through the preaching of the Gospel "the human race might become the Family of God, in which the fullness of the Law would be love."[5] Given the readings for today, it should be obvious that what we are seeking in the Word of God is not an anachronistic family model, but Spirit-guided discernment of the biblical values and attitudes that must be transplanted into our own homes and families in whatever cultural context we find ourselves, and under whatever government policies we live our faith.

In both the first and second readings, Abraham and Sarah are remembered. In the Genesis reading, the Lord appears in a night vision to Abram ("exalted ancestor"), not yet named Abraham ("father of a multitude"). In the first "conversation" between God and Abram, Abram questions God—but not abrasively—about the "reward" of descendants that God has promised him. If he remains childless, a man without heirs, who will carry on his name and keep his inheritance within the family? The only way Abram can see out of his dilemma is to make Eliezer, a slave born in Abram's house, his heir. But God assures Abram that he will not have to take this sociocultural option that was acceptable in that time. God will not only give Abram an heir; he will give him children of his own seed. As numerous, as fixed as the stars in the heaven, will Abram's offspring be. And without anything to depend on but the word of God, Abram believes in God's promise.

The second part of this reading shows us that Sarah's cynical laughter, when she glued her ear to the tent at Mamre and heard the stranger Lord's promise of a son (Gen 18:12-15), has now turned to exultant joy when she gives birth to her and Abraham's son, Isaac ("he who laughs"). Not only does the child in the womb come to full term; Abraham's (now "the father of a multitude") and Sarah's faith also has to mature. God is always creatively involved with a child's parents in the conception of human life. If we wonder at God's power shown in Sarah's and Abraham's parentage in old age, we might also wonder at the way in which God works in our own time through the "miracles" of modern medicine that give new promise to those longing for parenthood. With the responsorial Psalm 105, the call to remember the wonders God has done and the experience of God's fidelity in our history, becomes a present song for our worshiping community. Our remembrance of God's goodness, our seeking of his presence, may be distracted and inconsistent; God's remembrance of us is forever and always. "God's time is not our time; God's fidelity is beyond our imaginations."[6] The faith of Abraham persists as a model into the New Testament, and even into the First Eucharistic Prayer where he is described as "our father in faith." The Letter to the Hebrews proclaims three significant events in Abraham's journey of faith: his physical journey into the unknown with no security except the call and word of God; his extraordinary journey into parenthood when Sarah conceives a child in their old age when they are both "as good as dead" as far as their fertility is concerned; and the journey to Mount Moriah when Abraham is called to sacrifice Isaac, the child of the promise, in what would seem to be, in figurative biblical language, the snuffing out of the promised numerous "stars" of their descendants and the ravaging of the uncountable "grains of sand" of their offspring (cf. Gen 22:17). But Abraham trusts not in the promises, but in the Promise Maker. Just as in the conception and birth of Isaac, Abraham's God is a God who brings life where there seemed to be no life, so Abraham believes it will be in the death of Isaac. And so Isaac is "given back" to Abraham, a symbol of our surprising God's fidelity to bring life out of what seemed to be a situation of death. How often families need Abrahamic faith when loss or disillusionment invades their lives; when we struggle to believe that:

> Everything that happens in the unbelievably complex fabric of family life, the light and the dark of it, has God's life-giving heartbeat within it, God's loving signature set upon it. And we go to Mass to remember and to celebrate together

the extraordinary revelation that no moment is "merely" human or worldly, but rather a piece of grace; every threshold a door to heaven.[7]

Today's gospel is the account of a devout family event for the family of Jesus who are living in fidelity to the Mosaic covenant. Five times Luke repeats that Mary and Joseph bring Jesus to the Temple for the rituals that are in accordance with the teachings of Leviticus 12:1-8 about purification, and the redemption of the firstborn described in Exodus 13:13-16. Luke's Gentile origins may account for the confusion about "their" (Mary's and Jesus') participation in the ritual of purification that was for the mother only, and not the child. It was a ritual rooted in the Jewish belief in the sacredness of blood that, with the breath, was recognized as a mysterious life force. As such, any flow of blood was to be kept separate as far as possible from the secular activities of life. Because this was impossible in the case of childbirth, the purification ritual was required. The family that could not afford to offer an expensive lamb for the ritual could offer, as Mary and Joseph do, a pair of turtledoves or two young pigeons, one as a burnt offering, the other as a sin offering (cf. Lev 12:6-8). But this offering is not to be understood as saying that marriage and sexuality are sinful. They are fundamentals of human life that are affirmed and revered in the Old Testament, and to marry is still one of the basic *mizvot* or good works binding on Jews. A whole biblical book, the Song of Songs, is a lyrical hymn to sexual, erotic love, and referred to in Benedict XVI's encyclical, "God Is Love," significantly issued on the first Christmas Day of his pontificate.[8]

As a continuing remembrance of the Exodus and the passing over of the firstborn of the Hebrews by the angel of death, every firstborn male child was to be dedicated to God. By the ritual of the redemption of the firstborn, parents symbolically "bought back" or "redeemed" their child. Both this and the purification wove the remembrance and praise of God's salvation into the precious fabric of human life. This is always the point of ritual observances, and in the pressure of our modern-day living many religious rituals have been lost or so reduced to superficial and secularized events where a "nice traditional church wedding" or christening is a one-off participation in a church setting. After that, God can comfortably be dismissed from the everyday. We need to rediscover the treasury of the church's rituals appropriate for our twenty-first century,[9] and encourage ritual makers and text writers to create new ones: for the family life cycle, for lamentation and rejoicing, for the celebration of the presence of God among us in the holy place of our home.

The presentation of Jesus in the Temple is also an intergenerational meeting. Like a prophet of Israel, the devout and holy Simeon is drawn by the Holy Spirit toward this poor and apparently ordinary family. The aged prophet meets with the forty-day-old child; the firstborn who is carried obediently into the Temple for his ritual redemption is the One who will be the redeemer for all who are born of woman. The hope of Israel comes with no messianic fanfare. Simeon personifies the true, believing, hoping, and Temple-attending Israel who respond to Jesus. He can now welcome death since he has welcomed the One who will be the salvation of all nations. Then, standing in what would have been the Women's Court, Simeon speaks not to Joseph but to Mary. He announces that the sword of discerning judgment will cut through her mother's heart as she shares in the joy and pain, the acceptance and rejection, the falling and rising of those who accept or reject her son.

In his gospel narrative, Luke often sets a man and a woman together to express the human response to Jesus. Anna, described as a prophetess, is also a representative of devout and expectant Israel. She is both a woman in the past tradition of the prophetic women of the Old Testament like Miriam (Exod 15:20), Deborah (Judg 4:4), Huldah (2 Kgs 22:14), and Isaiah's wife (Isa 8:3), and also the first of the widows of the future early church whom Luke frequently mentions in both his gospel and the Acts of the Apostles (e.g., Luke 18:3; 21:2; Acts 6:1; 9:39-41). This is probably an indication of the important role these women played then, and a reminder to us that old age has a wisdom that should be enabled to speak out and be listened to now. Anna is a woman who has experienced three stages of family life: unmarried girlhood, marriage, and widowhood. Her constant prayer and fasting in the Temple have given her insight into the mystery of this child, one of so many whom she has seen pass in and out of the sacred precincts, and she speaks forth to those around her, proclaiming that here is the One who will bring to Jerusalem true freedom from captivity and alienation.

After this Temple encounter, Jesus, Mary, and Joseph return home to everyday life in Nazareth, to Jesus' growth in human maturity that delights his parents, to the unobtrusive and ordinary environment of blessing where the child grows in the wisdom and grace of God that will characterize his adult ministry. Today we celebrate the wonderful truth that it is parents who are chosen to midwife the mystery not only of the birth of their children, but also of their growth to adulthood. There will be unrelenting demands and incomprehensible sorrow in their parenthood, but also unspeakable joys and the revelation of God's incarnate beauty and grace in their children and their family love. These are precious gifts that must be reverenced and supported in church and society and, when absent, call forth a ministry of compassion.

Octave of Christmas

Solemnity of the Blessed Virgin Mary, Mother of God

• Num 6:22-27 • Ps 67:2-3, 5-6, 8 • Gal 4:4-7 • Luke 2:16-21

For many people, New Year's Eve is a time of celebrations not too far removed from the raucous festivities that ushered in 1 January when Julius Caesar reconstructed the civil calendar in 45 B.C.E. The church presents us with an alternative celebration. In today's gospel there is excitement as the shepherds hurry into Bethlehem to pour out what they have heard and seen to anyone who would listen to them. But at the center of this movement and ferment is Mary, the still point around which it all revolves. She says nothing, but in her heart she treasures and ponders all that is happening. The word that Luke uses here for "ponder" is *symballo*, a word in the Greek that literally means to "throw together." With Joseph at her side and her child lying in a manger wrapped in the swaddling cloths that bind both king and commoner (cf. Wis 7:4), Mary, the contemplative woman, silently holds and "throws together" in her heart the events of divine conception and human birth, heavenly hosts and hillside shepherds. Years of seeking to understand lie ahead of her as the first and most faithful of the disciples of Jesus. In her pondering and remembering, Mary is a model for our *lectio divina*, our reading of the Word of God and the conversation between that Word and events of our own lives.

As we gaze on this peaceful woman, we can appreciate how appropriate it is that 1 January has been chosen by the church as the day on which we pray for world peace. Like her, we are called to gaze on the child who is the Prince of Peace. It is his reign, not the Pax Romana, not the Pax Americana, nor any other political maneuvering, that will make the words of the responsorial Psalm 67 a reality in our hearts and in our world, so that God's way is known upon earth and all nations will learn God's saving power. Then humanity will be a people of praise, and all the nations will be "glad and sing for joy." The responsibility for peace is now in our hands. What the poet wrote after the devastation of the 1939–1945 World War still applies to our own century:

> Into our hands
> Mary has given her Child:
> Heir to the world's tears,
> Heir to the world's toil,
> Heir to the world's scars,
> Heir to the chill dawn
> Over the ruin of wars.[10]

The second focus of this day is the child's circumcision and naming. The rite of circumcision, celebrated eight days after birth, is called the "covenant of circumcision," and marks the male child's formal entry into the covenantal Jewish community (Gen 17:10-11). Every circumcision is a call to Abraham's seed to renew and live the covenant, but in Jesus the rite cuts deepest. The covenant made in his flesh, the blood shed for the first time from his foreskin will one day flow from raw wounds of the crucified Savior for the salvation of the world.

At the same time as circumcision, the naming of the child is celebrated. For a Jewish family, the name of the child is both a remembrance of previous generations and a hope for those yet to be born. We have no record of what words were spoken in the first-century rite, but the contemporary prayer is that God will: "give a pure and holy heart to N., a heart wide open to comprehend Thy Holy Law, that he may learn and teach, keep and fulfill Thy Laws." However the rite was expressed in Jesus' time, he was the most excellent son of his ancestors, the most obedient to God's Holy Law and, as "savior," the ultimate expression of his Name for the sake of the world.

The reading from the Book of Numbers is twinned with the gospel because of the emphasis on the name of the Lord that is three times called down or "put upon" the people of Israel in the priestly blessing given by the descendants of Aaron. The people are known to God and know themselves as God's people in an intimate relationship. This blessing is a gift from God, but is infinitely surpassed by that gift which is named Jesus, Savior.

Paul writes of this blessing of the Incarnation when the messianic hopes of Israel take flesh in Jesus. This happens in the fullness of God's own good time. The simple description of Jesus as "born of a woman" is Paul's sparse "infancy narrative," proclaiming Jesus as belonging to the human family; "born a subject of the Law" declares his Jewish identity, so dear to Paul; and the Spirit of Jesus makes those who welcome him into sons and daughters of "Abba," no longer needing the guardianship of the Law because of their new maturity in Christ. Adoption, inheritance, liberation: this is the gracious activity of God through Jesus, the Christmas gift we are called to unwrap and discover its surprises—not on one day, but on every day of our Christian lives.

Epiphany of the Lord

• Isa 60:1-6 • Ps 72:1-2, 7-8, 10-13 • Eph 3:2-3a, 5-6 • Matt 2:1-12

The gospel of the visit of the Magi is a narrative where the Spirit works through poetry, storytelling, and symbol. Seekers, stargazers, strangers, lead us not only to the revelation of the Christ Child but also to an anticipation of what the Child's life would hold: death and resurrection, rejection by his Jewish opponents, and acceptance by Gentiles. T. S. Eliot says it so well in his own poetic reflection that he places in the mouth of one of the wise men many years after their visit:

> . . . were we led all that way for
> Birth or Death? There was a Birth, certainly,
> We had evidence and no doubt. I had seen birth and death
> But had thought they were different; this Birth was
> Hard and bitter agony for us, like death, our death.[11]

What the wise men are doing we must all do: gaze at the biblical horizon on which the Christ is located, and then merge our own lives with that horizon. For the Magi, their visit to the Child meant the death of something of their old certainties, their old gods, their old astrological wisdom. And it also meant the birth of new appreciation of the grace of searching for truth across the boundaries of culture and religion, new allegiance to a poor and helpless king of the Jews, new insight into the workings of manipulative human power.

The first human word spoken in Matthew's gospel is the one the wise men address to Herod: "Where . . . ?" It is also the response of Herod when he summons the chief priests and scribes and his Jerusalem supporters (generalized to "all Jerusalem"). But the two questions are spoken from very different hearts. Herod is panic-stricken at the thought of losing his power to another "king of the Jews," and is desperate to know "where" this threat lurks. It is some of the same coterie that Matthew will later describe Herod as summoning to help him to plot the death of Jesus, and who will mock him on the cross (Matt 26:3-4; 27:41-43). In contrast, the wise men, Gentile (perhaps Persian) seekers and aristocratic scholars, have no concern with status or ethnicity; their "Where . . . ?" is a sign of their genuine search for the new king so that they may come to pay him homage. They also have the humility to come to Jerusalem to add to their foreign and pagan wisdom the wisdom of the Hebrew Scriptures to help them in their search. In the wolfish company of Herod and his cohorts, Matthew sees the wise men as witnesses to the later call of Jesus for all his disciples to be "wise as serpents and innocent as doves" (Matt 10:16).

The search of the wise men from the East begins with a sign in the skies and the guiding wisdom of pagan astrology; it ends with a Child of earth to whom they are led by both the star and the light of the Hebrew Scriptures. Whether Matthew intended it or not, later tradition has seen in the gifts the Magi bring a hint of the paschal mystery: the myrrh for embalming, the frankincense for fragrancing of sacrifices and burning before the Holy of Holies, the gold a fitting gift for a king.

Their human "dreams" fulfilled by their visit to the Child, God touches their spirit in a dream that warns them of Herod's hypocrisy so that they do not return to Jerusalem to tell him the "where" of Jesus, but return to their own country by another way.

When we place the Magi in our Christmas crib, they are usually dressed in opulent robes and have black, yellow, and brown faces. For the number or the physical appearance of the wise men we have no biblical evidence, but the truth that their visit declares, and the symbolism that their presence in the crib proclaims, is the gospel truth that Jesus is king for all the nations of the earth. This is what we pray for in the words of the responsorial Psalm 72: the establishment of God's kingdom of justice and peace throughout the world so that the rights of the poor and helpless are respected and the cries of the needy are answered.

In the story of the revelation of Jesus to the Magi, what is revealed to us about our own eagerness or reluctance to seek God? What is our own ability to listen to the Word of God, our own discernment of hypocrisy and hunger for power, in ourselves, our world, our church? What is our own attitude to strangers and our appreciation of their wisdom? Do we make the refugees and asylum seekers welcome in the parish or as neighbors, or do we regard them as a threat to jobs, property values, national security, our own comfortable and myopic spiritual wisdom? How do we respond to the young people who are searching for their own stars to guide them in their "where" and "when" of something more in their lives? Where and when must there be both a "birth" and a "death" in our Christian lives as we gaze on the Christmas Child and recognize the mystery of the adult Christ for adult Christians?

Gift-bearing strangers to Jerusalem also travel through the prophetic reading from Isaiah. The heart of sixth-century B.C.E. Jerusalem expands and throbs with joy, for she is called to be a witness to the glory of God that is shining upon her. Israel has endured the long night of exile, but now God comes to her and she rises up, exultant in the knowledge that she is no longer abandoned. Her sons and daughters, perhaps the second generations with little desire or resolve to return from Babylon, or those constrained to remain in exile after the time of the official return, are now coming back. But not only are they returning; with them come people from other nations bringing their wealth. Camels, gold, and incense flow into Jerusalem, but this exotic wealth is not only, or primarily, a tribute offered for Israel's prosperity and security. As with the Magi many centuries later, it is above all for the worship of God whose light and glory rises in the darkness and is recognized among the nations. Isaiah never had the privilege of gazing on the face of Christ or knowing the name of messiah, but his hope was large and passionate and joyful over the new birth of Jerusalem's glory, the resurrection of the city from the death of exile.

The Letter to the Ephesians proclaims "the mystery hidden for ages" from Isaiah and the generations before God's gracious revelation in Christ. The emphasis is again on the truth that, regardless of ethnic origin or social status, all people are called to be heirs of the same promises made in Christ Jesus. The biblical authors, be they Matthew, Isaiah, or the author of this Letter, never had small and narrow visions. What the readings announce at Epiphany is a large worldview and a church that in the intention of God is one and universal and in which all hostilities, exclusivism, and alienation have no place. We are still seekers and travelers who need the guidance of God to that place. We hope that we have enough dreamers among us who are determined to pursue this dream despite fears and hostilities, even within our churches. We are called to make more than a "courtesy call" to the Epiphany crib.

The Baptism of the Lord

First Sunday in Ordinary Time

• Isa 55:1-11 • Isa 12:2-6 • 1 John 5:1-9 • Mark 1:7-11

This Sunday is a "bridge" from the close of the Christmas season to Ordinary Time, and so is also called the First Sunday of Ordinary Time. The theme of revelation that was celebrated with the manifestation of the Christ Child to shepherds and wise men is continued with the baptism of the adult Jesus by John the Baptist. It is the realistic challenges of the Child grown to messianic adulthood that call us to the costly grace of discipleship.

John the Baptist is part of the stirring excitement of a new beginning of the Good News that Mark announces in the first verse of his gospel. He is the precursor, the one going before Jesus to prepare his way. But despite the crowds that are flocking to hear John and accept his baptism of repentance, the Baptist immediately focuses attention away from himself and onto the mightier one who "is coming after me." The distance between himself and this as yet unnamed coming one who will be *the* beginning, is emphasized by John's comparison of himself with a household slave well down the servile pecking order, and the only one who could be asked to perform the menial task of taking off his master's sandals. John also contrasts his baptism of repentance with that of the one he announces who will baptize "in the Holy

Spirit." The Old Testament backdrop to this drama may be Ezekiel 36:25-26, where the prophet promises the renewal of God's people by cleansing with water and putting a new spirit within them.

Mark also describes Jesus' arrival from the humble and unimportant village of Nazareth, in Galilee, in case anyone doesn't know it. Although he is without sin (cf. 2 Cor 5:21), Jesus puts himself in solidarity with the crowd and with sinful humanity. He bares his human body and at this, his first public appearance, chooses to go down into the waters of the Jordan to be baptized by John as a representative of our collective guilt. As he rises up, the heavens are torn open, and the action of God is manifested in the descent of the Spirit "in the form of" a dove and the voice addresses Jesus as "my Son, the Beloved, with whom I am well pleased." In the person of Jesus, this is the beginning of a new age, a new relationship of earth and heaven, of the whole of creation and our human condition. As Joel Marcus comments: "God has ripped the heavens apart irrevocably at Jesus' baptism, never to shut them again. Through this gracious gash in the universe, he has poured forth his Spirit into the earthly realm."[12] Here is the answer to the cry of the exiles to God: "Oh that you would tear open the heavens and come down!" (Isa 64:1). But there is no mountain quaking, no violent cosmic disturbances in this rending; it is a "gracious gash." The symbolism of "like a dove" is perhaps a memory of the spirit/wind of God that brooded birdlike over the face of the primeval waters at the first creation (Gen 1:2). It is also a witness to the gentle action of God that descends upon Jesus to empower him, like the prophets, with gentle service of the poor (e.g., Isa 42:1-5; 61:1) and our humanity that is impoverished by our sinfulness.

The word spoken by the Father at the baptism of Jesus is addressed to Jesus, not the Baptist or the crowd. The voice of God affirms Jesus as "my Son," with memories of Psalm 2:7, a royal coronation psalm, and then as "the Beloved" upon whom God's favor rests. In the humble setting of the Jordan River, a humble man from a humble Galilean village is baptized by the humble precursor and proclaimed by God as one with royal dignity. Three times in the testing of faith at Mount Moriah, Abraham refers to Isaac as his "beloved son" as Isaac and he face the sacrificial knife out of obedience to God (LXX Gen 22:2, 12, 16). The cost of Jesus' allegiance to his Father as yet hovers only as gently as a dove; in the not-too-distant future it is the carrion crow of death that will descend upon Jesus before he is unbound in the resurrection because of his obedient love of his Father.

This gospel is a declaration of who Jesus is to Mark's church, a statement of their self-understanding as disciples of the new messianic times who are sons and daughters of the Father because they are baptized into the Spirit-filled and Beloved Son, and commissioned to serve in his name. Throughout Mark's gospel, those who follow Jesus will struggle to understand and accept the implications of accepting one who is Son and Beloved, to understand what is revealed to Jesus as he rises from the waters: that humanity, despite its sinfulness, is loved with the prodigal love of God. The first human being in this gospel who professes faith in Jesus as the Son of God and recognizes the heavens torn open in the torn body of the Crucified is the Gentile centurion. We are caught up in this same struggle of faith. Baptism demanded everything of Jesus—as it does of us.

At the end of the Babylonian exile, Isaiah proclaims the word of God that calls the people to new faith and repentance. First, the people are invited to "come" to the water, the precious gift without which we cannot live. This water is a symbol of God's salvation that is offered freely and may be freely refused. So creative is God's word that it continually expresses itself in new ways. Like a street vendor, or like Lady Wisdom inviting the simple to enjoy the hospitality of her table, the next imperative is to "buy" and "eat" the nourishing gifts of God, and to "listen" for God's word as a source of rejuvenation and refreshment for the returning exiles. There will be times in our lives when we, too, will be "exiles" who need to return to God with the confidence that God will always take pity on us and forgive us. As we hear in the gospel, the water that receives Christ, the Word that affirms him, and the Spirit who descends on him, are the sources of our salvation to which we are invited to come, but that secret is not yet revealed to Isaiah.

For sixth-century B.C.E. Judah, God announces through the prophet, salvation will come not just from a physical return to Jerusalem, but through return to the homeland of their hearts where God has planted the covenant made with David and his house. God continues to do new things, for this covenant is now offered to all the nations through the witness of the people to the goodness of their nurturing and nourishing God. The last loving command, addressed to those whose hearts have not yet returned to God, is to "seek the Lord." This command is not punitive, but surprising in divine compassion and rich in forgiveness. With the imagery of falling rain and snow that water the earth to make the seed fruitful, Isaiah declares that God's word effects what it intends and gives a fruitful yield in the lives of those who listen to and obey it.

Our response to this reading is the joyful "song of the well," and is one of the "psalms" ("songs") found outside the Book of Psalms. In what seems to be a liturgical assembly, praise is offered for God's salvation that is compared to, but offers so much more than, life-giving water. In the future, which Isaiah of course cannot see, Jesus will become for us the fountain of salvation from which we will drink of the Spirit. In our Sunday assembly we are privileged to come and drink of this salvation from the deep wells of Word and sacrament, and praise God for these gifts. How joyfully do we respond? If someone wandered into our assembly, would they recognize that "great in your midst is the Holy One of Israel"?

The First Letter of John is by an anonymous author, sometimes referred to as "the elder," and probably writing in the tradition of and after the Gospel of John at the end of the first century c.e. In today's reading, the incarnate Son of God, Jesus Christ, is proclaimed as the hub of salvation. If we love God, it is through Jesus Christ who has shown us what love is; if we are claimed by God as sons and daughters, it is because of our obedience that is witnessed to us by Jesus Christ; if we are able to participate in eternal life, it is through the death and resurrection, the ultimate expression of Jesus Christ's love of God and humanity. This is our faith, to be expressed in active love and witness, which overcomes the aspects of the world that want nothing to do with God. The author stresses the importance of witness: the witness of the "water and blood." This is most probably an echo of John 19:34 where the blood flowing from the pierced side of the crucified Christ is mingled with water, a sign of the Spirit (John 7:38-39), providing a corrective to those who placed all the emphasis on water and Spirit at the baptism of Jesus as the key to understanding his salvific action.[13]

Faith and obedience, love that is willing to die to overcome death: this is made flesh among us in the witness of Jesus. These are the challenges for us to live as water-drenched people of God, baptized into Christ.

Notes

1. Normand Bonneau, *The Sunday Lectionary: Ritual Word, Paschal Shape* (Collegeville, MN: Liturgical Press, 1998) 111.

2. George Mackay Brown, "Poem for *Shelter*," in *The Collected Poems of George Mackay Brown*, ed. Archie Bevan and Brian Murray (London: John Murray Publishers, 2005) 152.

3. Daniel O'Leary, "Home's a Holy Place," *The Tablet*, 20 May 2006, 11.

4. Vatican II, Decree on the Apostolate of the Laity (*Apostolicam actuositatem*), art. 11.

5. Vatican II, Pastoral Constitution on the Church in the Modern World (*Gaudium et spes*), art. 32.

6. Irene Nowell, o.s.b., *Sing a New Song: The Psalms in the Sunday Lectionary* (Collegeville, MN: Liturgical Press, 1993) 10.

7. O'Leary, "Home's a Holy Place," 11.

8. Benedict XVI, Encyclical Letter *Deus Caritas Est*, 25 December 2005, art. 6.

9. For example, *The Book of Blessings: The Roman Ritual 1987* (New York: Catholic Book Publishing, 1990).

10. Carryl Houselander, "The Reed," in *The Mary Book* (London and New York: Sheed and Ward, 1950) 158.

11. T. S. Eliot, "Journey of the Magi," in *The Complete Poems and Plays* (London: Faber and Faber, 2004) 104.

12. Joel Marcus, *Mark 1–8*, The Anchor Bible 27 (New York: Doubleday, 2005) 165.

13. Cf. Raymond E. Brown, s.s., *An Introduction to the New Testament*, The Anchor Bible Reference Library (New York: Doubleday, 1997) 388.

3

The Season of Lent

If the drama of the liturgy is respected, when the catechumens who are to be baptized at Easter celebrate the Rite of Acceptance they are marked with the sign of the cross, not just on their foreheads, but on their heart, hands, and feet. It is as embodied men and women that we journey to God, and as Christians whose humanity is enveloped in our only boast, the Cross of Christ (cf. Gal 6:14), that we come to share his risen life. During this Rite the catechumens are also given a cross—not as a fancy piece of jewelry (one actress is reported to own four hundred cross accessories!), but as a reminder of the way they have started to walk in company with their crucified and risen Lord into whose death all disciples are baptized. To have the catechumens in our midst during Lent, on the last stage of their journey to baptism, is the most significant reminder for a community of the grace of our own baptism and the responsibility we have to continue our own journey of discipleship and witness to its joy.

On Ash Wednesday, we too are marked with the cross of ash as we begin our annual Lenten journey. It is a day that seems to draw more people than usual, a day when even those who are irregular church attenders seem to sense that they can line up without any feeling of unworthiness, presenting themselves (as the alternative ritual words announce) to: "Remember, O human one, that you are dust, and to dust you will return." With all the other Christians whose spirits are dusty and grimy, we affirm our shared need to "Repent and believe in the Good News/Gospel," and are marked with this identity.

We are familiar with ashes. On our TV screens they come into our homes on the agonizing faces of victims of war and terrorism against the backdrop of their burned-out buildings, and on the irreverent tongues of those who threaten violence that reduces hope to ashes. In contrast, on the faces of heroic firefighters and emergency workers, ash has new dignity, a humble witness to self-sacrifice and love of neighbor. Since the last Ash Wednesday, something has almost certainly and personally turned to "ash" for us: when illness struck, when a loved one died, when friendship was betrayed, when illusions about ourselves or others were destroyed . . . so much ash.

And yet ash is also fertile and protective. After a bushfire ravages the countryside, new life springs from cracked seeds and mulched branches; to keep the embers in the hearth warm until morning, there was an old Irish ritual of *grieshog*. The woman of the house would cover the last embers at night with a soft blanket of ash to keep them warm until morning when she would then brush away the ash and rekindle the fire with her breath.

Ash Wednesday calls us into the Lenten weeks of keeping warm the embers of our Christian discipleship through a renewed commitment to prayer, to fasting, and to almsgiving, so that the breath of the Easter Jesus may rekindle in us the fire of our baptism, and "Alleluia" may truly be our song of praise for what God has done, is doing, and will do for us in Christ. The Sundays of Lent retain their character of "Sundays," of commemorations of the resurrection of the Lord, and so the reminder that Lent is a preparation for the celebration of Easter is woven like a golden thread through the season's darker days.

In Year B, the Old Testament readings proclaim the roots of salvation history (that will flower at the reading of the Easter Vigil) as we listen to the accounts of the fidelity of Noah, Abraham, Moses, the surprising choice of Cyrus the Persian as an instrument of God's salvation, the promise of a new covenant, the Song of the Suffering Servant. Each week the second reading proclaims the paschal mystery of Christ and the significance of our baptism into this mystery to which we will again commit ourselves at the Easter Vigil. If there are adult candidates for Easter baptism, on the Third, Fourth, and Fifth Sundays of Lent the gospels of Year A (John 4, 9, 11) may be proclaimed as these are of major importance for Christian initiation.[1] On the First and Second Sundays, Mark's account of the wilderness temptation and the Transfiguration lead us into the passion and glory of this season.

First Sunday of Lent

• Gen 9:8-15 • Ps 25:4-9 • 1 Pet 3:18-22 • Mark 1:12-15

On the one hand, this Sunday's story of Noah has often been trivialized. It may recall images of wooden toys, school concerts of costumed animal performers, or animals parading graphically and gleefully across the pages of children's Bible picture books. On the other hand, we are also familiar with more meaningful, contemporary, and adult images of "the ark." The L'Arche

(French, "ark") communities founded by Jean Vanier are places of salvation for people with disabilities who might otherwise be swept away by the floods of social unconcern. In Thomas Keneally's book, *Schindler's Ark* (filmed under the title *Schindler's List*), he tells the story of Oscar Schindler, the hard-living German entrepreneur, who deliberately used all his entrepreneurial skills with the Nazis to obtain Jewish workers for his factory, the "ark," where he gave them as much protection as was possible in the shadow of Auschwitz.

The symbol story of Noah, probably based on the memory of some great flood, is a story about our promise-making God. Out of the deluge of human sinfulness that threatens to plunge the world back into primeval chaos, the God of steadfast love and kindness delivers the just man, Noah, his family, and the living creatures that were with him in the ark. Out of the waters God brings a new and liberated earth, washed with his mercy. God makes a cosmic, overarching promise to all humanity, to all generations, and to the whole of creation: never again will God destroy all flesh with water. As a reminder of this, God will set a multicolored bow in the sky. But the one who is to be reminded by this rainbow is *God*. In this context, remembering becomes a divine responsibility. God is imaged as the loving Divine Archer who hangs in the sky a bow that is not taut and targeted for destruction, but is unstrung and beautiful, joining heaven and earth with the radiant and elusive bridge of light of which the Book of Sirach says: "Look upon the rainbow and praise the One who made it" (Sir 43:11).

The universal Noahic covenant has radical consequences for our obedience to God, for our responsibility to the generations of all nations who are yet to be born, and for our ecological reverence for the earth. It is not about enclosing ourselves, metaphorically, in a safe floating box and sailing away, mindless of the suffering of humanity and the cosmos. Under the sign of the rainbow we are called this Lent to gather, to remember, to hope in God's promise and mercy, and to respond to this.

The First Letter of Peter sweeps us, with the speed of rising floodwaters, into the mystery of Christ and his saving death. Just as Noah and those with him were saved through their obedience to God, so Jesus passes obediently, safely, through the flood of pain and the storm of death into resurrection life. After three days, God's fidelity arches over Jesus' tomb, heaven and earth are joined, and all is made new and free in the Risen One. Likewise, proclaims this Letter, all who go into the flood of baptismal waters are saved for new life in and through the living "ark" of Christ. Because we share in the Christ-life, we too will also have to engage with the "powers and dominations" of our own personalities and society: the addictions, the seductions of consumerism, the violence we do to ourselves, to one another, and to our fragile planet.

Every year on the First Sunday of Lent, the gospel proclaimed is the wilderness temptation of Jesus. Mark's account is honed to three short verses following immediately and urgently after the baptism of Jesus. Jesus is "driven" into the wilderness, says Mark. We often describe people as "driven"—by ambition, lust, desperation—but what drives Jesus is the Holy Spirit. He is tossed into the physical and spiritual space where, before he begins his public ministry, before he proclaims one word of the Good News, he must struggle with two consequences of his baptism: his naming as Son of the Father and his solidarity with sinful humanity represented by the crowds on the Jordan's banks who were called by John to a baptism of repentance. Now there are no crowds; Jesus is alone with the Spirit of God and the spirit of evil, with the wild beasts and the angels, with communion and conflict, with the struggle—that will persist throughout his life and death—to be faithful Son. He is alone with the memory of his ancestors and their wilderness wandering in what for them was not only a place of God's revelation and promises, but also a place of their temptations and failures. Jesus will show himself to be the most faithful Israelite. The opposition between human sin and divine presence, between the "angelic" and the "beastly," were starkly exposed in Jesus' own psyche. And if we are honest and mindful, we know them in ourselves and in our own struggles to be faithful sons and daughters of our same Father.

The English artist Stanley Spencer (1891–1959) painted a "wilderness series" about the life of Christ. In one of these paintings he depicts Jesus sitting on the desert sands with a "wild beast." But the beast is not a roaring lion or a skulking tiger. In his cupped hands he holds a small but deadly scorpion. Jesus is no wraith-like ascetic, but very much a plump "flesh of our flesh" man. Spencer may be suggesting that the really dangerous beasts are those small ones that can slither insidiously into our lives; the persistent sins and small infidelities that, almost unnoticed, can inject a paralyzing venom into our discipleship. Alternatively, we might read Spencer's painting, and Mark's account, positively: as a vision of peace and harmony in a restored creation in the hands of the New Adam on whom angels wait in service. As with the Noah narrative, here again is a cosmic scenario, a prelude to (or perhaps a summary of) the vulnerability and conflicts that Jesus will face as "wild beasts" challenge him and finally crucify him, and as angels minister to him and announce his resurrection triumph over death and evil.

Jesus comes out from his wilderness experience strengthened for praise and pain and mission. The arrest of John the Baptist is the first storm that breaks over Mark's gospel, but over it rises a Galilean rainbow of hope as Jesus proclaims his first words: "The time is fulfilled, and the kingdom of God has come near, repent and believe in the good news." On Ash Wednesday, the last words of that proclamation were an alternative that was pronounced as we were signed as baptized disciples of the Tempted One, and called to Lenten mindfulness of the struggle between sin and grace, success and failure, into which we too are tossed.

The desert sand is not under our feet but in our hearts. Its grit is the daily irritations and indefinable loneliness we often feel. We need these Lenten weeks of heightened awareness of the importance of uncluttered spiritual and physical space where we can come to grips with our pain, where we can discover the beauty of God and our sisters and brothers under the surface sands of our busy lives, and where we can allow our ears to be "dug out" (Ps 40:6) by closer listening to the Word of God in our Sunday liturgy. We may then become much wiser about the spiritual baggage that we, as wilderness travelers, need to keep or discard in the trek toward Easter. That God may make known to us the way of love and truth, show us the right paths by which we may return when we have strayed, and make us humble and poor enough to accept the richness of divine mercy, is our prayerful response in the words of Psalm 25.

Second Sunday of Lent

• Gen 22:1-2, 9a, 10-13, 15-18 • Ps 116:10, 15-19 • Rom 8:31b-34 • Mark 9:2-10

This Sunday's readings center on two beloved sons of loving fathers: Isaac, child of the promise to Abraham and Sarah; and Jesus, the Beloved Son in whom the Father is well pleased. The binding of Isaac has become a paradigm of Jewish martyrdom, from the sacrifice of the mother of the Maccabees and her seven sons (2 Macc 7) to the murder of six million Jews, one million of them under the age of twelve, who were not delivered out of death during the Nazi years of 1933–45. In his book *Fear and Trembling* (1843), Kierkegaard described this narrative as a story about the faith that drives us to dread before the self is yielded to God. For its full dramatic impact, we should prepare for this portion by reading the whole narrative from Genesis 22:1-18 on which the Lectionary has used its "scissors."

Isaac is the child of destiny, the one on whom rested Abraham's and Sarah's hopes of descendants who would be as many as the stars of heaven and innumerable grains of sand. How can Abraham reconcile these bright promises of God with the dark command to sacrifice Isaac? Is Abraham . . . should Abraham be ready to jeopardize his own personal significance as "the father of many nations" by snuffing out the light and laughter of his life and lineage? And yet Abraham simply answers God with the prophetic, painful response: "Here I am." He is ready to trust, not in the promises made through Isaac, but *in the Promise Maker himself*, believing, as we all must when an incomprehensible disaster occurs, especially when we lose those who seem so necessary to our present and our future, that God has other ways of keeping his promises. "I kept my faith, even when I said, 'I am greatly afflicted,'" we respond with the words of Psalm 116. God takes the risk that Abraham will respond obediently; Abraham takes the risk that God will provide. Neither will fail each other.

Abraham takes up the most poignant weapons with which he is to fight his way into obedience to God: the wood with which he will make a fire for the burnt offering of his son, and the knife with which he will kill Isaac—and along with him, kill the hopes of his posterity. "My father," "My son," are the painful heartbeats of the climb up Mount Moriah. We like the end of the story: the sacrifice stayed, the ram substituted for Isaac. We would much prefer to have just the salvation and blessing part without the testing—but that is not God's way, then or now. It is well to remember that God did not want the sacrifice of Isaac or any other child (considered an abomination in Israel [cf. 2 Kgs 3:27]), and especially his own Son. What killed Jesus is what continues to crucify today: disregard for human life and human dignity, lust for power, materialism, violence. What gives life is faith and love. God wanted to know if he was the first in Abraham's life; God still wants to know this about us.

After this episode, the Genesis narrative has no more direct speech between God and Abraham. Like two old lovers whose faith in each other has survived so many crises, silence speaks most eloquently between them.

In the gospel, Mark recounts the climb of another Son up a mountain where he is transfigured—or perhaps "transformed" is the better word to use. It is six days after Jesus' first prediction of his passion followed by Peter's uncomprehending response, and Jesus' attempt to teach his disciples that true discipleship will mean suffering and death out of which new life will be born (Mark 8:27–9:1). So God provides a fleeting, encouraging glimpse of the outcome of Jesus' life and death. Jesus takes Peter, James, and John up a mountain, a place of privileged biblical revelation, to be alone with him and to attempt to give them some insight into the depths of the mystery veiled by his humanity. Here, "in the seclusion of the place and the security of the company, Jesus is able to be more fully himself."[2] These are the three disciples who will also go with Jesus into the Garden of Gethsemane where he will pray in the dust, his body wound into the agony of generations like a protruding root of the olive trees among which he lies. On the mountain it is very different. The presence of God erupts through Jesus' humanity, clothing him with its dazzling glory. Then two of his ancestors, Moses and Elijah, appear in conversation with him. They, too, are men who had experienced suffering, revelation, and transformation on the mountains of Sinai and Carmel (e.g., Exod 34:29-35; 1 Kgs 19:1-11). They are also representatives of the Mosaic Teaching/Law and prophets who will sustain him in the ordeal that is to come.

Before the glory, Peter panics and does what we so often do when confronted with the radically new and disturbing in our lives; he falls back into the security of the familiar. He suggests that they build three tents or booths, stay with the messianic expectation which, from their childhood, Jesus and the disciples had celebrated in the Jewish feast of Booths (or Tabernacles). A many-faceted feast, it had developed into a commemoration not only of the Hebrews' desert wanderings when they lived in fragile, temporary dwellings, but also of the dwelling of the *shekhinah*, the cloud of the Presence in the Jerusalem Temple. After the destruction of the first Temple, the feast became permeated with a longing for the coming of the messiah who would again raise up the fallen booth of David and repair its ruins (cf. Amos 9:11). That the messiah would come in the temple of Christ's body, ruined in passion and death and raised up in glory for the life of the world, was beyond the imagination of the disciples. Peter exclaims that: "Rabbi, it is good for us to be here"—but, comments Mark, Peter was speaking out of ignorance and fear. It is not good to be frozen in such a glorious moment, forgetful of the suffering that will lead to another high place and time of passion. Not only the three disciples who witnessed Jesus' transfiguration, but every disciple in every age has to learn that following Jesus is not about comfort and security but about daring to hammer the tent pegs of our lives into the mystery of Christ, with a readiness to strike camp and move on when he calls.

It is God, not Peter, who takes the initiative. The cloud of the divine Presence tents over the disciples, and in it the voice of the Father affirms that: "This is my Son, the Beloved. Listen to him." At Jesus' baptism the affirmation of Jesus' sonship was addressed to him alone, not to the crowds; now God speaks also to the disciples—and not only to those who are the characters in this narrative, but to all who must listen to him, who, like ourselves, will often hear but not understand, see but only recognize the surface reality of Jesus' mystery, and so thrash around in attempts to escape the demands of the One who is both Son of Man (Mark 8:31) and Son of God.

Then it is all over, and the disciples are left with "only Jesus," no longer transfigured. They themselves are still confused, and so Jesus orders them to tell no one of what they have experienced "until after the Son of Man had risen from the dead." It is obvious that they have not understood what has happened on the mountain, and so their telling would be both confused and confusing; the transfiguration is only a preview of the glory of Jesus to which he must go by the way of passion and death. To announce Jesus' glory without the cross would be both premature and theologically inadequate. Coming to terms with the scandal of this "Isaac" who is delivered out of death and given a glorious resurrected future will be a painful and slow climb.

In 1516–17 Raphael painted an extraordinary work, now in the Vatican Gallery, which he simply called *Transfiguration*. The upper section of the painting is of Jesus' transfiguration on the mountain; below is the healing of the epileptic boy. With his artistic and spiritual insight, Raphael, like the gospel writers, recognized both events as "transfigurations"; both are related. Baptized into the Transfigured One, we are called to lead transfiguring lives for the sake of our sisters and brothers, especially those who are suffering on the plain of our everyday life and encounters. It is to such a plain that Jesus and his disciples descend immediately after the gospel of the transfiguration, to the healing of the epileptic boy (Mark 9:14-29).

In the second reading from his Letter to the Romans, Paul says simply, yet with profound and unshakeable faith, that if God is with us, no one and nothing can be against us. This is a summary of Paul's deep conviction that he wishes to convey to his Roman communities. God's love for the Beloved Son surpasses even that of Abraham for Isaac, for God's Son is given up to death and is delivered only on its other side when he rises in glory. This death and deliverance was an outreach of love "for all of us," and again we have an echo of the Abrahamic story and Paul's earlier reference to the promises made to Abraham as the father of many nations, Jew and Gentile alike (Rom 4:16; Gen 17:4-6; 22:17-18). God has justified, has set the seal of approval on the life, passion, and death of Jesus Christ who now intercedes for us. And if he has died for us he will surely not condemn us.

In our doubting, our puzzlement over what "rising from the dead might mean," we need the faith of Abraham, of Paul, of Jesus himself. Our future may be surprising, will certainly involve suffering, but with profound trust in God who is "for us," nothing in the end will be against us. This is the Easter faith that sustains us and urges us as we travel through the weeks of Lent. The words of Oscar Romero to his Salvadoran people have a special relevance for all who are today threatened with violence or any other disfiguring threat: "This Lent, which we observe amid blood and sorrow, ought to presage a transfiguration of our people, a resurrection of our nation."[3]

Third Sunday of Lent

• Exod 20:1-17 • Ps 19:8-11 • 1 Cor 1:22-25 • John 2:13-25

The saying, "You keep the law and the law will keep you," is overturned in today's first reading of the Exodus version of the Ten Words—the Decalogue or Ten Commandments. Obedience to the commandments is a response to God's love that has already been shown to Israel by their liberation from slavery. Such obedience is not a kind of ethical trade-off: you do this and I'll do that. Rather, the commandments are for the sake of freedom from slavery: from the worship of false gods, including ourselves, and from distorted relationships with God and one another. The contemporary "gods" such as nationalism, racism, sexism, individualism, consumerism, militarism, and numerous addictions, attract slaves, not free worshipers. The God of the Decalogue is not domesticated, not a slogan or a formula, not to be manipulated as a patron of politics or projects. Likewise, communities who are obedient to the Decalogue are called to live as a grateful and liberated covenant people, bound together by their obedience to God. This is expressed in loving and just human relationships within the family and society, with the acceptance of clearly defined boundaries and an awareness of human limitations, including sin.

The responsorial Psalm 19 is part of a litany of praise to the Teaching/Law. The images are rich and evocative. The Law, the words of God, are light and truth for our guidance. They are more desirable to possess than gold, and as sweet to our heart as the honey oozing from the honeycomb is to our mouth. These words wait for the fullness of interpretation by Jesus, the Word.

On this Sunday we have the first of the three scrutinies for those who are preparing for Easter baptism, and from the time of St. Augustine (354–430) the Ten Commandments have been a significant aspect of catechesis. "These chosen ones open their hearts honestly to confess their failures and be forgiven," are the words of the concluding prayer of the scrutiny. If we are gathered with the elect for this rite we, the already baptized, are also called to scrutinize and cleanse the deep, personal sanctuary of our hearts during the days of Lent, and to worship "in spirit and truth," as Jesus tells the Samaritan woman in the alternative gospel from the Year A cycle (John 4:5-42).

A very different portrait to a healing and gentle Jesus is painted by John in today's gospel. We find it easy to admire—even if we do not imitate—the compassionate Jesus, but an angry Jesus armed with a corded whip, driving traders and moneychangers out of the Jerusalem Temple and upturning their tables, may shock us. This gospel does not actually use the word "angry," but Jesus' actions are played out against the backdrop of the "zeal" of Psalm 69:9, and the burning passion of the psalmist for God and the house of God, the Temple, that Mark places in the mouth of Jesus. This is the zeal that will consume Jesus in the hot noon of Calvary.

The cause of Jesus' anger is not so much the money exchange or animal trading in the outer court of the Temple. Foreign coinage that bore pagan or imperial images could not be accepted for the half-shekel tax for the up-keep of the Temple sanctuary, and so it had to be exchanged for acceptable Temple currency with which to pay this tax and also buy sacrificial animals. John writes that: "The Passover of the Jews was near," and so those flocking to Jerusalem to celebrate this feast from all over the Roman Empire needed to buy the animals required for participation in the Temple worship and the domestic rituals. They could do this most conveniently at the Temple. Jesus is not unaware of the need for the money exchange, nor so naïve as not to know that petty pilfering and profiteering can be involved in these transactions. Something much more radical is happening: the reclamation of the holy place from marketplace to his Father's house; from empty, atrophied ritual to living worship.

In the gospels we see Jesus angry in other situations also: when confronting the diseases that seize on human bodies, when little children are kept away from him, at the death of Lazarus. Jesus' mission is to reclaim creation from sin and death so that it may become "kingdom." By his "parable in action," Jesus momentarily terminates the Temple worship, reclaims it from chaos and commerce, and cleanses the privileged piece of creation that is his Father's house of prayer. No doubt a few hours later the tables were again in place, animals led back in, coins exchanged—with plenty to talk about!

Yet the disturbing Jesus does not disappear from the scene; he has more "table turning" to do. He stays to answer the criticism of his opponents who can see no further than the Temple built over forty-six years by human hands, or refuse to imagine or tolerate any alternatives to the religious practices and institutions that they consider faultless and unchangeable. In this Jesus stands in the line of the Hebrew prophets like Isaiah, Jeremiah, Hosea, and Amos, who angrily and zealously denounced triumphalism and absolutism in worship (e.g., Isa 58:6-9; Jer 7:4-7; Hos 6:6; Amos 5:21-24). Jesus, too, will suffer the fate of so many prophets before and after him: rejection, persecution, even death. Jesus dares to name himself as the new and living temple in which the divine presence dwells. Ultimately, the sanctuary of his body will be destroyed in his passion and death, only to be raised again in three days. It is only after these events that his disciples will remember and understand Jesus' words.

The contemporary church cannot consider itself beyond the reach of Jesus' whip or overturning hands. When church leaders connive with unjust and tyrannical civil leaders, when fundraising takes precedence over faith raising, when we refuse to tolerate or even imagine alternatives to religious practices and institutions (even when some of these are obviously in their death throes), when nostalgia for past liturgical practice resists the leading of the Holy Spirit into the future envisaged by Vatican II, then ecclesial "cleansing" is needed by prophets driven by that Spirit of Jesus. And like Jesus, these men and women may often be torn down and destroyed—but ultimately raised up by him. For us who are living stones in the Temple of Christ's Body, Lent is also a time for cleansing the deep personal sanctuary of our hearts, for driving out of our lives whatever clutters our discipleship, blocks our ears to the Word of God and the prophets, and distracts us from trading justly and lovingly with the gifts God has given us.

As Paul tells his church at Corinth, Jesus Christ crucified, devoured by his zeal for God even unto death, is a *skándalon* (Gk., "stumbling block") to Jews, and foolishness to Greeks who try to make sense of divine realities through human wisdom. Paul does not intend to dismiss reason and intellect. These are also gifts of God, but in the focus and context of this reading they are proclaimed as inadequate for understanding the wisdom and power of God that came among us in Jesus Christ, crucified and risen from the dead, and the ultimate witness to God's love for and involvement in humanity. The paradox of the Cross is a mystery that all disciples, and not only the Corinthians, find it hard to make sense of. But when we seek in faith and love to accept it, the Cross makes sense of us, and what may appear to be a stumbling block to our salvation by the crucified and risen One becomes a stepping-stone. Every Lent urges us and energizes us to continue this lifetime search.

Fourth Sunday of Lent

• 2 Chr 36:14-16, 19-23 • Ps 137:1-6 • Eph 2:4-10 • John 3:14-21

Today we hear one of the most well-known and best-loved verses in the whole of John's gospel, a verse that proclaims God "so loved the world that he gave his only Son, so that everyone who believes in him may not perish but may have eternal life." These words are spoken in the context of the night visit of Nicodemus to Jesus. Nicodemus, a Pharisee and Jewish leader and teacher, avoids the daylight that might reveal him as associating with a man who is unpopular with the religious institution, and so arouse suspicion of Nicodemus' own motives and stance. To be unafraid or unashamed of professing our friendship with Jesus by the way we live every day always brings hard demands. The German theologian Eugen Drewermann gives us a memorable image of ourselves when, in the words of the gospel, we "prefer darkness to light," to that light which is the only Son of God, given for its salvation to the world that God loves so much:

> . . . it can happen that we become like bats, like night-flying creatures who are so accustomed to the dark that our whole biorhythm is attuned to these shadowy periods, as if our eyes would be hurt and our whole lives would be turned inside out if we were dragged out of our caves and the hidden and fearful forms of our existence were exposed to the quiet regions of light and the brightness of day.[4]

But we often prefer the false safety of darkness to the light of Christ that exposes, for example, our selfish, racist, sexist, or violent selves. We all have our own caves that we need to name. Lent is designed to drag us out of their darkness into the Easter light of Christ through prayer, fasting, and the "almsgiving" of the gift of ourselves as well as the offer of material assistance to our sisters and brothers in many kinds of need.

To help the night visitor, Nicodemus, to come into the light of understanding something of his mystery and mission, Jesus uses a good catechetical approach: he talks the language of his listener. He reminds this "teacher of Israel" (John 3:10), who is very much in the dark, of a story from their own Hebrew Scriptures (Num 21:4-9). In the wilderness, the people grumble against God, and are struck with a plague of serpents whose bite could cause death. The people come to Moses, admit their sinfulness, and ask him to intercede for them with God. When he does so, God tells Moses to forge a bronze serpent, fix it and raise it up before those who are stricken. If they gaze on it they will be saved. This seems a great paradox: healing and life from gazing on a creature of death! But they obey and are healed.

In our humanity, we are all bitten by death; yet, Jesus tells Nicodemus, the God who is love wants to give us life that never ends. And so the flesh of the Son of Man will be brutally, senselessly twisted around the wood of the cross, will be forged by the fire of his passion and death and raised up for our salvation. In John's gospel, "raising" or "lifting up" always has the double sense of crucifixion and exaltation, death and resurrection, for the two movements are inseparable. To gaze with the eyes of faith on this mystery and commit ourselves to it will mean eternal life. Jesus does not come to judge, but just as turning on a light exposes what is hidden in darkness, so it is when the light of Christ shines upon us to expose both good and evil. The cross that will be raised up and venerated on Good Friday will give way at the Easter Vigil to the raised Easter Candle, marked with the cross of fragrant "nails" of incense, from which we catch fire and rekindle our baptismal commitment to the saving and universal love of Jesus Christ.

The reading from the Second Book of Chronicles describes the sixth-century B.C.E. darkness that had fallen over the Jewish people. The Temple was defiled, the prophets ridiculed, the word of God ignored, repentance rejected, and the people taken into the Babylonian exile. Whether all the historical details given by Chronicles are completely accurate is not the point. What is the focus is the good news of salvation that is embedded in the bad. The author announces that God's compassionate love for his people is steadfast; that a non-Jew, Cyrus the Persian, can be an unknowing instrument of God's salvation and allow the Jews to return from exile to their own land; that the rebuilding of the Temple is central to Jewish life and identity. But as we heard in last week's gospel, one day the destroyed and rebuilt Temple will be the Body of Christ into which we are baptized.

In his own way, the author of the Letter to the Ephesians repeats this Sunday's emphasis on the rich and merciful love of God that is shown us through the death and resurrection of Jesus. Three times it is stressed that it is only *with* Christ that we are brought to life, raised up, and given a place in heaven. The mystery beyond our imagining but accessible to our faith is that God sees and loves in us the image, the *eikōn*, of his Son. We must not deface the work of art that we are in Christ. What is called in this Ephesians reading the "immeasurable riches of God's grace in kindness towards us in Christ Jesus," makes us into a holy work of art. Lent is the time for the restoration of our priceless worth.

"How could we sing the Lord's song in a foreign land?" asks the psalmist in the responsorial Psalm 137. In the "foreign land" of much of our contemporary culture we might ask the same question. Often we may feel weak and vulnerable, fragile Christians whose discipleship can be so easily damaged. And yet, like the psalmist, we pledge ourselves to remember that God will not fail us. Over and above the psalmist's joyful trust, we have the assurance of God's steadfast love that, in the fullness of time, has been revealed to us in Jesus Christ.

Fifth Sunday of Lent

• Jer 31:31-34 • Ps 51:3-4, 12-15 • Heb 5:7-9 • John 12:20-33

A distinguished citizen once came to Nan-in, a Zen Master, seeking the meaning of life. The visitor began to tell Nan-in all about his own ideas, his achievements, his interests. As he continued his panegyric to himself, Nan-in graciously placed a beautiful cup in front of his guest and began filling it with tea. Even after the cup was filled, Nan-in continued to pour tea into it. The distinguished visitor quickly moved away from the overflowing cup, saying to

Nan-in, "The cup is overflowing! No more will go in!" Nan-in replied, "Like this cup, you are overflowing with your own opinions and achievements. How can I show you Zen unless you first empty your cup?"

The gospel of this Sunday proclaims the paradoxical wisdom of emptying in order to become full, of dying so that we may be raised to new life. This is the "hour" of radical obedience and exaltation for which, from Cana, through controversies, festivals, and miraculous signs, Jesus has been waiting: an hour that in today's gospel sees Jesus sought by new "first disciples," those beyond Israel, to whom the evangelist refers as "some Greeks." They were probably Greek-speaking Jews who had come up to Jerusalem to celebrate the Passover. They approach Andrew and Philip, two of Jesus' original disciples who are apparently approachable and good at bringing others to Jesus. (Remember Peter, Nathanael, and the boy with five barley loaves and two fish.) Although these seekers may have been Jews from far-flung places, John uses this episode on the threshold of Jesus' "hour" to suggest the call of the Gentiles. Many nations who eagerly seek Jesus will be drawn into his mystery when he is lifted up from the earth on a cross; all those who will belong to the church that is meant to be multiracial and multicultural.

To explain the meaning of his "hour," Jesus tells the parable of a grain of wheat. When it is dropped into the earth, the seed shrinks, "empties" itself, and dies. But in the warmth and moisture of the earth new life breaks out of the husk and bears much fruit. "Fruit" in John's gospel means "life," and the hour is at hand when Jesus will be buried in the heart of the earth and rise from there to transformed and transforming life.

The larger world beyond Israel now includes us. If we wish not only to see but also to follow Jesus, we must choose to empty ourselves of self-centeredness, of the instinct for self-preservation at the expense of our sisters and brothers. Those insulated from others' suffering, eager for good connections, popularity, and status, rather than finding and following Jesus, will lose their lives. From seeds buried in the warm love and service of others, and watered by fidelity to our baptismal commitment, the Christian community grows into the mystery of the death and resurrection of Jesus. This is not easy; it was painful for Jesus, and it is painful for us. Jesus' soul was troubled, we hear, but he embraces his hour of his own free will. He has already told the crowds that: "No one takes it (my life) from me; but I lay it down of my own accord. I have power to lay it down and power to take it up again; this charge I have received from my Father" (John 10:17-18). What Jesus has done, he proclaims, has always been for the glory of his Father, and he will die because of the way he lived. The Father's voice affirms Jesus' proclamation, declaring that Jesus is giving glory to God, and will be glorified because of this. It is a voice, says Jesus, that speaks not so much to reassure Jesus himself, but to bring faith and encouragement to the bystanders.

We are now the crowd assembled around Jesus. Do we understand his words or the Father's voice? Can we recognize his saving Cross at the epicenter of the tragedies that are born of sin, planted on the seismic fault lines that threaten to open and crack our world apart: the divides between rich and poor, peace and violence, north and south, east and west? Even more important, can we allow ourselves to be drawn to the exalted cross of Christ so that we ourselves may offer from the "right place" of the cross the fruit of healing reconciliation for the glory of God?

The reading from the prophet Jeremiah is taken from the two chapters that have been called "the little book of consolation" (Jer 30–31). At the beginning of the sixth century B.C.E., with the fall of Jerusalem and the exile of the southern kingdom of Judah into Babylon imminent, there seemed to be little with which to console the people. The northern kingdom had already collapsed; fear and despair seem to grip the people and empty them of hope, and they wonder if their promise-making God has deserted them. But Jeremiah assures them that "the days are surely coming" when God will pour new life into them. One day the kingdoms of the north and south will be reunited and again relate to God as one community because God will make with them, or "cut," a new covenant. There have been many previous covenants: with Noah, with Abraham, Isaac, and Jacob, with Moses at Sinai, with Joshua at Shechem. All were God's initiative; all came at times of crisis and transition for God's people, and are described in terms of intimate relationships. Like a parent leading a child "by the hand," God led the people out of Egypt; God was "a husband" to them, as close to the people as if they were his own flesh and blood.

Now, says Jeremiah, God will make a covenant with his people that will be even more intimate: a covenant that will be cut not onto tables of stone, but onto their "hearts"—the biblical way of describing the most profound depths of personal and communal existence and will (cf. Jer 29:13; Ezek 36:26). There God will inscribe the promise of divine fidelity: "I will be their God, and they shall be my people." Then the people will have a new capacity to respond faithfully to God "from the inside out." This will require conversion of heart to God, who alone can truly forgive and forget their sinfulness.

"The days are coming," too, for the Christian community as we move closer to Holy Week and the remembrance of the new covenant that was made in the hour of Jesus' suffering and death and his glorious transition to resurrection. The "interiority" Jeremiah announces attains its fullest meaning in Jesus who *is* the new covenant, and in the Eucharist shares with us his Body and Blood—his crucified and risen person—through which we are given the promise of eternal life and resurrection if we respond to his most intimate love.

The author of the Letter to the Hebrews warns us not to sanitize the sufferings of Jesus. "In the days of his flesh," in his humanity, Jesus experienced pain and disappointment. He knew what it was to be vulnerable and afraid, to be troubled in the depths of his soul, as today's gospel tells us. That Jesus' prayer was heard by God and yet he suffered, places Jesus in solidarity with his sisters and brothers whose experiences are the same. Nor was he exempt from continuing to discern throughout his life, even unto death, what it meant to be "Son," just as we must continue to discern what it means for us to be sons and daughters of God in the Son. That Jesus learned obedience through suffering makes him both our intercessor and our model.

The verses from the impassioned prayer of Psalm 51, today's responsorial psalm, is a prayer that lives close to our deepest hurts and most intimate groans. We may know very little about the prayer of Jesus but, as an observant Jew, he certainly prayed the psalms from the prayer book of his people, the Psalter. It is our privilege to pray for a new and cleansed heart in words that have been prayed not only by believing Jews and Christians for thousands of years, but also to pray in the words that ran daily through the heart and were on the lips of Jesus and shaped his fidelity to his Father.

Palm Sunday of the Lord's Passion

Procession Gospel

• Mark 11:1-10

Through the gate of palms we today enter into the Great and Holy Week of the church's year. In the gospel for the procession we remember Jesus as he rides into Jerusalem, but liturgical "remembering" does not mean the staging of a pageant. It is not an artificial or slavish reenactment of a first-century event, but an invitation to participate in the mystery of our salvation as a *present* reality, as people who have been baptized into Jesus' death and resurrection. In Mark's gospel, Jesus tells his disciples to bring to him a tethered colt (Gk., *polōs*) that no one has yet ridden. This Greek word can refer to the offspring of various animals, including donkeys and horses. Mark's background to this description is probably Zechariah's prophetic words addressed to a joyful Jerusalem: "Lo, your king comes to you; triumphant and victorious is he, humble and riding on a donkey, on a colt, the foal of a donkey" (Zech 9:9). Mark may also intend us to remember Solomon seated on a mule, riding down to Gihon to be anointed king (1 Kgs 1:32-33). Jesus will make his symbolic journey into Jerusalem not on a well-trained and muscular warhorse, but on a gentle animal, not yet broken in, that he tells two of his disciples to untether. The donkey is to be freed for its first service—carrying Jesus into Jerusalem.

Immediately before this event, Jesus has healed the blind beggar, Bartimaeus, who, when he rose up to come to Jesus, had flung away his cloak that served him as an outer garment, a shelter from the weather, and a begging bowl for a few meager offerings tossed to him (Mark 10:46-52). Perhaps many of the crowd that accompany Jesus from the Mount of Olives are like Bartimaeus: the poor, the sick, the outcasts who have been touched by him and who join the crowd of jubilant pilgrims coming up to Jerusalem for the feast of Passover. And in the procession, here we are. . . . Are the blind eyes of our hearts a little more open, our moral paralysis a little more healed, a few more of our personal and communal demons cast out, our applause for those who ride for peace, not charge into war, a little louder because of our prayer, fasting, and almsgiving during the weeks of Lent?

In his *Sermon on Prayer*, Andrew of Crete (ca. 660–740) encouraged his community in their following of Christ in the way of Palm Sunday:

> Come then, let us run with him as he presses on to his passion. . . . So it is ourselves that we must spread under Christ's feet, not coats or lifeless branches or shoots of trees, matter which wastes away and delights the eye for only a few brief hours. But we have clothed ourselves with Christ—"for as many of you as were baptized into Christ have put on Christ"—so let us spread ourselves like coats under his feet.[5]

The branches that we wave today will wither, our "Hosannas" will be silenced by our infidelity. What will last will be the palms of justice for the oppressed, of mercy for the sinner, of compassion for the wounded, of patience with the young, of companionship for the old, that we take not just in our hands, but wave vigorously by our lives; what will be an eternally blessed shout is the praise-filled life we live out of our baptismal commitment to a crucified and risen Christ.

The Mass

• Isa 50:4-7 • Ps 22:8-9, 17-20, 23-24 • Phil 2:6-11 • Mark 14:1–15:47

So significant are the four Suffering Servant Songs of Isaiah that they are read every year as part of the Holy Week Liturgy, culminating with the Fourth Song on Good Friday. Today the Third Song is proclaimed. The Servant is not identified, and has been variously suggested as Zion, the exiled people, a prophet, or someone present or future who will endure great suffering. By the use of this ancient sixth-century B.C.E. text on Palm Sunday, the church directs our hearts to the memory of the Servant for whom Isaiah hoped and whose sufferings became brutally realized in Jesus.

The Servant speaks in the first person, describing himself as a listener to and learner from the Lord God, to whom he is completely obedient. To aid and sustain the weary, God calls for a person and his words, not a revolution or an army. This proves to be a risky and unpopular vocation that earns the Servant much abuse. But God stands by his Servant because the Servant is unwavering in his trust in God, and uncomplaining even in the midst of suffering.

What exactly the Servant says, we are not told. The early church had heard Jesus proclaiming the Good News to the poor, had seen him comforting the weary, knew that he had been beaten and scorned in his passion and death. It recognized, therefore, that the Isaian Servant's words and identity had taken on a new and deeper meaning in Jesus the Servant who was vindicated by God because of his fidelity that endured to the end of his life—and beyond, into risen and eternal glory.

We respond to this reading with the lamentation of Psalm 22 that moves from an expression of agony to ecstasy, from despair to hope, and from the derision of enemies to the praise of God in the assembly of God's sons and daughters. In this psalm are several verses that the gospel writers quote in their passion narratives. When they searched for words with which to express the truth of Christ's passion, death, and resurrection, Psalm 22 was in their memory and seemed to express the Christian faith in both the darkness of his crucifixion and the light that overcame the darkness in his resurrection (e.g., Ps 22:7-9 and Matt 27:39; Ps 22:1 and Matt 27:46; Mark 15:34; Ps 22:18 and Mark 15:24).

It is generally agreed that Paul found the magnificent hymn to Christ circulating among some early Christian communities, probably written by an early Christian poet—perhaps one of the "poor ones," the *anawim*—and incorporated by Paul into his Letter to the Philippians. The first movement of the hymn is Christ's descent into our humanity as a loving and obedient Servant. The culmination of this descent is his obedience unto death. Far more than the Isaian Servant, Christ is the suffering Servant who is unconcerned about divine status and power, and so is vulnerable, "even (to) death on a cross." Jesus' humanity is the most definitive, the most understandable Word that God can speak, the Word that reveals God as self-giving love for humanity. Because of Christ's loving obedience, God raises him and places all creation in submission to him—not a submission of fear and triumphalism, but one of compassion and fidelity that can transform submission into solidarity for the Philippians who, like Paul, were suffering because of their belief in Christ (Phil 1:29-30). Obedient service of God and humble self-giving in relationship rather than selfish preoccupation will also raise us up. Charles Cousar comments that the Philippians were realistic:

> . . . (they) knew only too well that all knees had not yet bent in obeisance, nor had all lips confessed Jesus as Lord. They, like Jesus, were living in a violent world and were facing opposition without and tensions within. But liturgy shapes life and moulds experience. Sunday after Sunday, the congregation should rehearse the promise and by it be nurtured in its vocation in the world. Jesus' scandalous death, which also characterized both Paul's life and the readers' lives was not the end. The future was in the hands of the servant Lord.[6]

Jesus dies because of the way he lived, and throughout the passion narrative Mark lays bare the contradictions and gospel paradoxes of Jesus' life, especially in his relationships with other women and men. To focus on these relationships may help us to listen more attentively to and identify with the understandings and misunderstandings of Jesus in the days of his passion and death. Of all the gospel writers, it is Mark who most urgently draws the sharpest portrait of Jesus as a suffering Servant and Messiah. Very early in his gospel the shadow of the cross is cast by the simmering criticism and opposition of his enemies (Mark 2:6, 16, 24; 3:6). Now, still in the shadow of secrecy and two days before the feast of Passover, the chief priests and scribes plan to have Jesus arrested and killed.

On the threshold of his passion, Jesus dines at Bethany in the house of Simon the leper, presumably a man healed by Jesus. There he affirms the loving extravagance of an anonymous woman who intrudes on the dinner and wastes her love on him by anointing his head with costly ointment as a prophetic sign of his burial. Not only does she pour the precious nard over his head in a symbolic gesture of kingly anointing, she also breaks the jar in order to do this. Like the poor widow whom Jesus has just praised for giving both her coins, "all she had to live on" to the Temple tax (Mark 12:44), this woman also spends her precious possession on Jesus. In contrast to those who criticize her for wastefulness and seem suddenly to become concerned about the possibility of selling such costly ointment for the poor, Jesus praises the woman's loving extravagance, for he is facing the ultimate poverty of betrayal and death. Wherever the Gospel is preached, says Jesus, what this anonymous woman has done will be remembered and told as Good News. As a dark foil to the woman's love, Mark immediately afterward recounts that Judas Iscariot goes to the chief priests—not to waste money and love on Jesus, but to get money by betraying him. Where do we stand? With the woman or Judas, especially in our materialistic and self-centered society?

At the Last Supper table, the dish is passed, the morsel shared, and the treacherous question oozes out of Judas, out of his inner darkness: "Surely not I, Rabbi?" It is a question we must honestly and painfully dare to ask and answer ourselves. The bread is taken, blessed, broken, given by Jesus to his disciples to eat. The cup is poured out, given, and drunk by them. A new Passover is celebrated, a new exodus out of the slavery of sin is promised, a new covenant is sealed in Jesus' blood "for many" (cf. Exod 24:8). Jesus' body is about to be broken and his blood spilled, but he promises the disciples another festive meal to be celebrated after his resurrection in the kingdom of God. And this promise is made to these obtuse disciples, so fragile in their faith that they will all desert him in the breaking of his body and the flowing of his blood, and even to the one who will betray him to this ignominy.

Singing psalms, the disciples (with the exception of Judas, who has other work to do) accompany Jesus to Gethsemane. Even though Jesus speaks to them of their imminent desertion of him, at the same time he assures his failing disciples of his unfailing presence, assuring them that after he is raised up he will go before them into Galilee. Peter crows about his fidelity, and the other disciples join in with similar protestations. Like the disciples, how well, or how little do we know ourselves? Are we inclined to put our trust in our own opinions of ourselves or in Jesus who knows what is in us?

In the Garden, Jesus' body lies in the dust, crushed into the agony of generations there among the olive trees. The last time Jesus and his disciples were on the Mount of Olives Jesus had told the disciples to watch for the signs of disaster, of the destruction of the Temple, but also to realize that this suffering would be the birth pangs of the new. Now Peter, James, and John, who had just professed their fidelity, distance themselves from Jesus in sleep. Sorrowful unto death in the face of his coming passion, agonizing over his disciples who will fall not only into sleep but into desertion, Jesus is a man of lamentation, of fearful communion with and painful obedience to his "Abba, Father" as he accepts to drink the dregs of the world's sin. The traitor's kiss smacks the disciples awake. There is a little pitiful swordplay, and then they run away from Jesus.

Mark paints a small and unique detail of tragic discipleship into the Gethsemane landscape. After the flight of Peter, James, and John, a young man who has been following Jesus is also grabbed, as Jesus was, by the arresting gang. He, too, flees from the prospect of sharing Jesus' suffering, leaving his linen cloth in their hands and rushing away naked. For Mark, this is the tragedy of those who once left everything to follow Jesus (Mark 1:16-20), but now leave everything to run away from him. Nakedness is a symbol of nothingness, of degradation and misery. Spiritually, that is what a disciple of Jesus becomes by refusing to share his destiny.

Jesus stands before his religious opponents for his Jewish trial and hears false witness offered against him. Now that it is his "hour" he accepts the messianic sonship about which he had earlier commanded silence; now he can solemnly say "I AM" to the personal reality of a messiah who will be both suffering and glorious. Jesus speaks the truth, and his enemies regard it as blasphemy. Peter, the leader of those appointed "to be with him" (Mark 3:14), has ventured into the high priest's courtyard only to spider in a dark corner and trap himself in his web of lies. While Jesus is on trial inside the high priest's palace, Peter is put on an ignominious and tragic trial by a servant girl who accuses him with the truth. And the cock sentences Peter who had a few hours earlier crowed about his fidelity. What will save Peter is his remembrance of the words of Jesus and his own bitter tears. It is what will save us who are listening and watching on this Palm Sunday.

Physically abused, Jesus is handed over to Pilate for his Roman trial. Pilate wobbles spinelessly between the demands of the agitators in the crowd, the demands of Caesar's friendship, and his own conscience. Jesus will say only one other thing about himself. As with his acceptance of messiahship before the high priest, when Pilate asks if he is the King of the Jews, Jesus accepts this title—in its truth, and not in the political sense that Pilate means, for soon he will reign from a cross, and there will be the "scandal" of the relationship of suffering to kingdom and kingship. Jesus will say nothing more. Pilate compromises by handing over Barabbas to freedom and Jesus to crucifixion. Made a fool king by the soldiers who scourge and crown him and ironically proclaim him as King of the Jews, Jesus is then led away. What of the "Pilate" in all of us: the compromises, the surrender to social and peer pressures, the reluctance to fall out of favor with important people?

There is only one person who helps Jesus to carry his cross, and how willing Simon of Cyrene was to be "requisitioned" is debatable. Jesus is stripped naked, humiliated, and his garments divided among the crucifixion gang. Under the beat of hammers, iron and wood scream out an agonized duet. Jesus' cracking bones are the chorus of the hymn of the world's salvation. A torrent of abuse which, ironically, is the profession of the truth, sounds over the silent One: from passersby enjoying the spectacle and feeling vindicated in their judgment of this charlatan who spoke about the destruction of the Temple; from chief priests and scribes who are glad to see the man who saved others by his upsetting compassion unable to save himself; from two criminals in whose company Jesus, the friend of the marginalized and sinners, is not ashamed to die. Dare we admit that we sometimes feel "It serves them right" when we see someone suffering? Do we really believe that it is not by coming down from the cross, but by sharing it with Jesus, especially when we are emotionally or physically abused, that we will be raised up with him?

Jesus' agonizing passover into death proceeds relentlessly. At the third hour (about 9:00 a.m.), he is crucified. At the sixth hour, it is darkness, not strong noon light, that falls over the whole earth as witness to the cosmic tragedy of Jesus' crucifixion (cf. Amos 8:9). And at the ninth hour (3:00 p.m.) Mark puts on the parched lips of Jesus the first words of Psalm 22: "Eloi, Eloi, lama sabacthani?" "My God, my God, why have you forsaken me?" Mark keeps these words in the Aramaic mother tongue of Jesus, for on the threshold of their new birth the dying so often revert to the intimacy of the language they first learned in their childhood. This is not a cry of despair, for no one sends out his or her passionate voice to a God in whom they do not believe. Through familiarity with the great psalmic laments, the readers of Mark's gospel know that what seems to begin in despair is a struggle that ends in triumphant hope; that agony ends in ecstasy, and threatening death becomes in the end an affirmation of life.

Some of the bystanders mistake Jesus' cry as directed to Elijah, and one of them offers him an anesthetizing mixture of wine and myrrh. But, thirsting for the salvation of the world, Jesus screams his human way into death with a wordless cry. As his last breath is torn from his body, Mark speaks of the symbolic tearing apart of the Temple sanctuary veil. Now anyone can look into a new sanctuary; there is free access to God through the new temple of Jesus' ravaged body. At Jesus' baptism, early in Mark's gospel, we heard that the heavens were torn apart and the Spirit of God descended on Jesus as the voice of God declared Jesus as Beloved Son. Now it is the voice of the Gentile centurion who is the first to look beyond the ravaged body, the first in this gospel to give a human voice to the profession of faith in Jesus as Son of God. Standing directly in front of the crucified and dead body of this man, he faces the way that Jesus dies—and in it finds faith. He is the first of the nations for whom the death of Jesus has brought conversion and the reversal of the insults and cynicism of those who taunted Jesus; the first of both Jews and Gentiles who will be living stones built by faith into the temple of Christ's body. How aware are we of being living stones in this holy temple?

Mark's passion narrative ends on the note of brave friendship. No class of people, rich or poor, Jew or Gentile, is excluded from following Jesus. Joseph of Arimathea, a respected member of the Sanhedrin, cares nothing for the opinion of his fellow councilors. He does what Jesus' disciples fail to do: he associates himself with the Crucified One. At his brave request, he is granted the body of Jesus by Pilate; he folds the dead body of Jesus in linen sheets and hurriedly lays him for his Sabbath rest in a rock tomb. Of the women who had earlier been "at a distance," Mary Magdalene and Mary the mother of Joses now come closer and see where the body is laid. Is the tomb the end of the story? Is this the reality to which God has abandoned his Beloved Son? We know what they did not know: Easter is coming.

Notes

1. Reflections on these gospels are found in Verna A. Holyhead, *Welcoming the Word in Year A: Building on Rock* (Collegeville, MN: Liturgical Press, 2007).

2. Michael Casey, *Fully Human, Fully Divine: An Interactive Christology* (Mulgrave, Victoria: John Garratt Publishing, 2004) 194.

3. Oscar Romero, *The Violence of Love*, compiled and translated by James R. Brockman, s.j. (Farmington, PA: The Bruderhof Foundation, Inc., 2003) 210.

4. Eugene Drewermann, *Dying We Live: Meditations for Lent and Easter*, trans. Linda M. Maloney and John Drury (Maryknoll, NY: Orbis Books, 1994) 67.

5. Andrew of Crete, *Oratio 9 In ramos palmarum*, in the Office of Readings for Palm Sunday, *The Divine Office*, vol. 11 (Sydney: E. J. Dwyer, 1974) 255.

6. Walter Brueggemann and others, *Texts for Preaching: A Lectionary Commentary Based on the NRSV Year B* (Louisville, KY: Westminster John Knox Press, 1993) 246.

4

The Season of Easter

The Easter Triduum

For forty days we have been carried in the womb of the Lenten church; now the time of new birth is upon us. And like all birth it is an extraordinary event of both intense pain and ecstatic joy. When we go to the Evening Mass of the Lord's Supper on Thursday evening, we begin the three-day (Triduum) feast of the celebration of Christ's Passover from death to life, a mystery of blood and breaking waters through which, every year, we are reborn more deeply into his mystery. One day is not enough for the celebration of this awe-inspiring mystery of the passover of Jesus from death to life, and our passover with him. For this we need three days—and then the seven weeks that follow them. And every Sunday of every week is the Lord's Day, a memorial of Easter that is to every week what the season of Easter is to the whole liturgical year.

These days of the Triduum—from Holy Thursday evening to Easter Sunday evening—are days when we do things that we do at no other time in the Christian assembly: wash feet, kiss wood, light fires, splash water. They are days of both treachery and euphoria, light and darkness; days of the smell of fragrant oils and our own humanity; days when the love of God for this fragile and wounded humanity is revealed in its extraordinary depth in the ordinariness of broken bread and poured wine, and the poverty and riches of a cross and empty tomb.

Holy Thursday

Evening Mass of the Lord's Supper

• Exod 12:1-8, 11-14 • Ps 116:12-13, 15-18 • 1 Cor 11:23-26 • John 13:1-15

In *Ah, But Your Land Is Beautiful!* set in the apartheid era, Alan Paton tells the story of the relationship between Reverend Isaiah Buti, the black pastor of the Holy Church of Zion, and Judge Jan Christiaan Olivier, the Afrikaaner who is the Acting Chief Justice of South Africa. The pastor asks Olivier if, as a witness to the possible and positive relationships between black and white South Africans to which they are both committed, he would come to Buti's all-black church on Holy Thursday night and participate in the washing of the feet of his parishioners. Mr. Buti tells Olivier that he will call the judge up to wash the feet of Martha Fortuin, who was a servant in Olivier's house when his children were young. Olivier agrees readily, saying: "She washed the feet of all my children. Why should I hesitate to wash her feet?" but says he will do it as a free and private person, as he cannot parade himself as a judge. On Holy Thursday night he wrapped a towel around himself, took a bowl of water, and knelt at the feet of Martha Fortuin. Not only did he wash both her feet; he took in his hands those feet that were worn and calloused with much serving, and gently kissed them. Then Martha and all the Holy Church of Zion in that place wept. But a young and ambitious reporter had, by chance, seen the judge drive up and enter the church, and followed him. His "story of the year" broke in newspapers the next morning, and Judge Jan Christiaan Olivier, like Christ, faced his passion and the wrath of the white supporters of apartheid and the ruin of his legal career.[1]

On this night when we remember the institution of the Eucharist the gospel chosen is not from one of the Synoptics that describes the words of institution; it is left to Paul in the second reading to hand on that tradition. In her wisdom, the church proclaims John's good news of the washing of the feet. It is a gospel that offers a radical challenge to the conventional ideas of leadership, a summary "parable in action" of Jesus' life of humble service that was a reproach to those who lusted after status, feared any religious or social change that would threaten this, and disregarded human dignity and equality, be it in first-century Palestine, twentieth-century South Africa, or in our own twenty-first-century social and ecclesial contexts. Not only is the foot washing a summary of his life of service, it is also a dramatic commentary on his death to which he goes forth from the supper room.

On this night, "the hour" is dawning, the hour when Jesus will show those whom he loved in the world how he will love them to the end. He begins to dispossess himself: tonight of his garments, tomorrow of his life. Tonight he himself lays aside his own garments, tomorrow his clothing will be ripped from him by others. Wrapping a servant's towel around himself, Jesus puts on a visible sign of his love; tomorrow, naked on the cross, he will be wrapped in nothing but his own blood. He is the Good Shepherd who earlier had said: "For this reason the Father loves me, because I lay down my life in order to take it up again" (John 10:17). In his hands, Jesus takes the holy vessels—a bowl of water and his disciples' dusty, soiled feet. These are the simple, human symbols of "all things" (v. 3) that the Father has put into Jesus' hands. Authority is about to be redefined in a new "transfiguration"— not dazzling on the mountaintop, but humbly on the floor, in terms of towel and basin and feet.

Jesus begins to wash his disciples' feet without any discrimination. Judas is there. He is not passed by; the community of disciples is never an elite gathering of the perfect. Peter protests about Jesus washing his feet. Does he suspect that a Master who gets down on his knees on the floor as a humble servant will expect the same of him? Would Peter be happier, safer, more in control if he was washing Jesus' feet? Then warned that the unwashed, those who do not accept Jesus as a servant, who prefer a different kind of saving messiah, will have no part with Jesus, Peter becomes typically, wildly enthusiastic about the washing of his hands and head as well. Jesus patiently explains to him that it is the quality of the relationship with the Servant Jesus, not the quantity, that makes a true disciple.

After the foot washing, Jesus puts on his clothes again and returns to the table to challenge his disciples about their understanding of what he has done. He reminds them that they rightly call him "Teacher and Lord," but he has just given them a subversive example of Lordship where there is a reversal of the servant and served status; a service that includes, as Jesus knows, both the struggling faithful and the blatantly betraying. "If I, your Lord and Teacher have washed your feet, you also ought to wash one another's feet," Jesus says. Jesus passes over to his disciples the command to do as he does. Their loving service is to be nondiscriminate and inclusive, a ministry to both those they consider faithful and those they think are unfaithful. Blessed by the loving service of Jesus, they are now called to be given, broken, consumed in the service of one another. This is communion; this is what Eucharist is all about; this is why the church chooses this gospel tonight. The way out of this room leads to Gethsemane and Golgotha, to the self-giving, the breaking, the consuming of the Servant in passion and death, and the affirmation of his love by the Father when Jesus passes over into his resurrection.

The reading from the Book of Exodus proclaims the significance of the Jewish people's annual remembrance of the first passing of the angel of death over the Hebrew homes that were marked with the blood of the lamb, and the consequent exodus of the Hebrews from slavery in Egypt to freedom. The Jewish people become a community of memory through the ritual Passover meal they eat together, the central focus of which was the sacrificed lamb.[2] At the first Passover, the meal was eaten quickly, travel clothes were the order of the night, and a traveler's staff was in their hands to help them on their urgent flight from Pharaoh in obedience to God who acts on behalf of the poor and oppressed.

Probably the ritual marking of doorposts originated in a nomadic ritual when herders were moving their flocks from winter pastures to places of spring grazing. Great care had to be taken of the young lambs and, for the sake of the whole flock's safety, a choice lamb was killed and its blood smeared on the tents to ward off any evil power. Just as liturgy continues to do, rituals are replanted in new contexts and take on a new significance. The marking of blood becomes a sign of God's protective love; the evil power is Pharaoh; Hebrews leave the political "winter" of slavery in Egypt for the "springtime" of wilderness freedom. Every year this liturgy makes of the past event a present reality—where the Jewish people affirm both their identity as God's saved and covenanted people gathered around the family table, and God's identity as their liberator who binds them to one another and to God. At the table, through ritual words and actions, the past is remembered into the present for the sake of their shared future. Our Eucharist is also a memorial that makes present the Passover of Jesus from death to resurrection, so freeing us from the slavery of sin and enabling us to pass with and through him into God's covenant love.

We respond to the Exodus reading with verses from the responsorial Psalm 116 and the repeated refrain from 1 Corinthians 10:16. This provides us with a bridge by which we pass from a "toast" to the joy of salvation, that may have been expressed by the offering of a libation poured out in the Temple, to the reading from Paul's First Letter to the Corinthians, one of the earliest traditions of the institution of the Eucharist. Psalm 116 is one of the psalms (Pss 113–118) that was sung as part of the Passover observance, possibly when the fourth and last cup was drunk. The one who offers thanks to God names himself or herself as God's servant who is bound to God by vows, promises made and promises to be kept. James L. Mays comments: "The psalm becomes the voice of Jesus and the congregation, the one providing the cup and sacrifice, the other united by them with him in his death and resurrection."[3]

Paul calls the communion cup "the cup of blessing that we bless." Through his death, Jesus drained the cup of the world's sinfulness to its dregs and his body was broken in death, but because of his absolute obedience to God he is raised out of that death to eternal life. Passover becomes Eucharist, "I" becomes "we." Those who eat the broken bread and share the cup of the new covenant become the Body of Christ in the present, called to proclaim his death and go forth to live this self-giving for one another until Jesus comes again at the parousia.

With the psalmist we might ask ourselves how we can make a return to God for all this love—we who are so self-centered and yet so often lonely;

so bent on success and yet so often failing; so eager for love and yet so often refusing it? It is only possible, as we proclaim at the end of every eucharistic prayer, in Christ, and through Christ, and with Christ, who witnesses to us the gospel paradox of eternal life and love that comes out of passion and death.

Good Friday

Celebration of the Lord's Passion

• Isa 52:13–53:12 • Ps 31:2, 6, 12-13, 15-17, 25 • Heb 4:14-16; 5:7-9 • John 18:1–19:42

This is the day of the hard baking and the brittle breaking, the crushing and outpouring of the body and blood of the crucified Servant, the day that is made "Good" for us because of his sacrifice. The first reading, the Fourth Suffering Servant Song, gathers us with the sixth-century B.C.E. bystanders as they gaze on the humiliated and disfigured one who is exalted in their midst. They are amazed that God has revealed his power toward his Servant not by saving him from his sufferings but in his sufferings. Nowhere else in the Old Testament is it so clearly proclaimed that God's strength is revealed in weakness. The bystanders realize that this truth is their salvation as, with a sense of poignant and painful wonder, the narrator confesses both the innocence of the Servant and the guilt of those who not only disregarded the sufferings of the man of sorrows but also shunned him because of them. This wounded healer is repulsive and yet fascinating, one from whom people hide their faces yet cannot resist a look at him. The painful, prophetic insight is that this dehumanized one is wounded and humiliated for the sake of others; that the people may shun the Servant, but the loving and innocent Servant embraces their sufferings and absorbs their sins so that they may find peace and healing. This is what it means to be vulnerable—without aggressive violence, without revolutionary protest, like a lamb being led to slaughter. Because of this, what God promised in the first verse of the song, the prosperity of the Servant (53:13), will now be kept. What the Servant has surrendered—reputation, friendship, his very life—God will return to him abundantly in a long life, many heirs, and his peaceful exaltation over his enemies.

As the Christian community, under the guidance of the Spirit, sought for words with which to proclaim the paradox of a crucified and risen Messiah, they could find no more appropriate language than this Fourth Suffering Servant Song, and no more appropriate day on which to proclaim this Song than on Good Friday when we are faced with our own discernment of the raw mystery of the crucified and exalted One.

After this reading we break our amazed silence with Psalm 31, a psalm of the suffering person's enduring trust in God to intervene against the wicked who threaten the just and discarded one. In Luke's passion narrative (Year C), the evangelist can do no better than to express the hope of the dying Jesus with a verse from this psalm that he puts on his lips as Jesus' last human prayer to his Father: ". . . into your hands I commend my spirit" (Luke 23:46; Ps 31:5). It is this Lukan verse that is our repeated refrain to the responsorial psalm. As servants of God, baptized into the death and resurrection of Jesus, we too are called to commit into God's hands all our "times," our life and our death, and find in God the love, courage, and hope we need.

The reading from the Letter to the Hebrews proclaims Jesus as the high priest who, though he has been exalted to the highest heaven, is able to intercede for us with incomparable efficacy because in his humanity he was completely one with our human condition. In the Synoptic wilderness accounts, Jesus is shown to withstand the temptations to be a very different kind of messiah, and these are the temptations he would face throughout his whole life, and even in his passion and death. "Although he was Son," although he was personally without sin, "in the days of his flesh" Jesus suffered the torments of body and soul as he experienced the depths of human vulnerability and limitations. He cried out to his God with the passionate and agonizing entreaty that characterize Jewish and psalmic prayer such as we have just prayed in the responsorial psalm. For his unqualified obedience, his prayerful trust in his Father, Jesus is exalted and made the source of our eternal salvation. This is the constantly recurring faith of all the New Testament writers, no matter how they may choose to announce this Good News and with what different portraits and metaphors. Today we have the confession of Jesus as the high priest who has entered the heavenly sanctuary, but this exaltation does not make him distant from us; nailed to the altar of the cross, it makes him the unique and quintessential mediator for humanity before the throne of grace.

Now we are prepared to listen to the most solemn proclamation of the Word of God in the passion narrative of John. In this gospel it is as if the eyes of the church are piercing, almost impatiently, the darkness of crucifixion in order to glimpse the mystery that John announced in his Prologue: the glory of the Word who became flesh and dwelt among us to show us "the glory as of a father's only son, full of grace and truth" (John 1:14)—the "I AM" who is infinitely more than water, bread, light, death, and life for those who have eyes to see. And those who do see will pass over with the Son into the intimate love the Father has for his only Son "who is close to the Father's heart" (John 1:18).

From the garden of the arrest to the garden of royal burial, the Johannine Jesus is not one to be subservient to his enemies nor domesticated by our memory. In John's portrait of Jesus, the darkness of suffering is there, but just as in the traditional painting of holy icons the dark colors are scratched away by the artist to reveal the foundational gold layer, so John reveals the burnished gold of Jesus' passion, and studs his cross with the truth of his victory that found expression in the "jeweled" cross, corpus-free, of the early centuries of the church's art and literature. "The light shines in the darkness, and the darkness did not overcome it" (John 1:5). So today we more appropriately venerate a bare cross and recognize the strong Christian insight of that powerful eighth-century Old English poem "The Dream of the Rood" (in Old English "rood" means "cross"), the vision of the cross as "the glory tree":

> Stained and marred,
> stricken with shame, I saw the glory tree
> shine out gaily, sheathed in yellow
> decorous gold; and gemstones made
> for their Maker's Tree a right mail-coat.[4]

As Jesus' passion begins in Gethsemane, there is no identifying and treacherous kiss. At his own initiative he goes forward to meet the arresting troop. He announces himself as the "I AM (he)" to their unwilling and prostrating confusion. Yet Jesus uses the power of the divine name not for his own protection, but for his disciples. "No one," he has already said, "will snatch them out of my hand" (John 10:28b). The parade of the people of the passion has begun, and perhaps one way of focusing on this long gospel is to reflect on what these people represent—to us and in us—as they move on and off the stage of this tragic and yet triumphant drama.

Jesus is bundled away to his Jewish trials before Annas, the father-in-law of Caiaphas, the high priest, and then Caiaphas himself. These men are the self-confident upholders of law, frozen in objectivity that they maintain is responsible, humane, and incorruptible. Yet they are entrenched in nepotism, in cultivating opportunist political relations with the occupying forces. It was Caiaphas who pronounced his belief that it is better for one person to die for the sake of damage control than for a whole nation to perish (cf. John 11:49). Ironically, he did not realize the deepest truth of what he said. Such people are still with us, in church and society—and often they are still within us.

Jesus is on trial inside and Peter goes on trial outside in the courtyard of Caiaphas, the high priest. Huddled by a charcoal fire and cornered with Jesus' enemies, his heart is frozen with fear. While a dignified Jesus has been sent bound by Annas to Caiaphas, Peter is undergoing an undignified trial by a servant of the high priest who accuses him of being one of Jesus' disciples. On Peter's repeated denial, the cock's crow passes a guilty verdict at the dawn of the darkest day of Peter's life. Who among us has not blustered, excused ourselves, betrayed something of precious friendship, and suffered the consequent agony of disillusionment with ourselves? In John's passion narrative there is no Jesus who passes by Peter, no account of Peter's tears and remorse at what he has done. That must wait until after the resurrection (cf. John 21:9-22).

Then Jesus is parceled off to Pilate, and we meet the functionary, the bureaucrat, who wobbles his spineless way through life not interested in truth, because if you believe nothing you can do anything with the power you are given to administer, and go to any lengths to safeguard that power. Pilate, the would-be neutral man, becomes a victim of his own compromise, and falls into the ignominy of listening to the clamor of the crowd and bargaining for the release of either Jesus or Barabbas. When that fails, Pilate makes a last bid for his conscience. He will make fools of "the Jews" in the person of one of them. Perhaps they will be moved by the sight of this broken man, or at least realize that he should not be taken seriously and so forget the whole unfortunate incident. Pilate has Jesus dressed in purple for scourging, crowning, and clowning. What is meant as mockery should be recognized by John's community, and by all Christian communities, as a prophetic proclamation of Jesus as the true king of both Jews and Gentiles. Pilate then brings Jesus forth, and summoned by the words "Here is the man!" we behold the heights and the depths of our human potential for good or evil. It is Pilate's last attempt to free himself from the web of guilt his own compromise has spun, but he is trapped in fear of losing favor with Caesar, the old deranged emperor Tiberias, who brooded in Capri over the slightest suspicion of treason. Before the threat of the loss of self-advancement to "friend of Caesar," the privilege of Roman senators, the lower equestrian-ranked Pilate surrenders Jesus to judgment. The tragic drama of reality and illusion is summarized in the cry, "We have no king but Caesar!" It is echoed in those who refuse to recognize their King, and all of us have probably been tempted at some time by whispers of such betrayal. Pilate's denial of his own conscience, and his lust for ingratiating himself with imperial and religious leadership, can also haunt us.

John's gospel differs from the Synoptic accounts by weaving into the passion narrative the thread of the Lamb of God motif, the name by which the Baptist first pointed out Jesus to his first disciples (John 1:29). As Jesus is handed over for crucifixion it is the Day of Preparation for Passover, the day on which, at about three o'clock in the afternoon, the minor priests in the

Temple would ritually slaughter the Passover lambs for eating after sunset at the paschal supper. It will be at this hour, says John, that the true Lamb of God will be slaughtered.

Self-possessed and undefeated, carrying his own cross unaided, Jesus advances purposefully toward the accomplishment of his Passover. On the cross Pilate puts the inscription that ironically names the One who had put him on trial: "Jesus of Nazareth, King of the Jews." Written in Hebrew (the language of Jesus' own people), Latin (the language of Roman governance), and Greek (the language of trade and commerce), what Pilate intended as no more than a salve to his conscience becomes a proclamation of Jesus' universal kingship for all future believers. At Golgotha, Jesus is raised up as king upon the throne of his cross. He takes his painful place of honor between the "two others" whom John names neither as criminals nor insurgents; they are simply two shadows who wait in anonymous attendance upon the One who reigns and judges from the cross.

Then comes the radical dispossession of the man who, like the buried grain of wheat that surrenders everything to the earth, now surrenders everything so that new life may come forth. Dispossessed of his clothing by the soldiers, Jesus begins to give away all that is most precious to him. With the painful breath of the dying, Jesus speaks to the woman and man who are his ideal disciples. In the Fourth Gospel, these two are never given their family or personal names; they are always described in terms of their relationship with Jesus: as "mother," or the "disciple whom Jesus loved." It is the hour of patient pain and separation that, by gospel paradox, will become the hour of new communion as this woman and man are given to each other by their dying son and master. Here is the model for the Johannine church and for every Christian community: disciples called by the naked and crucified Jesus, given to and welcoming one another as gifts of Jesus under the shadow of an exalted cross; faithful followers who are the folds of the robe of flesh with which Christ continues to clothe himself until the whole Christ is formed at the end of human history.[5] After this dispossession, "Jesus knew that it was all now finished," but there is one final obedience for which he thirsts. At the cry, "I thirst," there is the typical Johannine misunderstanding from those who do not believe, and soldiers offer Jesus cheap sour wine, holding it on a sprig of hyssop to his lips. Once again John evokes the "Lamb of God" memory, for it was with the fern-like hyssop that Exodus 12:22 describes the sprinkling of the doorposts of the Hebrews on the night of their feast of freedom. Having drained the cup of suffering, Jesus dies—not with the loud cry of the other gospel narratives, but with the quiet triumph of one who has accomplished that for which he came into the world. In his death, Easter is already on Golgotha. Jesus hands over his spirit/breath that will animate the new creation; his expiration is our inspiration.

In this narrative there are no other cosmic signs. The signs are all in the body of the Crucified One, the new Temple. No bones of this Paschal Lamb are broken, but when his side is lanced the last drops of mingled blood and water flow out (cf. John 19:34). Breath, water, blood: all are given for safe-keeping to his church, newborn from his pierced side, to be offered to us in the holy hospitality of baptism and Eucharist and the love of the Spirit that binds us together with each other and with Jesus.

The firstfruits of the death of Jesus are harvested as two disciples, Joseph of Arimathea and Nicodemus, come out of doubt and darkness to carry off his holy seed of flesh in an expensive cortege, fit for a king, and lay him in the heart of earth. There, in the most ancient mothering arms of death, Jesus awaits the new embrace of resurrection.

We go up to touch the cross's mystery, to feel the wood and recognize that our lives are grafted onto it for fruiting into resurrection: adults walking independently; parents carrying their children on their shoulder or leading them by the hand to this mystery, and wondering, perhaps, how it will be lived in their lives in the years to come; young people, glad of the activity; the frail aged and those with disabilities heading with determination toward what they are so familiar with; rich and poor, weak and strong—all are embraced in the outstretched arms of the Crucified and Risen One. This is "Good" Friday; this is Easter Triduum; this is our Easter faith.

Today the church is even dispossessed of the eucharistic action and we receive the bread that was consecrated at last evening's Mass. We leave the church in silence to move into our own Day of Preparation for the night of nights, the preparation that will allow Jesus to burst forth from the tomb of our hearts—a day that, as Karl Rahner writes, will, in one sense, continue until the day of the cosmic Easter:

> And this day takes place beneath the freedom of our faith. It is taking place as an event of living faith that draws us into the colossal eruption of all earthly reality into its own glorification, the splendid transfiguration that has already begun with the resurrection of Christ.[6]

The Easter Vigil

• Gen 1:1–2:2 • Gen 22:1-18 • Exod 14:15–15:1 • Isa 54:5-14 • Isa 55:1-11 • Bar 3:9-15, 32–4:4 • Ezek 36:16-17a, 18-28 • Rom 6:3-11 • Mark 16:1-7

This is the night of fire and water, of story and song, of bells and lights, of images that we need because it is so difficult to surface the right words to express its deep and overwhelming mystery. The moon above us is newly full. Casting off the sophistication of artificial lighting, we gather like our ancient forefathers and foremothers around the pile of dry wood and fallen twigs, and light it (preferably) with fire struck from the dead material of flint. We rob the lighting of the Easter fire of much of its symbolism when we reduce this moment of liturgical drama to a flick of a match, and the time of its lighting to before the people gather around the wood.

In the spark that springs from the stone tonight, the wonder of fire that eons ago brought warmth and light to a frozen people blazes out—but tonight it is the symbol of the light of Christ that warms our frozen hearts and transforms the darkness of our lives with the faith that death and the grave will never finally extinguish the living spark of our humanity.

Our song accompanies the flame and names the mystery: "Christ our Light!" "Thanks be to God!" Lest we forget the unbreakable bond between crucifixion and resurrection, the presider traces a cross on the paschal candle; but tonight it is pierced with five fragrant "nails" of incense. The current year and the Alpha and Omega are also traced on it, a reminder that for this year, as for every year, Christ is the Beginning and the End of our lives. Then we stumble, or push (just a little) our way into the dark womb of the church to exult in the Light of the world. Around the self-consuming pillar of fire we listen to the stories, the same stories year after year, of our family history that affirm our identity and enable us to remember again the inheritance that has been handed down to us from the First Adam to the Second Adam. If we are privileged to listen to these stories in the presence of those about to be baptized, about to join us in this family history, there will be added joy and significance in our listening.

In the first reading from Genesis, the Word of God broods over the primeval chaos and new life springs forth to the repeated rhythm of God's speaking, naming, seeing, and blessing. It is all "good." And then into the world prepared by God's creative wisdom, humanity is called forth: male and female, equal and complementary, created uniquely in the image and likeness of God and entrusted with stewardship of creation. And it is "very good." Then on the seventh day there is the "Sabbath," the day of contemplative, mutual presence of God to all that has been created.

The reading of what in the Jewish tradition is called "the binding of Isaac" describes what certainly does not seem at first to be good. God seems to ask the impossible and the abhorrent of Abraham when he tells him to take his son, Isaac, the child of the promise, the hope of his and Sarah's lineage, and sacrifice him on Mount Moriah. Abraham trusts in the Promise Giver, even when the promises seem about to be destroyed. He responds to God with the simple, prophetic "Here I am." "My father," "My son," is the painful heartbeat of the climb, but there is no struggle, no argument. Abraham carries the dangerous knife and fire; Isaac the wood. Yet God does not want child sacrifice (cf. Ps 106:37-39; Ezek 23:36-39), and Abraham's obedience and trust are rewarded not only with the life of Isaac, but with the promise of descendants as numerous as the stars of heaven and the grains of sand on the seashore. Abraham is the pioneer of our faith, witnessing to us a hope against hope (Rom 4:14-16) that would be realized in the obedience and deliverance of an only Son whom he would never see in this world.

At every Easter Vigil the story of the passage of the Hebrews through the Sea of Reeds is an obligatory reading, for it is part of the foundational faith of Jesus the Jew and the Jewish people, "the rich root of the olive tree" (Rom 11:17) onto which Christians have been grafted. God the Liberator uses as instrument of deliverance his words of command to Moses to stretch out his arm and staff over the sea to make a safe and dry way for the people's passover. God's messenger, the guarding angel, accompanies them, and the pillar of cloud by day and of fire by night is both guide for the Hebrews and a buffer between them and the Egyptians. Pharaoh, considered divine by the Egyptians, and his pursuing army are overcome by the God of the Hebrews, and the religious establishment and the military might of Egypt is thrown into the watery chaos. When we respond with the canticle of Moses: "I will sing to the Lord, for he has triumphed gloriously," we remember the waters of the flood of death that overwhelmed Jesus, his passage through these, and the glorious triumph of his resurrection. It is into this death and resurrection that we have been baptized.

Isaiah uses familial imagery, inevitably patriarchal and with a male bias in that era, to acclaim God's faithful love of his bride, Israel. God's love is as intimate as the marriage covenant, despite God's disappointment because of bride Israel's unfaithfulness; despite temporary separation, anger, and upheavals, the loving relationship is reestablished. And not only is it reestablished, but it is recreated and transformed into an everlasting love by forgiveness, integrity, and peace. Tonight we celebrate the new covenant that Jesus has made with us by his faithful love and acceptance of us, even when, through our sinfulness, we are unfaithful covenant partners.

In the other reading from Isaiah, the love that God offers is compared to water for the thirsty, food for the hungry, wine and milk for the poor. Through the words of the prophet God tells the people to "come, buy and eat," to accept and nourish themselves with God's abundant love so that they may live. The covenant God made with David is extended as a free gift of grace to all who listen to God and are open to God's mysterious ways. The people are called to seek the Lord, to call upon him, to know how near he is, and the wicked and the unrighteous are invited to a change of heart and return to the Lord whom they have deserted, but who is always ready with abundant pardon. We cannot understand the depths of God's wisdom or love, but if attended to the words that proclaim this will work their unfailing creativity. But nowhere and in no one does God's word and will achieve fulfillment as it does in Jesus, the Word made flesh and the Covenant Maker in his own body and blood.

The reading from the prophet Baruch, Jeremiah's secretary (Jer 36:4), is both a hymn of praise to God's Wisdom and an admonition to the people to listen to this Wisdom who is a gift of God to Israel. This Wisdom is practical, not speculative. If they are attentive to her she will lead them out of their exile of sin and companion them back to the youthful love and peace of their earlier relationships with God. "Turn," "seize," "walk," are vigorous words that Baruch uses to encourage the people to make the right and wise choices in life-and-death situations. Such were the choices made preeminently by Jesus who reveals God's wisdom made flesh among us (cf. Mark 6:2; Matt 11:19; Luke 11:31).

The regeneration of the people after they had defiled themselves by their infidelities of idolatry and violence is proclaimed symbolically by Ezekiel. First he describes it as a ritual washing that cleanses them of any defilement, and then as a biblical "heart transplant." Only God can be the surgeon who delicately removes the people's hearts of stone and replaces them with new and tender hearts that beat strongly with love for their God. Then God will breath his own resuscitating spirit/breath into the exiles to enable them to continue to live strongly and obediently according to his laws: "And you shall be my people, and I shall be your God." For us, as a Christian assembly, this is the great night of the memory of our washing and regeneration in the waters of baptism, and our life-giving inbreathing by the Spirit.

Paul is very explicit about this. In the waters of baptism we go down into the death of Christ so that we may rise up with him to new life. Through his crucifixion Christ put to death the slavery of sin for the sake of our freedom; in his descent into the waters of death he transformed them into a means of life. On this Great Night we will again affirm our identity that we *are* the baptized, and we renew our promises to live as people who make their exodus out of sin in Christ and to stand in solidarity and mutual affirmation with the elect who will go down tonight into the waters. After this reading, for the first time since Ash Wednesday, we respond to the Word of God with the joyful "Alleluia!" for once again we remember that we are truly Easter people, and this is our song of praise for the love of God in Christ that has no end.

In Year B the gospel is from what most commentators hold to be the ending of Mark's gospel (Mark 16:1-8), with the exception of verse 8. It proclaims that there is no place for triumphalism in the Christian community, for it is a gospel of "little ones," of women who were considered so insignificant that their witness had no social or religious validity. By the end of the day of crucifixion, Mary Magdalene and Mary the mother of Joses had edged closer to the tomb, their hearts as heavy as the stone rolled in front of it, their hopes as dead as the tortured bundle of flesh and bones that Joseph of Arimathea laid there (Mark 15:47). For two days they have nursed their pain of life without Jesus. On the third day, "just as the sun was rising," just as light begins to mingle with darkness and overcome it, Mary Magdalene, Mary the mother of James, and Salome come to the tomb to do that something more (that women seem to be so good at) to the hurried and minimal burial rite. They come with spices to anoint the body of Jesus, and ask the desolate question of women who have no men around to help them roll away the stone. But then they see that the stone has already been rolled away and the tomb is open. Entering it, they find that there is a man there—a young messenger of God. What he announces to them means that the tomb is no longer a place of death; it is the place for beginning to talk of life. After he has offered the women the assurance that Jesus of Nazareth has been raised, he gives them their mission: to go and witness to the disciples that Jesus is going before them into Galilee. Peter especially is mentioned, for he is now a different kind of "little one" whose pride and self-assurance have been cut down by his betrayal and watered by his bitter tears. Galilee was the place of the first call, the first following, the springtime of discipleship. Now after the winter of failure and death, the disciples are called back to a second springtime. The risen Jesus goes before us, too, to call us back with compassionate and forgiving love to our "Galilees": to a second, a third, how many more seasons and places of new life.

It seems fitting that in all the gospel accounts of the resurrection, although in different ways, it is women who are entrusted with its proclamation. The passion narratives are about the work of men, but in so many of the bloody events of history, again and again it is women who are not only those who give birth to life, but are also the protectors of life.

Perhaps verse 8 is not read because those who selected the reading did not want any note of "terror and amazement" (v. 8) to sound on this night. Yet this may in fact be our great consolation, as it was for the persecuted Markan church: that in spite of all our failures and fears, like the women at the tomb, we too have to entrust ourselves to faith in the message that Jesus of Nazareth is risen; we are the women. Jesus is not with us as he was before because he has gone ahead of us, too, has reached the risen and glorious end of his journey, and waits there for us to be with him. The absence of Jesus is promise, not failure. The very fact that we have "a gospel according to Mark" witnesses to a believing community in which the women had eventually struggled through their own terror and found their faithful voices. For over two thousand years, down to our own times, fearful and fragile communities have found hope in the affirmation of God's power working in our weakness through the Crucified and Risen One whom we celebrate on this night of nights, have been liberated then from their fear, and have joyfully witnessed with their lives to "the good news of Jesus Christ, the Son of God" (Mark 1:1).

The Sundays of Easter

Unlike Advent or Lent, the Easter season is not a preparation for a great feast but a prolongation of it. For fifty days we celebrate the "Great Sunday" of the feast of Christ's resurrection. This is the most joyous space of the church's year, the time of radical hospitality when we remember that in Jesus' resurrection God has welcomed the whole of creation—all peoples, times, and seasons—into the glorious freedom of God's children. The restless Spirit of God urges us to keep heading into this joyful space, rejoicing especially with those who have entered it by baptism at the Easter Vigil.

Second Sunday of Easter

• Acts 4:32-35 • Ps 118:2-4, 13-15, 22-24 • 1 John 5:1-6 • John 20:19-31

So important is today's gospel that it is proclaimed on the octave of Easter in Years A, B, and C. Perhaps this is because, like the disciples on the evening of that day called the "first" of the new resurrection timeline, we also are so often imprisoned in fear and disillusionment—with ourselves, with our church, with God. It is often at such times that the risen Christ will appear in our midst in ways we do not expect.

Dispirited and terrified after the death and burial of Jesus, confronted with their own cowardice and with hearts and minds closed against the resurrection proclamation of Mary Magdalene, the disciples huddle together behind locked doors. They are a more inclusive group than the Twelve (become Eleven through Judas's treason); and they are Jews. This latter fact is often forgotten when John speaks of fear "because of the Jews," and in the context of the widening separation between the church and synagogue at the end of the first century when John is writing his gospel. It is not only the doors that are locked; fear has locked their own hearts. But for the risen Jesus there are no locked doors or prisons. Suddenly, the Tomb Breaker, the Free and Freeing One, stands among them in his glorified humanity. He does not come among them as the powerful One, but as the wounded. He shows them his hands and side, for he carries his wounds to the other side of death. Jesus then offers them his first Easter gift: "Peace be with you." These are not a sedative; they are words that preface the second gift of a dynamic mission, a sending out of the disciples from behind their barricades of fear, for: "As the Father has sent me, I also send you." Biblical peace is much more than a cessation of war; it is wholeness and holiness of spirit, soul, and body. Its biblical opposite is chaos, and the disciples on that Easter eve were certainly a community in chaos.

Then Jesus breathes on them, and the word used here for "breathe" is used nowhere else in the New Testament. To biblical memories it has all the privileged nuances of the enlivening spirit/wind/breath that hovered over the chaotic void of Genesis (Gen 1:2); all the wonder of God's inbreathing into the clay of our humanity (Gen 2:7) with the mission to multiply, fill the earth, and steward it. It is the ultimate expression of the prophetic breath that Ezekiel sent over the valley of dead bones (Ezek 37:1-10). In this Easter room there is a new creation of men and women who are raised up out of their fear and despair by Jesus. They recognize themselves as forgiven, and in this recognition comes another aspect of their mission: the disciples' responsibility to offer to others the gift of forgiveness that they have received. This is a gift and responsibility not only for the ordained ministers of the church, but for all who have been baptized into the risen Jesus and received his Spirit. We celebrate the sacrament of reconciliation as a most privileged moment of reconciliation, but there are the more frequent—and related— celebrations of reconciliation: the daily forgiveness of our sisters and brothers, the speaking of the hard words, "I'm sorry," and the gracious acceptance of another's offering of apology. In these occasions Jesus is also standing in our midst, unlocking our hearts, helping us to break out of what can become death-dealing animosities or sometimes almost cherished victimhood that we are loathe to release to forgiveness.

To be individuals and communities of forgiveness is to create peace. In his book, *The Gift of Peace*, the late Cardinal Joseph Bernardin wrote of the last three years of his life before his death from pancreatic cancer in 1996. In this very personal memoir, he tells of an experience of the healing power of peacemaking and forgiveness that, he said, could be nothing but an empowering gift of God's love. Bernardin describes the reconciliation (that he initiated) with Steven Cook, the man who had falsely accused him of sexual abuse. Steven was dying of AIDS, and at their meeting he offered, and Bernardin gently accepted, an apology that the cardinal described as simple, direct, and deeply moving. Bernardin offered Steven a gift, a Bible in which he had inscribed words of loving forgiveness. Then he showed him a hundred-year-old chalice, a gift to the cardinal from a man he did not even know, but who had sent him the chalice and asked him, one day, to celebrate Mass for Steven Cook. That was to be the day. Word and sacrament opened both their eyes to the deeper significance of the gifts of peace and forgiveness. Bernardin described that meeting as the most profound and unforgettable experience of reconciliation in his whole priestly life.[7]

Thomas has not been in the room when the risen Jesus appeared to the disciples, and so has missed out on any personal encounter with him, the words of missioning, and the bestowal of the gifts of peace and forgiveness in the Spirit. John makes Thomas a foil for our own need of these gifts and our struggles with doubt and faith. Often the comments about Thomas concentrate too much on him as a doubter (which he is never called anywhere in the gospels) and too little on his desire to touch the source of Life. John's gospel shows him to be the kind of person who blurts out the questions or comments others are too timid or too embarrassed to speak. He is ready to go along with Jesus en route to Lazarus's grave and die with him (John 11:16); and he is honest enough at the Last Supper to say that none of the disciples have any idea where Jesus is heading (John 14:5). The disciples to whom the risen Lord appeared on Easter eve announce the resurrection to Thomas in the same words as Mary Magdalene spoke to them: "We have seen the Lord!" And they are just as unsuccessful in convincing Thomas as Mary had been with them. Like all disciples, Thomas needs a personal experience of Jesus before he will believe. Until then, he is locked in his own criterion for faith: he wants Jesus to be "touchable."

So eight days later, on the next "first day of the week" according to the resurrection timeline, the risen Lord of the Sabbath stands again in the midst of his disciples, greets them with his peace, and then turns to the individual who is most in need of this. For eight days Thomas has wrestled with the dark stranger of doubt, and is wounded by this struggle. The wounded, risen Jesus and the wounded disciple stand before one another. Jesus invites Thomas to stretch out his hand to the wounds of his hands and side. But there is no physical touching. Jesus' personal presence and self-offering to Thomas touch him and demolish all doubts. Here is "the way, and the truth, and the life" that Thomas is seeking, and he responds with the most profound and personal assent of faith in all the gospels: "My Lord and my God!" For the future generations who will listen to this gospel in the presence of the physically absent Jesus, the last beatitude that

Jesus then addresses to Thomas is our greatest hope: "Blessed are those who have not seen and yet have come to believe." It is to hand on such life-giving faith, says the evangelist, that he has written his gospel.

In his *Asian Journal*, Thomas Merton wrote:

> Faith means doubt. Faith is not the suppression of doubt. It is the overcoming of doubt, and you overcome doubt by going through it. The man of faith who has never experienced doubt is not a person of faith. Consequently, the monk is one who has to struggle in the depths of his being with the presence of doubt, and has to go through what some religions call the Great Doubt, to break through doubt into a certitude which is very, very deep because it is not his own personal certitude; it is the certitude of God Himself, in us.[8]

Christ took his wounds into the grave and did not disown them in his resurrection. Because of his wounds, Jesus is now credibly in touch with wounded humanity: with the wounded in body and spirit, those hurt by society, the victims of domestic and global violence, those suffering from their own addictions, those abused by our disregard and complacency. And we know only too well our own woundedness. Such wounds reveal our need for one another and, therefore, the potential for the building of a compassionate, healing community that witnesses to the love of the Wounded Healer.

In the somewhat idealized reading from the Acts of the Apostles, the early Christian community is described as a gathering of unity in heart and soul, of deep and genuine solidarity, where the Christians tried to discern what was happening in each other's heart, walk in their shoes, and express this solidarity by a practical readiness to share their material resources so that no one of them would be in need. (For evidence that all was not perfect, read on to the story of Ananias and Sapphira in the next chapter!) And as yet, the early Christian community does not have the resources for an outreach beyond themselves. This would be a later challenge (cf. Gal 6:10), as it is now for us who are confronted with "Make Poverty History." Luke suggests that the best of the Hellenist and Jewish traditions have been absorbed into the Jerusalem community: the Hellenist ideal of friendship suggested by the unity of "one heart and one soul," and the Jewish tradition of Deuteronomy 15:4-5 and the commandment to share possessions with the needy. Christian unity is translated into a love that does not deny the right to possessions, but opposes possessiveness in favor of the community of goods. In the reception and distribution of goods according to need, the apostles are again the accepted leaders. Their ministry of the Word and their ministry to the needy are rightly complementary. And all this is made possible because the community is empowered and emboldened by their faith in the risen Christ who has sent his peacemaking and healing Spirit upon them.

The responsorial Psalm 118 is the last of the "Egyptian Hallel (Praise)" psalms (Pss 113–118) that were sung at the great Jewish festivals, and especially at Passover, in eager expectation of the coming of the messiah. In the church's liturgical use of Psalm 118, it becomes a grateful hymn to the limitless love of God that has been revealed in Christ. "The day that the Lord has made" is above all the day of Christ's resurrection. The raising up of Christ, the rejected corner-stone, as the foundation of our lives is God's doing, and a marvel in our eyes, because for those built on him and into him the inevitability of death is transformed into the hope of eternal life. Despite the cracks, the holes, the wounds, we can say in Christ: "I shall not die but I shall live." This verse continues to present us with an ongoing mission to "recount the deeds of the Lord."

In the First Letter of John we are caught up into a spiral of believing, knowing, and loving. In such a few verses we are circled so swiftly through references to the love of God for us, our love of God, the love of Christians for one another, and our attitude to the world, that our listening and understanding may be threatened by spiritual giddiness. Yet the author supplies us with "the still point of the turning world"[9]—Jesus the Christ and the Son of God, revealed not only in the water of his baptism (John 1:33-34) but also in the water and blood of his death (John 19:34). We are to entrust our lives to this Jesus Christ whose victory over death and dehumanization is affirmed by the Spirit.

Third Sunday of Easter

• Acts 3:13-15, 17-19 • Ps 4:2, 4, 7-8, 9 • 1 John 2:1-5a • Luke 24:35-48

This Sunday's gospel follows the appearance of the risen Jesus to the two disciples on the way to Emmaus. The Emmaus meal was a welcoming event; the meal with the risen Jesus in Jerusalem will be a missioning event. Despite the witness of the two disciples who have hurried back from Emmaus and the news of Jesus' appearance to Simon, the eleven and their companions are still startled and terrified when Jesus appears among them and greets them with peace. They think he is a ghost! In this Gospel of Luke, as in John's narrative last Sunday, Jesus makes clear to them the reality of his glorified human presence, his full embodied existence, by showing them his wounded hands and feet, inviting them to touch him, asking them to give him something to eat, and then taking the piece of grilled fish and eating it before their eyes.

In Luke's Last Supper account, Jesus was among his disciples "as one who serves" (Luke 22:27); now he is among them as one who is to be served. Just seeing with their human eyes is not enough. As Jesus had done in the passion predictions during his ministry, as he had done for the disciples on the way to Emmaus, as the two messengers at the tomb had done for the women on Easter morning, Jesus now opens the eyes of the Jerusalem disciples' hearts so that they may understand the Scriptures. Luke mentions the threefold division of the Hebrew Scriptures: the teaching of Moses (the Pentateuch/Torah), the Prophets, and the Writings (represented by the psalms). These were the Scriptures that had nourished Jesus throughout his life, and with them the Christian Scriptures stand in continuity, not supercession.

Jesus tells his disciples clearly that they cannot stay in this Jerusalem house of ecstatic joy, listening to his words and serving him at table. This experience must burst through the doors in the service of those outside, people of all nations who are waiting to hear the good news of repentance and forgiveness of their sins. At the first meal with Jesus that is recorded in Luke's gospel, the great banquet that Levi hosted for Jesus, Jesus spoke of the *metanoía* (Luke 5:32), that life-changing repentance that turns one's life around, and which Levi had just experienced in his call to follow Jesus. At that meal, Jesus had addressed the call to repentance to the tax collectors and sinners; at this last meal after his passion and resurrection:

> . . . the same message had to be preached to all the nations, beginning with Jerusalem. Jesus' passion–resurrection transformed the table of Jesus the prophet into that of Jesus Christ the Lord and made it the springboard for the church's universal mission. Jesus' message at this point in his final discourse looks directly to the story of the church on mission in the Acts of the Apostles.[10]

This is what the disciples are to witness. And we, who at this Sunday Eucharist also sit at the "transformed table" of Jesus, share in the same urgent mission. As individuals and as church, we must admit our own sinfulness, continually turn to Jesus in repentance, and then go out in the strength of the Eucharist we have received to bear credible, outreaching witness of the need for conversion to the following of Jesus in our own small or larger worlds. Many places in our contemporary world are obviously not founded on repentance and forgiveness, but on war and entrenched animosities that we may publicly lament, or rationalize, or even excuse, while at the same time still allowing violence and bitterness to inhabit our hearts. If we are to be disciples who take seriously Jesus' Easter greeting of "Peace be with you!" and who offer this peace to one another around the eucharistic table with a present and future intent, we need to create a space in our lives and our hearts where such peace with God and with our sisters and brothers can truly be at home.

In the first reading, we hear that this is exactly what Peter is doing with the people of Jerusalem. His sermon is spoken in response to the healing of the lame man at the Beautiful Gate (Acts 3:1-10), the first of the "wonders and signs" (Acts 2:43) worked by the disciples and witnessed by the crowds that gathered at the Temple at the hour of afternoon prayer. Peter is adamant that it is not the personal power or piety of the disciples that has cured the man, but God who is at work in them: the God of their ancestors, of Abraham, Isaac, and Jacob, and the prophets—and of the servant Jesus whom God has glorified. The risen Jesus and his messianic community are now the "place" of God's saving activity rather than any building. At first hearing, Peter may seem to be speaking in a very condemnatory anti-Judaism manner, placing the responsibility for the death of Jesus on his Jewish listeners, and there is certainly a paradox and irony present that is still a challenge to Jewish-Christian relations, despite Vatican II's most solemn declaration of the abhorrence of any displays of anti-Semitism.[11] Because of their ignorance of who Jesus really was, Peter excuses any of those who have some guilt by implying that if they had understood how Jesus stood in the line of prophetic succession, especially that of the Suffering Servant tradition, they would have acted differently. This is the purpose of Peter's sermon: to emphasize life, not death; repentance, not blame; the forgiving power of God that can raise anyone from their sins, just as God raised the Sinless One from the grave. The word of God expressed in this sermon of Peter is also for our enduring instruction.

We respond to this reading with a selection of confident verses from Psalm 4. Like Peter and John, we are frail disciples who can do nothing without the grace of God revealed to us in Christ; like the people of Jerusalem we are often people of faulty judgment of good and evil, especially as this is expressed in others. And so we call out to the God of justice to teach us right relationships with one another and with our society; to help us to recognize the divine presence (God's "face") in which we will find that true happiness that makes for human wholeness and peace.

The author of the First Letter of John is both a wisdom teacher, addressing his readers as "my little children," and also a down-to-earth realist about the community of disciples, the church. It is a gathering not of the perfect, but of pilgrims who are seeking perfection, "that continual reformation of which she (the church) always has need."[12] Cerebral knowledge about Jesus is not enough. As with the Jerusalem disciples, we need an experiential knowledge of him: to be able to serve him, to experience his forgiveness, to eat with him at table, to have an awareness of his wounded presence to us. Such experience comes to us now through our attentive listening to and praying of the Word of God, through the healing sacraments of the church, and through our service of our sisters and brothers, especially those who are the wounded members of Christ's Body. This is faith become obedience to God's commandments that will lead us forward on our pilgrimage into the love of God in Christ. And when we fail, Jesus, the Just One who still bears the wounds of his passion, is our mediator.

Fourth Sunday of Easter

• Acts 4:8-12 • Ps 118:1, 8-9, 21-23, 26, 28-29 • 1 John 3:1-2 • John 10:11-18

In John's gospel we find fewer parables than in the Synoptics, but John has given us the wonderful "I AM" statements that function in much the same way as parables, while also reminding us that in Christ is the revelation in the flesh of the "I AM" of the burning bush (Exod 3:14). This Sunday's gospel presents us with one of the most loved images of Jesus when he says of himself that "I am the good shepherd . . ." We are sometimes seduced by images of a smiling Middle Eastern shepherd with a cuddly, clean, and fluffy lamb tucked under his arm. Much less romantic and more accurate and robust is the earliest known statue (ca. 60 C.E.) of the Good Shepherd at Caesarea Maritima in Israel. The legless remnant has a huge, heavy sheep draped around the shepherd's shoulders. To carry such a load would be no easy task! In 1 Samuel 17:34-35, 37 we have another vigorous Old Testament description of a shepherd in the context of King Saul's attempt to dissuade the young David from fighting against the mighty Philistine warrior, Goliath. David argues his case for the fight with a graphic description of how he kept sheep for his father:

> . . . whenever a lion or a bear came and took a lamb from the flock, I went after it and struck it down, rescuing the lamb from its mouth; and if it turned against me, I would catch it by the jaw, strike it down and kill it. . . . The Lord who saved me from the paw of the lion and the paw of the bear will save me from the hand of this Philistine.

As our Good Shepherd, Jesus fights for us, saves us from the gaping jaws of whatever or whoever seeks to grab and destroy our discipleship and wound the "little flock" of the Christian community. He shepherds us with his loving care so that we may "have life and have it more abundantly" (John 10:10). In parts of the world where flocks of sheep are numbered in the thousands, and shepherds are on horseback or motorcycles, we are in a very different cultural context from that of the first-century world of the parable. But in this larger scenario we probably regard sheep as rather stupid and smelly animals, with a tendency to a mob mentality. We might think that to regard ourselves metaphorically as Christ's "flock" or "sheep" is hardly appropriate or complimentary—and yet it might be a very accurate image of our following of Jesus!

In one of his magnificent Easter sermons (ca. 387 C.E.), John Chrysostom describes the confrontation of Christ with death. Death pounces upon the body of Christ but finds itself lighting upon God; as gulping down earth and choking on heaven. It is the risen Christ who is the snatcher of abundant life for his sheep, reducing death and its sting to nothing.

In contrast to the Good Shepherd is the hireling who is concerned primarily with his own self-interest: his reputation, remuneration, and safety. Through the prophets, God had denounced the shepherd leaders of Israel who had prostituted their pastoral ministry. "I myself will be the shepherd of the sheep," God promises his people (Ezek 34:15; cf. Isa 40:11; Jer 31:10). There are still some political, social, and ecclesial "hirelings" with us, but there are also the magnificent shepherds who are willing to lay down their life for their sheep. In *Oscar Romero: Memories in Mosaic*, by Maria López, the memories of two hundred people who had lived, prayed, and worked with such a shepherd—Archbishop Oscar Romero—have been collected. Here is one of such mosaic pieces:

> One morning in rainy season when the skies were heavy with the day's rain, a man in rags, with a shirt full of holes and hair made curly by dust, covered with dust, was cleaning the (Romero's) tomb carefully with one of his rags. The sun had just come up, but he was already active and awake. And even though the rag was dirty with grease and time, it left the tombstone clean and shiny.
>
> When he was done he smiled with satisfaction. At that hour in the morning, he hadn't seen anyone, and no one had seen him. Except for me. I saw him. When he left to go out, I felt I needed to talk to him.
>
> "Why do you do that?"
>
> "Do what?"
>
> "Clean Monseñor's tomb."
>
> "Because he was my father."
>
> "What do you mean . . . ?"
>
> "It's like this. I'm just a poor man, you know? Sometimes I make some money carrying things for people in the market in a little cart. And sometimes I spend it all on liquor and end up lying hungover on the streets. . . . But I never get discouraged. I had a father! I did! He made me feel like a person. Because he loved people like me, and didn't act like we made him sick. He talked to us, he touched us, he asked us questions. He had confidence in us. You could see in his eyes that he cared about me. Like parents love their children. That's why I clean off his tomb, because that's what children do."[13]

As a child, as a son, Jesus the Good Shepherd lives, dies, and is raised to life in the power of the mutual love between him and his Father. Into this love Jesus gathers his disciples so that they may also share in it.

The writer of the First Letter of John is overwhelmed by the love God has lavished upon us, a love that is beyond all our human imagining. In faith we believe this is a love that transforms us now into God's own likeness, a likeness that will be brought to full realization in the not-yet end time. Especially at difficult times in our lives, this may be the huge hope to which we must surrender, and the only faith that keeps us going on our way of discipleship. By the unmerited gift of God's love for us, we are recreated and transformed as God's children. Empowered by this love, our responsibility is to live confidently and courageously in a world that will certainly not always love us because it does not know or believe in the love of God.

In the first reading, Peter and John are experiencing such hostility as they stand before the Sanhedrin, the supreme religious and lay council of the Jews. The context of the reading (Acts 3:1–4:4) is the arrest of the two apostles after they had healed the lame beggar at the Beautiful Gate of the Temple, and had the temerity to go to Solomon's Porch, with the man leaping and jumping around them, to address the crowd! Peter proclaims to the crowd that this miracle is not because of their own power, but because of the power of God working through them. God had done much more than raise up a lame beggar from his mat and change him into an exultant dancer; the God of whom Peter speaks is the God who raised Jesus from the dead.

The Sanhedrin is not concerned with the miracle, which is undeniable, but with the question of in whose name (in whose personal power) this was done. In his defense, Peter is living out what Luke had written in his gospel: that his disciples would be brought before religious and civil authorities, but they were not to worry because what they were to say at that time would be given to them by the Holy Spirit (Luke 12:11-12). Peter repeats that it is "by the name of Jesus Christ the Nazarene" that the man was healed, adding a rebuff to those who had plotted against Jesus: "whom you crucified." Peter then quotes from Psalm 118, select verses of which are today's responsorial psalm. He personalizes one of its verses, addressing it to the Sanhedrin and confronting them with the accusation that Jesus is "the stone that was rejected by you, the builders." To this rejection, God responded with the exaltation of Jesus. (Once again, we must be careful not to read into this text any global condemnation of the Jewish people. After all, it is Peter, a Jew, who is speaking about Jesus the Jew.) Like all Scripture, the words are also addressed to us, the present hearers, and to our temptations to reject Jesus in some aspects of our lives.

With Psalm 118 we also can personalize the words of the psalmist and sing of the enduring love of God shown to us in Jesus the Good Shepherd: rejected, wounded unto death, exalted in his resurrection, and become the cornerstone of our faith. As God's children, and brothers and sisters of Jesus, with great humility we rejoice in the unimaginable but glorious hope of what we will become when we see God "as he is."

Fifth Sunday of Easter

• Acts 9:26-31 • Ps 22:26-28, 30-32 • 1 John 3:18-24 • John 15:1-8

Today and next Sunday the gospel readings are from the Last Supper discourse of John. Chronologically, the Last Supper took place before Jesus' death and resurrection, yet we hear them after Easter. This is a reminder that we are not remembering and celebrating events in their strict historical sequence, but that we are immersed in a liturgical mix of time and timelessness; we are celebrating the mystery that is always and everywhere the reality of the resurrection of Jesus. As we listen to the Johannine account of the last meal of Jesus with his disciples, we are, here and now, at the table with Jesus and the community of disciples, tangling our lives with him, the True Vine, and with the branches of all the baptized.

We hear much shouting of would-be people of power: fanatical tyrants, political agitators, self-righteous politicians. We may even add to this chorus our own small voices on matters personal, ecclesial, or social. But what Jesus speaks about at table is the power of love and of gentle growth. He gives us another image of the great intimacy and interdependence that exists between himself, his Father, and his disciples: "I AM the vine, and my Father is the vinegrower"—and we are the branches. The vine and vineyard were familiar images to the people of God in the Old Testament. Israel was the vine brought out of Egypt and planted by God the Vinegrower in its own soil (Ps 80:8-13). The prophets, too, spoke of Israel as a vine (e.g., Ezek 17:6, 8; Hos 10:1; 14:7), and Isaiah sings a plaintive "love song of the vineyard" (Isa 5:1-7) that should never be read as an infidelity versus fidelity—a comparison between Judaism and Christianity—but rather as a reminder that both communities need to be pruned of unproductive branches because neither bears the fruit they should. So significant was the image of the vine that on one facade of the Jerusalem Temple sanctuary was carved an ornamental vine with golden clusters of grapes as big as a human hand. And the early Christian community painted the vine on the walls of the catacombs in memory of Christ, the True Vine.

The image of the vine is a radically nonhierarchical image of the people of God, for all the branches are so intertwined that when looking at a vine it is almost impossible to tell where one branch begins and another ends. All tangle together as they grow from the central stock, undifferentiated by anything but their fruitfulness. Such is the relationship of Jesus to the new community that grows from his death and resurrection. Such communities are also to be branching out, hospitable communities that live by and bear fruit ("fruit" being the Johannine word for good works) through the surging sap of Christ's risen life. Without the stock there would be no fruit-bearing branches; without the branches there is no fruit-bearing vine.

To remain healthy and productive the vine must be pruned by our Vine Grower God. Those in whom the baptismal sap rises have already been pruned by the words Jesus speaks, but we must continue to accept not only the short, sharp pain of God's snipping from our lives the small and withering infidelities, but also be willing to endure the longer agony of more drastic pruning that is sometimes necessary. This is not to make of the Vine Grower a ruthless tyrant, because what is done is done out of love for the vine. In his passion and death, the Christ who knew no sin was made sin for us (cf. 2 Cor 5:21), and suffered in faithful hope that most drastic pruning of his passion and death so that the branches of the vine, his community, might thrive through his resurrected life. Sometimes what needs to be pruned in our lives is the parasite runner of individualism that wants to go its own way, or the sucker that feeds on self-interest; both draw life away from the vine. At other times, our vinedressing God recognizes our potential for greater fruit-bearing, and with this the need for heavy pruning. After such pruning, a vine may bear no fruit for several years, but it remains rooted and waiting, confident in the tending of the Vine Grower, until both are rewarded with a tremendous, bursting yield. When we yield such a harvest of good works, says Jesus, we give glory to the Father and are confirmed in our discipleship.

The use of verses from Psalm 22 as the responsorial psalm shows us the thanksgiving aspect of this well-known lament, familiar to us in the liturgy of Holy Week. Now in the Easter season we pray our belief that hope can come out of despair, ecstasy out of agony, and life out of the death of heavy pruning when we remain faithful to the fulfillment of our baptismal vows.

For people like the Israelites who had once been a wandering people, vine-yards symbolized a place where one was at home and at peace. Under one's own vine, hospitality was offered and its wine drunk. In the Old Testament, such hospitality became an image of the cosmic hospitality of God to which Israel looked forward in the messianic times (1 Kgs 4:25; Isa 36:16; Mic 4:4). Eight times in the eight verses of today's gospel John uses the word "abide" (unfortu-nately and more prosaically sometimes translated as "remain"). In the gospel it becomes a word that continues and surpasses the tradition of being at home and nourished under one's own vine. Now we can be "at home," indwelling and belonging in the most secure of homes: in Jesus, the true Vine.

In the first reading from the Acts of the Apostles, we have a moving example of Saul's (Paul's) "homelessness" when, after his conversion, he attempts to join the Jerusalem community of disciples. Will the graft of this one-time persecutor onto the true Vine really take? There is heavy suspicion of Saul, and Barnabas (whose name means "son of encouragement") must speak for him, entwine Saul in his belief in him, and have Saul accepted as a fruit-bearing branch. Yet Saul very soon has to endure pruning from some of the Hellenists to whom he preaches boldly and argues in the name of Jesus, and who consequently are now determined to kill him. This pruning is the affirmation of the successful graft of Saul, and he is sheltered by the Christian community and taken to his home city of Tarsus.

What are we better at: sheltering or judging one another, welcome or suspicion? How practically aware are we of our parish's newly baptized members who need to be supported by today's "sons and daughters of encouragement" after their Easter grafting onto Christ? How welcoming are we of the "strangers" who come into our Christian community, perhaps with a strange language, strange dress, strange customs, perhaps as refugees fleeing from new pharaohs? Do we greet them as precious members of a church that can never be monocultural but is called by Christ to reach out to the nations?

The First Letter of John continues to emphasize the love that Christians should practice. It is not a love like that of Mrs Jelleby that Charles Dickens describes in *Bleak House*: a "telescopic philanthropy," because she could see nothing nearer than Africa! She loved Africa, in general, but didn't take care of her own children. We may profess that we do love humanity, but our spiritual telescope cannot see those nearest to us who are in need of our practical love. If our love is just empty words and posturing speeches, can we really be at home with God? Moreover, the life of faith will not be without dilemmas of conscience; such inner conflict bears witness to the fact that we are not just passive people. Even though we may sometimes make the wrong decisions, in our failures we have the assurance of God's love for us even as we fail. In our successes and obedience, we need to have the humility that recognizes that this is the work of the Spirit within us.

Sixth Sunday of Easter

• Acts 10:25-26, 34-35, 44-48 • Ps 98:1-4 • 1 John 4:7-10 • John 15:9-17

The heartbeat of today's gospel and of the second reading from the First Letter of John is "love." As disciples, we are called to feel this pulse and make our lives beat in rhythm with it. The love commandment that Jesus gives to his disciples depends on God's limitless love for the world (John 3:16). This love is made incarnate and dwells among us in Jesus, the one who is "close to the Father's heart" (John 1:18), and so Jesus' own relationship with his Father, his own life and death, become the norm of the costly love he asks of his disciples. This must not be a cramped or grudging love, but joyful and expansive, encompassing the world for which Jesus was sent.

One of the most priceless human gifts is friendship. It allows us to disclose ourselves to and receive from another in complete openness and trust. Before a friend we can think aloud; with a friend we can participate in one another's joys and sorrows, hopes and fears; through a friend we can survive loneliness, indifference, hostility. Small wonder, then, that in today's gospel Jesus calls his disciples by this most precious of names: "my friends." Drawn into and abiding in the mutual love of the Father and the Son, disciples are no longer called servants but friends. By his death Jesus "befriends" the whole world, and it is to such loyal befriending and fruit-bearing in steadfast love that Jesus commissions his disciples.

The Johannine community was to live as friends and so, throughout his gospel, John introduces us to various occasions of friendship: John the Baptist, the precursor and "the friend of the bridegroom," who like a best man hands over the Bride Israel to Jesus (John 3:29); the family at Bethany, especially Lazarus, the friend for whom he wept at his grave and for whom Jesus was the Tomb Breaker (John 11:35-44); Pilate, who at a critical moment preferred to be a friend of Caesar rather than Jesus (John 19:12); the disciple beloved of Jesus (John 13:23; 19:26; 21:7); and Peter, the forgiven friend who will lead and shepherd the community of the forgiven (John 21:44ff.). As we gather around the table of our eucharistic supper, we hear that we have been chosen by Jesus as his friends and commissioned to befriend the world in and with the love he has shown us.

The love of God knows no barriers, as Peter discovers in the first reading from the Acts of the Apostles. To really appreciate the significance of this event for the early Jerusalem church, it is helpful to read the verses immediately preceding this reading in Acts 10:9-16. While at midday prayer on his own rooftop, Peter is startled by the vision of a kind of "tablecloth ark" being lowered from the heavens and containing, without distinction, animals that are regarded as both ritually clean and unclean according to the Jewish dietary laws (cf. Lev 11). In response to the voice telling him to "Get up, Peter, and eat," Peter protests that, as an observant Jew, he has never eaten anything unclean or profane, but he is left with this threefold proclamation ringing in his ears: "What God has made clean, you must not call profane."

No sooner has the cloth been snatched away than three Gentiles, and so "unclean" men, arrive to invite Peter to the house of another "unclean" Gentile, the Roman centurion Cornelius, an upright and God-seeking man. The no-doubt-bewildered Peter then embarks on what Dan Berrigan has described as "a tumultuous voyage through the white water of the Spirit."[14]

This voyage into unchartered waters begins with hospitality: with Peter's hospitality to his three (presumably Gentile) visitors. The next day, in the company of some of the Jewish Christian believers from Joppa, they all go to Cornelius's house. Peter's entry into this Gentile household is catching a wave that will sweep the church into a new inclusiveness, into the recognition that not only is there no food that is "unclean" but, more significantly, there is no person who is to be regarded in this way, because God shows no partiality with those who are God-seekers. And so before Peter has finished speaking to Cornelius and his household, before he has the chance to baptize anyone, the Spirit takes over and descends on the whole gathering. This outpouring of the Spirit is witnessed by the Jewish Christians that accompany Peter, and Peter proclaims to both them and the Gentiles that since the Gentile household had shared the same Pentecostal experience as they had, the membership of the Gentiles in the Christian community should now be ritually confirmed by baptism in the name of Jesus.

Then as now, God's love is a universal, barrier-breaking love, but are we as ready as Peter to accept this? Do we recognize God's presence in unexpected people and places, in their often stumbling, inarticulate search for God? Can we accept that what we may insist are legitimate, unchanging religious practices may be only thinly disguised elitism or rationalization of our reluctance to change, despite the urgings of the Spirit? God's love is neither safe nor conventional.

The most startling, profound, yet simple naming of God is proclaimed in the reading from the First Letter of John: "God is love." It is from this Letter that Benedict XVI took the title and theme of his first encyclical, and he returns frequently to this conviction. As he wrote:

> In a world where the name of God is sometimes associated with vengeance or even a duty of hatred or violence, this message is both timely and significant. For this reason, I wish in my first encyclical to speak of the love which God lavishes on us and which we in turn must share with others.[15]

The Letter is addressed to the "beloved," those with whom God has taken the initiative, who are parented by God's love, and this self-giving love is the source of human love. Like today's gospel whose heartbeat is love, so love beats strongly in this reading—named nine times in its four verses. It is love that is expansive and global, yet also intimate and personal, revealed most fully in Jesus, the Son of God and our brother.

In what has been called the photographic event of our time, invitations were sent at the turn of the millennium to 192 countries inviting photographers to submit entries that captured and celebrated the essence of humanity's "Moments of Intimacy, Laughter and Kinship" (M.I.L.K.). Ultimately, seventeen thousand photographers from 164 countries entered with over forty thousand photographs. As well as becoming an international traveling exhibition, the winning photographs are published as three books entitled *Family, Friendship and Love.*[16] As love always does, the M.I.L.K. images reach across all continents and races, youth and age, poverty and affluence, to reveal the heart of humanity and, surely, the heart of God. The viewer has no idea if the God of Jesus Christ is known or unknown to the six-year-old "policeman" in the slums of Calcutta who is holding up his hand to stop the traffic so that three blind men, their hands on one another's shoulders, can safely cross the road; whether any prayers are being murmured by the 84-year-old woman saying goodbye to her dying 92-year-old friend; or what is the faith of the parents welcoming their womb-wet, wailing newborn. But the Christian gazing on these photographs, or on such realities in our everyday lives, can surely say: "God is love," for here is the presence of Christ who:

> . . . plays in ten thousand places,
> Lovely in limbs and lovely in eyes not his . . .[17]

Seventh Sunday of Easter

Feast of the Ascension of the Lord

• Acts 1:1-11 • Ps 47:2-3, 6-9 • Eph 1:17-23 • Mark 16:15-20

While the 1969 reform of the church's liturgical calendar retained the feast of the Ascension in the Easter season, the integrity of the fifty postresurrection days, the "Great Sunday," has been restored to the status it enjoyed in the early church. The Ascension is one of the many-faceted Easter jewels that crown the liturgical year, and today's readings reflect this light. In favor of this integrity, in most places the feast of the Ascension has been transferred from the forty-day interrupting marker of "Ascension Thursday" to the Seventh Sunday of Easter, and symbolically the paschal candle is no longer extinguished on the Ascension but continues to be lit until Pentecost Sunday.

In their different ways, all the gospel writers want us to appreciate the threshold moment of Jesus' exaltation into heaven. Luke ends his gospel with one account of the ascension of Jesus happening on the evening of Easter day, and begins the second part of his good news, the Acts of the Apostles, with another account forty days later. Perhaps Luke is using these two accounts to stitch together the farewell reality of Jesus in his glorified humanity (Luke 24:50-53) and the mission of the church, his Body, which in his Spirit must continue his presence and work in the world (Acts 1:9-11). Luke addresses the Acts of the Apostles to "Theophilus" ("Lover of God"), perhaps a patron of the early Christian community. Gathered today around the Word, we are also the intended readers, all called to be "lovers of God."

Mark narrates that Jesus is risen. He has appeared to his followers during forty days—a biblical number symbolic of both fullness and transition—and has instructed them about the promised coming of the Holy Spirit. He explains this coming in baptismal terms. Water had been the baptismal medium of the Baptist, but this new baptism will be in the outpouring of the Holy Spirit. So the disciples wait for this unimagined and unimaginable outpouring, still captive to curiosity about times, dates, the possible relationship of Israel to the kingdom about which Jesus has so often spoken, and an implied hankering for knowledge of their own positions in this kingdom. Jesus deflects their desire for such answers into a concern for mission—the witness to him that the disciples will be called and empowered to give beyond Jerusalem, beyond Judaea and Samaria, to the very ends of the earth. The disciples are still a wounded community, wounded by Judas's treachery, by Peter's betrayal, and by their own cowardice. Yet it is in the midst of such failure, false expectations, and incorrigible personal ambitions and wishes for quick solutions, that Jesus will call them to mission.

The narrative of the Acts is less concerned with the ascension as a personal event for Jesus and more concerned with the experience of the disciples as they witness it. Saying goodbye is always difficult, even though the experience may be mixed with some joy. We rejoice when a daughter or son moves out to begin the university course or start the job or begin the married life they've been dreaming about, and yet there is an emptiness in the home they leave; we watch the mixture of pride and fear of the families of defense force personnel as they wave off their loved ones to active duty in war-ravaged countries, wondering if and when they will see them again; we see a friend off on a long holiday to a distant place, or a move to a new home, both of us promising to "stay in touch," and hoping that we will. But there is no doubt that the ascending Jesus will stay in touch with all his disciples, down through the ages; no disappointment of the hope that where the Head has gone, the body of believers will be called to follow.

The Lukan description of the Ascension might be translated colloquially as: "For heaven's sake! . . . What on earth are you doing?!" For heaven's sake, say the two messengers in white (reminiscent of the two at the empty tomb) to the gawking disciples, don't just stand there looking up to heaven. There is an earth to be transformed into God's kingdom before Jesus returns! Behind this scene it seems that there are Luke's memories of Elisha and Elijah (2 Kgs 1:9-14). Only after Elisha had witnessed Elijah's ascension to heaven in the chariots of fire, could he put on his master's prophetic coat and be filled with his spirit. Only after the ascension of Jesus and the disciples' clothing with his Spirit can his disciples of all generations take up their prophetic role and work with deep desire to make the world ready to become the new heavens and new earth when Jesus comes again. Of this commitment and expectation Pierre Teilhard de Chardin wrote in 1957:

> Successors to Israel, we Christians have been charged with keeping the flame of desire ever alive in the world. Only twenty centuries have passed since the Ascension. What have we made of our expectancy? . . . We persist in saying that we keep vigil in expectation of the Master. But in reality we would have to admit, if we were sincere, that we no longer expect anything.
> The flame must be revived at all costs.[18]

Despite our possible problems with seductive "space-age imagery" rather than biblical imagery, the ascension of Jesus is a feast of expectation that reminds us to continually open our hearts to the Spirit who revives in us our sense of mission.

In the words of Psalm 47 we respond to this responsibility with shouts of praise and words of faith: "God goes up with shouts of joy; the Lord goes up with trumpet blast." In the Temple liturgy of Rosh Hashanah (literally "the head of the year"), this psalm was sung seven times before the *shofar* (ram's horn) blasts that announced the Jewish New Year. As we sing it today, it is our privilege to know that the risen and ascended Jesus has inaugurated the reign of God in the new era of the church.

For some reason, the Lectionary omits verse 14 from today's reading of the "longer ending" (and third post-resurrection appearance of Jesus) of Mark's gospel. It is considered an inspired but later addition to Mark 16:8, for the comfort and strengthening of the communities on mission. And so as we gather liturgically around the table, we may not realize that Jesus' commission to go and proclaim the Good News of his resurrection to the whole of creation is also given to the wounded Eleven "at table." Nor do we hear how Jesus upbraids them for their lack of faith and stubbornness—something that is surely a great consolation for ourselves as wounded, struggling disciples in whom the flame of missionary desire can flicker or even be extinguished. Yet like the Eleven, we are also people entrusted with the mission of proclaiming the Gospel now that the physical presence of Jesus has ascended to heaven and is no longer with us. We too are sent to do new wonders, speak new words with the fire of the Spirit on our tongues, offer new healing to our sisters and brothers, and cast out contemporary "demons" from ourselves and others. And all this continues to be "in the name of," in the personal power of Jesus into whose Body we are baptized.

The author of the Letter to the Ephesians, a close associate of Paul and writing in his name, speaks as a "prisoner in the Lord." Paul encourages Christians to unselfishness and gentleness, patience and peace. These are the "chains" that are more important than those in which he is imprisoned, the bonds that will create unity among them. This unity is sevenfold: one body, one Spirit, one hope, one Lord, one faith, one baptism, one God and Father of all. Practically speaking, to live lovingly and eagerly in such unity requires humility, gentleness, long-suffering, and forbearance with one another. And lest we think this is too great a demand, we are reminded that the risen and ascended Christ has sent upon us the gifts that make such relationships and ministry possible. Paul is confident that the risen and ascended Christ has taken captive the powers that oppose the Christian community, and will also equip the church with the grace that will enable his body to grow to full and cosmic maturity. Diversity of gifts among its members is no threat to, but rather the strength of, such unity. In our own times, when stability is under threat in precious relationships such as marriage, Paul longs for a stability that is not passively entrenched in the old and familiar, but is vital and ever new, the growth of the Body of Christ. To again quote Pierre Teilhard de Chardin for whom such growth has cosmic consequences:

> Since Jesus was born, and grew to his full stature, and died, everything has continued to move forward because Christ is not yet fully formed: he has not yet gathered about himself the last folds of his robe of flesh and love which is made up of his faithful followers.[19]

Pentecost Sunday

(For readings for the Vigil of Pentecost, see *Welcoming the Word in Year A: Building on Rock*, pp. 83–87)

Day Mass

• Acts 2:1-11 • Ps 104:1, 24, 29-31, 34 • Gal 5:16-25 • John 15:26-27; 16:12-15

With Pentecost, the Easter season comes full circle, embracing us in the mystery of the risen Christ, firing our hearts with new images, and impelling us as with a strong wind to make the Good News a daily reality in our own and others' lives. In today's first reading, Luke is groping for a way of describing the Pentecost experience, and again he uses images. The house where the apostles are gathered is shaken "as if" by a great wind, and something "like" tongues of fire divides and rests upon each of them. Then in four verses Luke rushes us with gale-force speed into a description of the first effects of the Spirit who sets in motion preaching, prophecy, mission, conversion, and worldwide outreach—at least to the then-known Mediterranean world.

With fire on their tongues and with boldly prophetic breath, the disciples immediately go out to speak to those who are gathered in Jerusalem for the Jewish feast of Pentecost (Shavuot or feast of Weeks). Luke makes this feast the backdrop for this new drama. It was one of the major pilgrim festivals, celebrated fifty days, or seven complete weeks, after the feast of Unleavened Bread/Passover. The latter marked the harvesting of the barley, while Pentecost was the time of the wheat harvest. As Israel became less of an agricultural society, Pentecost also developed liturgically into a commemoration of the giving of the Torah/Law on Mount Sinai. In the Exodus account of the event (Exod 19:16-18) there is also the presence of fire and the violent shaking of the mountain.[20] Luke's theological creativity links this Jewish tradition with both the new harvesting of the post-Pentecostal Christian community and the new law of the Spirit given by the risen Christ. Those to whom the disciples speak are described as "devout Jews from every nation under heaven living in Jerusalem." After Luke had described the descent of the Spirit on Jesus at his baptism, he traces the genealogy of the generations of his Jewish ancestry back to Abraham, and even to Adam (Luke 21–38). After this "baptism in the Spirit" of the apostles and their companions, Luke gives us a table of nations from which the Jews had gathered at this Pentecost. The promises and hopes of his people that were harvested in Jesus will now be carried to the ends of the earth by his disciples who are sealed in their identity and mission by the Spirit of Jesus, but it is the Jews of Jerusalem and the Diaspora who are the first to be gathered into the Christian community. The language of the Spirit is that of a particular human group, with their recognizable Galilean accents, because God always works through real people, never obliterating our human characteristics. But the effect is of God, reversing the divisions of Babel, as all those to whom the apostles speak hear them in their own language.

Pentecost is a continuing event that dares us: dares us to become a community of fire that will keep the flame of passion for God, and for the world which God loves, burning strongly even through the darkest days and nights. It dares us to become a community of strong wind that blows the Good News of the risen Christ through the cracks and crevices of our fractured lives. And if we, like that first Jerusalem community, persevere in prayer and community, the Spirit will also enable us to speak in intelligible tongues to the men and women of our own times and cultures. This is not just a personal challenge; it is a challenge for the church, especially its leaders, from the pope down, and especially in their ecclesial statements. We will all make mistakes; at times we may be "out of breath" because life rushes us into so many distractions, temptations, and social changes. But God will never fail us; if we are open to the Spirit, the community of believers will never suffocate.

This is what Paul affirms in his Letter to the Galatians. He tells them how they can discern whether or not they are being led by the Spirit, keeping in step as a community, walking in the way of Jesus Christ, and keeping the law by which we are called into freedom (cf. Gal 5:1, 13-15). Such freedom in Christ and his Spirit is the whole context of this chapter of Galatians. If our rebellious human nature is self-centered and self-indulgent, Christians will not yield a harvest worthy of the kingdom of God. Paul lists specific examples of such sinfulness for a practical review of life: sexual depravity, religious infidelity, social discord, addictive and disorderly behavior. In contrast, if our lives bear the fruit of the Spirit, if we try to create social harmony and peace, and if we are servants of one another, practicing something of the sacrificial love that Christ showed most fully by his crucifixion, then we will be ingathered into the reign of God. As Richard B. Hays comments: "The church at its best has been willing to take the gamble that Paul recommends, wagering its future on the guidance of the Spirit, trusting God and performing without a safety net."[21] Does the church have too many "safety nets" stretched out over our world today? Do we as individuals prefer to perform too safely as Christians?

The part of the farewell discourse that we hear in today's gospel gives us the Johannine perspective on the coming of the Holy Spirit. The Spirit is one of the great gifts of that last night of gifts: the night of the service of humble foot washing, of friendship, of shared bread and cup. John names the Spirit as "Paraclete," which can be translated as Advocate, Encourager, Counselor—all names that offer enormous hope to the disciples. Moreover, the Spirit is both the memory and the future of the church, not only recalling to our minds and hearts what Jesus has said and done, but also guiding and urging us into future openness to the fullness of truth. Those who believe, nostalgically, that the pilgrim church was already perfect in some past golden age, need to listen to the highest teaching authority of the church reminding us that until the end of human history: " . . . as the centuries succeed one another, the Church constantly moves forward towards the fullness of divine truth until the words of God reach their complete fulfillment in her."[22] New encounters with the words of Jesus will be necessary in changing social and cultural situations. The Paraclete will be our guarantee of new tongues in which to speak intelligibly to people in these new situations, and of new hearts that can keep alight the flame of Pentecostal passion to ignite the love of God in our world. The Easter flame was struck from hard flint to enkindle the Easter Fire; it is now from the hard flint of our hearts that this same flame must continue to be struck.

In the select verses of today's responsorial Psalm 104 we pray: "Lord, send out your Spirit, and renew the face of the earth." The psalm praises God's provident creation of the myriad forms of life, and in this interdependent web of life, humanity is also situated. We praise God's provident care for all this creation, and not only for our own species' existence. The gift of our physical life is placed together with the gift of our spiritual life. It is in our embodied and interdependent reality, not in some superior dream world, that the Spirit works to bring humanity to the existence for which it is created.

Pentecost is not only what we often refer to as the birth of the church; it is the celebration of *being* church. The Easter season has come full term, and now we must continue through the season of Ordinary Time to live what we are born to in the waters of baptism: the new life of the risen Christ.

Notes

1. Alan Paton, *Ah, But Your Land Is Beautiful* (New York: Charles Scribner's Sons, Paperback edition, 1983) 229–240.

2. After the destruction of the Temple in Jerusalem in 70 c.e., Jewish sacrifices could no longer be offered, and since then the paschal lamb at the Seder meal on Passover Eve is represented by a roasted lamb shank bone only.

3. James Luther Mays, *Psalms: A Bible Commentary for Teaching and Preaching* (Louisville, KY: John Knox Press, Interpretation series, 1994) 372.

4. "The Dream of the Rood," in *The Earliest English Poems* (Harmondsworth, Middlesex: Penguin Books Inc., Penguin Classics, 1966) 106. Used with permission.

5. Cf. Pierre Teilhard de Chardin, *Hymn of the Universe* (London: William Collins Sons & Co. Ltd., 1965) 121.

6. Karl Rahner, *The Eternal Year* (London: Burns Oates, 1964) 94–95.

7. Joseph Cardinal Bernardin, *The Gift of Peace* (Chicago: Loyola Press, 1997) 38–40.

8. *The Asian Journal of Thomas Merton* (New York: New Directions, 1973) 306.

9. T. S. Eliot, "Four Quartets—Burnt Norton," in *The Complete Poems and Plays* (London: Faber and Faber Limited, 1969) 173.

10. Eugene LaVerdiere, *Dining in the Kingdom of God: the origins of the Eucharist according to Luke* (Chicago: Liturgy Training Publications, 1994) 184.

11. Vatican II, Declaration of the Church on Non-Christian Religions (*Nostra aetate*), art. 4.

12. Vatican II, Decree on Ecumenism (*Unitatis redintegratio*), art. 6.

13. María Virgil López, *Oscar Romero: Memories in Mosaic*, translated by Kathy Ogle (London: Darton, Longman and Todd, Ltd., 2000) 423.

14. Daniel Berrigan, S.J., *Whereon to Stand: The Acts of the Apostles and Ourselves* (Baltimore, MD: Fortkamp Publishing Company, 1991) 135.

15. Benedict XVI, Encyclical Letter, *God Is Love*, Rome, 25 December 2005, art. 1.

16. Published by PQ Blackwell, Auckland, New Zealand.

17. Gerard Manley Hopkins, "Inversnaid," *Poems and Prose of Gerard Manley Hopkins*, selected with an introduction and notes by W. H. Gardner (Harmondsworth, Middlesex: Penguin Books Ltd., 1982) 51.

18. Pierre Teilhard de Chardin, *Le Milieu Divin: An Essay on the Interior Life* (London: William Collins Sons & Co. Ltd., A Fontana Book, Sixth Impression, 1967) 151–152.

19. Pierre Teilhard de Chardin, "Pensées 58," *Hymn of the Universe*, 121.

20. In *On the Decalogue* 46, Philo Judaeus explicitly associates the giving of the Torah with speech from the flames, speech which became articulate language familiar to the hearers. See Luke Timothy Johnson, *The Acts of the Apostles*, Sacra Pagina Series, volume 5 (Collegeville, MN: Liturgical Press, 1992) 46.

21. Richard B. Hays, "The Letter to the Galatians," in *The New Interpreter's Bible*, Volume XI (Nashville: Abingdon Press, 2000) 329.

22. Vatican II, Dogmatic Constitution on Divine Revelation, art. 8.

5

The Season of Ordinary Time

Ordinary Time is divided into two parts: the weeks between the end of the Christmas season until the Sunday before Ash Wednesday, and the weeks after Pentecost until the last Sunday of the liturgical year, the Solemnity of Our Lord Jesus Christ, the Universal King. This is not a dull, uneventful season that we grind through with Macbeth's attitude of (substituting "Sunday"): "Tomorrow, and tomorrow, and tomorrow, creeps in this petty pace from day to day . . ." (Act 5, scene V, line 19).[1] These are weeks that are "ordered," not so much to mathematical sequence, but rather to the unfolding of the mystery of the Christ. Each Sunday is "the Lord's day," keeping us mindful of his mystery in much the same way as the early church did before the festal seasons developed. The Sundays of Ordinary Time are to each of our thirty-four weeks what Easter is to the whole liturgical year.

Timothy Radcliffe comments that:

> It sounds boring, something to be got through before the next exciting thing happens.
> But the word "ordinary" here refers to something basic to our humanity. We can only be human because we are ordered, meaning pointed, away from ourselves. We are ordered towards each other, and we are ordered towards God. Ordinary time is when we grow in the ways that we belong to each other and to the Kingdom.[2]

The liturgical color for Ordinary Time is green, the symbol of life and fertility, and after the high points of Christmas and Easter we remember, from Sunday to Sunday, that in the midst of the everyday our lives are being inserted into the life of the Incarnate and Risen One who transforms our ordinary existence with extraordinary and fertile possibilities.

In Year B, the gospels of Ordinary Time are from the Gospel of Mark, with the exception of the second Sunday, when John gently directs us toward the Baptist's encouragement to follow Jesus, and in the five weeks (17th to 21st Sundays) when John's Bread of Life discourse is proclaimed. Not having his own "year" in the three-year cycle, we are reminded in these weeks of the significance of John 6 for the liturgical assembly. The Markan portrait of Jesus is sketched with quick but sure strokes as he moves urgently through a dark landscape of sickness, sin, and evil. Very early in this gospel (Mark 3:6) the cross casts its shadow over the Servant Jesus. Like the first disciples, we meet a Jesus who calls us and sends us out to continue his mission of healing and confronting contemporary suffering, of facing controversies and demons in ourselves, our church, and our world. In Mark's gospel, Jesus meets much disbelief and opposition, especially among those who think they know him yet cannot accept his deepest personal truth. Such obtuse discipleship may often be our reality; but real, too, is the abiding and converting love of Jesus for those who fail.

The Old Testament readings distributed over these weeks are again chosen as fairly short but representative samples of the riches of the Scriptures of Israel, and with the conviction that "the New Testament cannot be properly understood apart from the Old Testament and the Jewish tradition which transmits it."[3] The readings are "moored" to the gospel in various ways: by an explicit reference to the Old Testament reading, by reference to a similar event or deed, by complementing or supplementing an idea or viewpoint proclaimed in the gospel or occasionally presenting a different viewpoint, or by providing the Jewish background to the words and deeds of Jesus. On a very few Sundays the gospel moorings seem to slip, but the Old Testament reading is still significant. The responsorial psalm verses often sum up the theme of the Sunday, and invite the assembly to an active engagement with the Word that has been proclaimed.

In Year B, as in all years, the second reading is semicontinuous and chosen from the Letters of the New Testament so that we may be exposed to the Good News of the mystery of Christ and the way it was lived in the early churches. To conform our lives to this mystery is the basic reason why we gather as a liturgical assembly. In Year B, the readings are from Paul's First and Second Letters to the Corinthians, the Letter to the Ephesians, the Letter of James, and the Letter to the Hebrews. There is less correspondence between these readings and the Old Testament and gospel readings, but the Scripture, in every year of the three-year cycle: ". . . is inspired by God and is useful for teaching, for reproof, for correction, and for training in righteousness, so that everyone who belongs to God may be proficient, equipped for every good work" (2 Tim 3:16-17).

On the two Sundays following Pentecost, the church seems reluctant to return to Ordinary Time and so celebrates the two solemnities of the Most

Holy Trinity and the Most Holy Body and Blood of Christ. These feasts suggest what Ordinary Time should be for us: the discovery of our true identity as a community of believers who are offered the hospitality of life in God, and who share communion in the risen Christ and one another through the sacramental bread that is broken and wine that is poured out for the life of the world.

The Solemnity of the Most Holy Trinity

• Deut 4:32-34, 39-40 • Ps 33:4-5, 6, 9, 18-20, 22 • Rom 8:14-17 • Matt 28:16-20

Ronald Rolheiser writes that:

> The most pernicious heresies that block us from properly knowing God are not those of formal dogma, but those of a culture of individualism that invite us to believe that we are self-sufficient, that we can have community and family on our own terms, and that we can have God without dealing with each other. But God is community—and only in opening our lives in gracious hospitality will we ever understand that.[4]

And so we need this solemnity that reminds us that God is a Trinity, a flow of relationships between Father, Son, and Holy Spirit—and ourselves. The Lectionary readings chosen for today, therefore, are about relationships of love. Deuteronomy takes us back to the beginning of human history and the great events by which God related to the Hebrew people. Through the spoken word ascribed to Moses, the human experience of the past is remembered and lives again for them in the present, so that they can identify with the exodus generation and the provident care of their liberating God now and through future generations. God's choice, therefore, is expansive: from Moses to his enslaved people and to us as hearers of the word who also need to commit ourselves to the daring claim that "there is no other besides him." Other idolatries are still with us, even if we do not call them "gods": the worship of individualism, of money, of the false comfort of addictions, of the pleasures that we hope may solve the problem of what to do with our pain—all of which trivialize both the dignity of humanity and the reverent wonder of God.

To choose such a God is not a matter of doom and gloom, as the responsorial Psalm 33 reminds us. God is a God of steadfast love of the cosmos, of humanity, as well as of those who have the privilege of knowing God's creating word and to which they respond with hope and trust.

For Paul, our relationship to God is trinitarian, although he does not use this later theological language. It is the Spirit who leads us into the freedom of God's children even more wonderfully than the pillar of cloud and fire led the Hebrews out of slavery. Now we can cry "Abba! Father!"—a naming of a relationship of intimacy that adopts us with the consequent status of God's sons and daughters in Christ the Son. The Christ who has suffered, died, and is risen is already in possession of his inheritance. Our sharing in this inheritance will mean sharing both his sufferings and his glory, but our cry to "Abba" is one that proclaims confidence even, and especially, in the face of weaknesses and difficulties in our journey of faith. It is the cry of Jesus in Gethsemane (Mark 14:36) that Paul has retained in the privileged Aramaic mother tongue of Jesus.

Today's gospel gives us the concluding words of Matthew. The risen and authoritative Jesus meets with the Eleven, wounded by betrayal and failure, still a very human mix of hopeful faith and hesitant doubt, of adoration and indecision. For our consolation, these are the disciples to whom Jesus entrusts the inclusive mission of making disciples of "all nations," without distinction of race or culture. With the authority of the risen Jesus, they are commissioned to baptize "in the name of the Father and of the Son and of the Holy Spirit," and to teach these new followers to obey everything that Jesus has revealed to them during his earthly mission. On their first missionary journey (Matt 10:1, 5-8) there had been no command to teach, but now that they have experienced not only Jesus' life but also his death and resurrection, they are equipped to teach the full significance of his instructions. We who have gathered to celebrate the Most Holy Trinity have been baptized and taught, called and schooled by Jesus through the mission of his church. We have been drawn into the divine-human communion of that first "trinitarian" moment of Jesus' baptism by John in the Jordan when the Father, Son, and Holy Spirit were named. Matthew gives us the solemn assurance that Jesus, Immanuel, "God-with-us" (Matt 1:23) as the personal promise of God, will be with the church until the end of human history. His is no "absentee lordship" but a presence of a servant Christ who wishes to liberate rather than dominate. His church, therefore, must also be a humble servant that remembers that its authority is not absolute but is derived from Jesus; a church that identifies with those who are a very human mix of faith and doubt; a church that avoids all triumphalism and insensitivity to the wounded people of our world.

And as we are the church, are *we* this kind of people? When we sign ourselves "In the name of the Father and of the Son and of the Holy Spirit," could we sometimes reflect on this rather than making a very perfunctory "brush and babble" gesture? Can we instead have something of the passion of John Donne's "Holy Sonnet XIV," where Donne expresses his faith that, to be truly free, we must be rescued from sin and then taken captive again—but this time by the love of the "three-person'd God":

> Batter my heart, three-person'd God; for you
> As yet but knock, breathe, shine, and seek to mend;
> That I may rise, and stand, o'erthrow me, and bend
> Your force, to break, blow, burn, and make me new.[5]

The Solemnity of the Most Holy Body and Blood of Christ

• Exod 24:3-8 • Ps 116:12-13, 15-16, 17-18 • Heb 9:11-15 • Mark 14:12-16, 22-26

We all know the importance of blood for life. Blood tests, blood disorders, blood transfusions are part of medical care and diagnosis. We talk about blood relationships and the fact that "blood is thicker than water" when reflecting on (sometimes surprising) familial loyalties. The loyalty that is symbolized by blood is central to the reading from the Book of Exodus that describes the dramatic ceremonial ratification of the covenant between God and the Hebrew people.

First comes listening, as Moses proclaims the commands of God to the people, and they respond with one voice that they will obey all that the Lord has decreed. The commands are put into writing, a "book of the covenant," as a recorded reference for the people and a source for future liturgical use. Then the stage for the renewal of the covenant is arranged: an altar is built to designate the presence of the Holy One, and twelve pillars erected as symbols of the totality of the people of the twelve tribes. As Israel is about to enter into a binding covenant relationship with God, some young Israelites who were not priests or Levites, and perhaps those who also stood at the threshold of the lifelong relationship of marriage or sworn loyalty in military excursions, are chosen to offer burnt offering and sacrifice oxen at the altar. To seal the covenant, half of the blood of the oxen is sprinkled first on the altar, the symbol of the deity, for it is God who initiates the covenant.

Then the book of the covenant is read again to the listening people; this is their second chance to decide if they will be faithful partners with God in this covenant. They profess their loyalty, and Moses sprinkles the other half of the sacrificial blood on the people as a most solemn twofold sign of their pledge as the covenant partners: that one will lay down life for the other, and that if one partner is unfaithful their life may be surrendered to the other. The gathering around the altar, the listening to the reading of the book of the covenant, and the sealing of the relationship between God and the people by the blood of the covenant constitute a solemn liturgical action. And in the verses immediately following the portion read today, the leaders of Israel ascend Mount Sinai with Moses to eat as well as drink in the presence of the God of Israel.

We, too, are gathered around the altar, listen to the Word of God, and participate in a sacrificial covenant, but it is a radically new covenant sealed in the Body and Blood, the whole and real personal presence of Jesus, who is given for us in sacrifice and sacrament. Mark details the instructions that Jesus gives his disciples for the preparation of what the evangelist understands as a Passover meal, a memorial (*zikkaron*) celebration of the great Jewish feast of freedom and hope that pulls the past into the present for the sake of the future. Two disciples had been sent into Jerusalem to prepare for Jesus' earlier and triumphant entry into the Holy City (Mark 11:1-7); two go again to prepare for the feast and find the people and place just as Jesus had told them. This sets the scene for today's different entry into Jerusalem, which is quietly assured and deliberate, a presence of Jesus in the face of death that continues throughout the whole supper narrative. The Lectionary cuts out the prediction of the betrayal of Judas and the frightened questioning of the other disciples that we have heard on Palm Sunday, and focuses on the theme of today's solemnity: the sharing of bread and wine.

In Mark's gospel, Jesus had twice before broken bread for the crowds, both Jews (Mark 6:34-44) and Gentiles (Mark 8:14-21), and again on this night he takes, blesses, breaks, and gives the bread to his disciples—but with the deepest significance, for Jesus says: "This is my body." The word used for "body" is *sōma*, meaning "person," not *sarx*, "flesh," and Jesus hands over to the disciples his "body," his person that is about to be handed over to others to be tortured, broken in a sacrificial death of selfless and inclusive love, which is the final act of his earthly mission and which the Father will affirm by his resurrection. Likewise, the cup is shared as "the blood of the covenant, which is poured out for many." Not only the Exodus covenant of the first reading is recalled, but also what Jesus had earlier told his disciples about himself and his mission, that: "the son of Man also came, not to be served, but to serve, and to lay down his life as a ransom for many" (Mark 10:45). Jesus tells his disciples that this meal will be the last he will share with them *until* they celebrate again in the freedom that is to be found on the other side of death, in the kingdom. Donald Senior comments:

> But coupled to the prediction of separation and death is a defiant "until" that bridges the chasm of death and projects Jesus into the banquet of the Kingdom. In spite of death he *will* share in the banquet on Zion for which Israel longed,

the banquet where the wine of the Kingdom would flow anew and God would brush aside the cobweb of death and wipe away all tears (Isa 25:6-8; 65:17-25). The verse is a stunning prediction of hope and victory planted in a story that rushes towards death.[6]

The disciples are fragile and vulnerable, as the next few hours of the passion will show. Just as this is a meal of hope for them, unworthy as they are, so the eucharistic sacrificial meal of Christ's Body and Blood is for us. We no longer celebrate this solemnity with elaborate processions, walking behind the monstrance. What is more important is our participation in the broken bread and the spilled wine when, in the blessed strength of Christ's Body and Blood, we go out of the liturgy to walk with our sisters and brothers and allow ourselves to be broken and given and consumed as we sacrifice ourselves in their service, just as Jesus sacrificed himself for us. Every parent, every friend, every unselfish person knows such giving and consuming.

In the most solemn rituals of the annual Jewish Day of Atonement, the high priest first sacrificed a bull and then, on this day only, entered alone into the Holy of Holies, "and not without blood" (Heb 9:7), to sprinkle its blood on the ark of the covenant, the mercy seat, in atonement for his sins and those of his family. After this the high priest sacrificed a goat and sprinkled its blood on the people. God and the people are ritually bonded in the blood (cf. Lev 16:1-19). The Letter to the Hebrews does not deny the spiritual effectiveness of these sacrifices, but the emphasis is on the "how much more" of Christ's sacrifice. Christ is the High Priest who goes, with his own blood, before the mercy seat of God in the heavenly tabernacle. It is a sacrifice "through the eternal Spirit," a one-and-only, never-to-be-repeated, and perfect act of sacrifice of himself. What he accomplishes for us is the purification of our inner selves, our consciences, and so we too become acceptable for worship before God, as we are doing at this Eucharist.

With the responsorial Psalm 116 we proclaim that God is our ever-faithful covenant partner who protects the lives of his people. This psalm was also one that was recited during the Jewish Passover ritual, perhaps in connection with the drinking of the fourth cup. For this reason it is also the responsorial psalm for Holy Thursday. "How can I repay the Lord for his goodness to me?" is the abiding question we might ask ourselves on this solemnity, a goodness that, in and through and with Christ, surpasses anything that the psalmist could have dreamed. At this Eucharist we raise the cup of salvation, the cup of the new covenant in Christ's Blood. Drinking from this one cup, we become one with the sacrifice of Christ, and this identity brings with it vocation: to be ready for the crushing that makes many grapes into the wine;

to share the cup that makes us, like Christ, responsible for the dregs of our society, those whose lives are costly in the sight of God.

Second Sunday in Ordinary Time

(The First Sunday is the Baptism of the Lord, which also completes the Christmas cycle. See pp. 25–28.)

• 1 Sam 3:3b-10, 19 • Ps 40:2, 4, 7-10 • 1 Cor 6:13c-15a, 17-20 • John 1:35-42

As we begin our journey through Ordinary Time, the first reading we hear is the well-known call of the young Samuel and, like today's gospel, it orients us to the significance of God's call and our response. Probably familiar from many of our childhood classrooms is the painting of a rather angelic, curly haired little Samuel enveloped in his nightshirt, innocent, wide-eyed and attentive to something or someone outside the frame of the picture. But there is much more to this "infancy narrative" of the prophet, many deeper implications for the new things that God will do for the people.

It is a crisis moment in the life and politics of Israel. The priestly family serving the temple at Shiloh has become spiritually exhausted and dissipated; the people lack any religious leadership; politics and society are corrupt. In the two verses before the Lectionary's choice, we are told that "the word of the Lord was rare in those days; visions were not widespread" (1 Sam 3:1-2). The old, half-blind priest Eli is representative of the enfeebled religious situation and enduring the tragedy of his objectionable family. This is the situation in which Samuel is serving his temple apprenticeship, having been offered to God by his mother Hannah, so long barren, in gratitude for the gift of her son. Through Hannah's piety, Eli's discernment, and Samuel's availability, what Hannah sang of so joyfully and gratefully (1 Sam 2:1-10) is about to be realized. God will raise up the poor and the needy and put down the rich and ambitious. The Word of God is about to fall on the fertile hearing of the young Samuel and find there the rich soil of obedience and prophecy.

As Samuel lies in the sanctuary, probably keeping night watch to ensure the lamp before the ark of the covenant does not go out, he three times hears a voice addressing him personally by name. Three times Samuel mistakes the voice as that of Eli. Only at the fourth time does Eli, old and physically half-blind, yet with the gifts of spiritual discernment and experience, realize that it is their persistent God who is calling the boy. He reveals this truth to Samuel, and also tells him how to respond. "Speak, for your servant is listening" are words that we, as baptized servants of the Lord, need to make our own, especially in times of religious indifference and social chaos. Like Samuel, our witness to God will then be blessed and fruitful as we grow in age and in the grace of our baptismal consecration as God's prophets.

In the responsorial Psalm 40 we identify with the person delivered from some disaster who praises God for this deliverance with a new song. One aspect of this newness is that the psalmist understands his gratitude not to consist primarily of a sacrificial thanksgiving offering, but rather in the vivid and vigorous imagery of allowing God to "bore" or "dig out" his ears so that he can always hear what the word of God asks of him. With another bodily image that reflects personal, attentive presence to God, the psalmist stands before God with "unsealed lips" for witness. As we pray in our liturgical assembly, we might reflect on what clogs up our ears so that we become deaf to God. What shuts our mouths against witnessing to God's saving action, above all in Christ?

For the next five weeks we read from Paul's First Letter to the Corinthians, and after that for four weeks from his Second Letter to this same church. Depravity and licentiousness are a reality for the city of Corinth, located on the gulf of Corinth and a center of commerce, and Greek, Roman, and Egyptian religious diversity. Paul is anxious to strengthen the morality of his young church living in the midst of a superficial cultural life with a population where the affluent were ambitious and socially mobile, and the poor were neglected. It had also earned the reputation of something of an ancient "Sin City," where sailors enjoyed themselves, often in sexual romps, during a few days of shore leave. The Christians were mainly poor and Gentile (1 Cor 1:26), with a minority of the more affluent, a disparity that was to challenge Paul's pastoral leadership, especially in regard to eucharistic unity (1 Cor 11:17-34).

If the second reading had commenced one verse earlier, it would be easier to put the text in context. "All things are lawful for me," is the catch-cry of some of the Christian community who are pushing Paul's teaching about freedom in Christ beyond its acceptable limits. In Paul's terminology, the body (*sōma*) is not just the physical entity, something we "have"; it is the whole embodied person, the self that we are, our whole human and personal reality, and something sacred. Christians, through their baptism, have been incorporated into the Body of the risen Christ, and are one with him. Sexual immorality (*porneía*) is related linguistically "to sell," and understood as "sex for sale" that violates and defiles the dignity of those who indulge in it, as well as defiling for Christians the intimate relationship between Christ and themselves. Bodily faithfulness is not just the contemporary concern about exercise, diet, substance abuse, or sex outside marriage. Ernst Käsemann comments that, for Paul, the body is "the piece of the world which we our-selves are and for which we bear responsibility"[7]—a holistic and Christian responsibility. Surrounded as the Corinthians were by dozens of pagan temples and shrines they would have been familiar with the idea of a temple as a dwelling place of the gods and places of sacrifice and prayer. Each Chris-tian person is a temple, a dwelling place of the Holy Spirit, purchased for God by the sacrifice of Christ and owing honor to God in Christ and through the Spirit. We are called to "glorify God in our bodies," in our sacred and pre-cious embodied humanity by which we can relate to others, since we are not disembodied spirits. Such relationship is to bring honor to the One who has purchased us at such a great price. In our present individualistic society this is a challenge, as it was so long ago to our Corinthian sisters and brothers.

The first of today's readings was concerned with listening to the call of God; the gospel begins with looking and gazing and responding to the call to discipleship. John the Baptist stands with two of his disciples, ready to decrease in personal significance so that Jesus may increase (cf. John 3:30). After his testimony there will be no hanging onto or hankering for his former disciples. John watches Jesus pass by; the eyes of John's heart penetrate to the reality of this man, and he points him out to his disciples as the Lamb of God. The Jewish religious experience of the lamb was as the sacrificial offer-ing that overcame the alienation of sin and created unity between the people and God. In whatever way the Baptist's disciples understood his words, they were spoken with an urgency that made them leave John and follow Jesus. Jesus himself turns and sees them. The word the evangelist uses for "sees" (*theásthai*) has the sense of gazing contemplatively and engagingly at these two followers. Jesus then asks them his first question in the Fourth Gospel: "What are you looking for?" It is a question that will persist throughout this gospel, from this first chapter to the garden of the resurrection morning, but by then the "What" has become "Whom" in the intimate encounter of Jesus and Mary Magdalene (John 20:15).

The two disciples ask Jesus, the Teacher (Rabbi), where he is staying, and he responds by inviting them to "Come and see." Their question is about a place; their experience is about abiding for the rest of the day in a relation-ship with a person, about the beginning of a new communion between the people and this Lamb of God. The "where" is not as important as the "with whom." The pattern of discipleship is established: through witness (of the Baptist), others follow and experience Jesus' truth for themselves. They in turn bring others to Jesus. One of the first two who followed Jesus remains anonymous, perhaps as a Johannine invitation to future readers to see a challenge to themselves in the following, seeking pattern of discipleship. The other is later named as Andrew, who announces to his brother, Simon Peter, that he has found the Messiah. Like the first disciples, we all see something different in this same Jesus, and Jesus recognizes the truth in us, just as in this first chapter of the Fourth Gospel Jesus' insight into Simon's role in the community of the disciples suggests his renaming as Cephas (Aramaic *kepha/* Greek *petra/* Rock).

This gospel proclaims that all discipleship is an active and involving relationship with Jesus: a following, seeking, staying, finding, and dialoguing with him. We hear how each decision to follow Jesus is a response to a statement about Jesus' identity as Lamb of God, Rabbi, Messiah, by people whose ears and hearts are open to the Word of God, who hear his invitation through the words of friend or stranger, through events of joy or sorrow, or who discern a moment of religious significance in the everyday. As Matthew Arnold wrote in "The Buried Life":

> But often, in the world's most crowded streets,
> But often in the din of strife,
> There rises an unspeakable desire
> After the knowledge of our buried life;
> A thirst to spend our fire and restless force
> In tracking out our true, original course,
> A longing to enquire
> Into the mystery of this heart which beats
> So wild, so deep in us—to know
> Whence our lives come and whence they go.[8]

Third Sunday in Ordinary Time

• Jonah 3:1-5, 10 • Ps 25:4-9 • 1 Cor 7:29-31 • Mark 1:14-20

In the wilderness Jesus has withstood Satan's temptation, and strengthened in spirit by this personal combat, he comes into Galilee, the "springtime" place of first preaching, first ministry, first calling of disciples. Yet there has also been a winter: the arrest and imprisonment of John the Baptist, which add urgency to Jesus' first spoken words in Mark's gospel. The time of God's reigning presence is at hand, and this Good News of God demands a response. "Repent and believe in the good news" may have been repeated as an early Christian baptismal call to the catechumens (the elect) as they descended into the Easter waters to rise up as God's new creation. At infant baptism our parents and our faith community made this response for us; the challenge is for us to say our own continuing adult "Yes" to this call, and grow in our discipleship.

Urged on by his sense of mission, Jesus passes along the lakeside, the Sea of Galilee. He "sees" Peter and Andrew, with a seeing that penetrates to their deepest selves and their future potential as his disciples whom, with all their successes and failures, he will make fishers of people to draw others into the kingdom. All that Simon and Andrew will become will be because of Jesus and, with contagious gospel urgency, "immediately" they follow him, leaving behind their nets, the source of their income. A little further on another two brothers, James and John, sons of Zebedee, are called while they are involved in their fishermen's task of mending nets. Once again the call and response is immediate and the dispossession is radical when they follow Jesus. It is significant that the first disciples whom Jesus calls are people who must leave what is indicative of their success in a brotherly and family venture: boats, nets, hired servants, parent. They follow Jesus, not hoping for a better lifestyle, but urged by his words to an unconditional obedience to him. From the beginning of his ministry, Jesus gathers a community around himself in a relationship of "brotherliness" that the call of two sets of brothers may also suggest.

Whereas our consumer society has to packet and market every commodity, every offer has to have a good sales pitch, even in some megachurches and by some TV evangelists, Mark's narrative of Jesus' call is stark and unadorned. Like any relationship, this is the "honeymoon" period.[9] Much of what they understand at this moment they will progressively forget, and compromises, obtuseness, status-seeking will replace following until, on the eve of Jesus' passion and death, the disciples leave everything to run away from him (Mark 14:50-51). The traditional prophetic calling accounts, such as that of Samuel or Elisha's call by Elijah (1 Kgs 19:19-21), are transformed because now it is Jesus who calls. Jesus does not issue orders to his followers like a charismatic military leader (e.g., Judg 3:28; 1 Sam 11:6-7); he offers no rallying call to a revolutionary war (1 Macc 2:27-28), but he does make promises. Do we live as though we believe these promises? How constant, how radical are we in our following of Jesus to which we are invited by our baptism? How discerning of its demands are we in our contemporary society, and has Jesus priority in our lives? Do we continually try to launch out into a shared mission with Jesus that will transform us from day to day and draw other people into a relationship with him, or do we cling to the safe and familiar?

The Book of Jonah is perhaps best understood as a "novella." It is a delightfully eccentric book, probably using an extended legend, a good story that becomes a significant vehicle to carry the biblical truths about the steadfast love of the God of surprises and the divine desire for people's repentance and conversion. It is twinned with the gospel reading because of the emphasis on repentance. But Jonah is a reluctant prophet, unwilling to preach repentance to Israel's hated Assyrian enemies in the city of Nineveh that is also described in terms of legendary greatness. Eventually delivered by sea mail to that city, courtesy of God and a whale, Jonah finally obeys and stalks through the city, halfheartedly proclaiming that destruction is threatening in forty days—if they do not repent. As the latter part of the book indicates, Jonah shows no enthusiasm when the Ninevites, from the king down, do readily find faith in God and repent of their evil ways in sackcloth and ashes. Such an eager acceptance of his message throws Jonah's own efforts to escape God into sharp relief, and he becomes a sulky prophet, jealous of the Ninevites' conversion. To us, this reading presents the challenge of both offering reconciliation to our enemies or those who have hurt us, and rejoicing when such reconciliation eventuates. Has the Jonah in us ever been secretly annoyed when someone seems to turn to God more readily than we do, or when someone we consider (very privately!) much further from God than we are, surprises and, dare we admit it, annoys us with their goodness and forgiveness? God continues to be a surprising God whom we must learn to recognize in events and people. Our mission is to evangelize, not to evade.

To understand what may seem disturbing words of Paul to the Corinthians, we must realize that he shares the early Christian expectation that Christ would soon return, and that influenced the way in which Christians of that time lived their ordinary lives. We may have experienced how, when a human event of great sorrow or great joy occurs, everything engages us in a different way because of this crisis, and we know that life will never again be quite the same. The second coming of Christ, that great event of decisive *kairós* time, should make Christians reevaluate their lives, says Paul. He does not tell the Corinthians to stop marrying, eating, mourning, rejoicing, buying, or selling. Ordinary activities have to continue, but they are not to engage in these "as though" these were the ultimate values or concerns in life because all these are transitory when seen in the context of the "not yet" future that God has prepared for us in Christ and that makes its present "now" claims on the way the Corinthians live.

Two thousand years later, we may be inclined to say "So what!" to Paul's words. Yet the same challenge is there: the challenge not to be so obsessed with the demands of society, so engrossed with things, so trapped by our superficial likes and dislikes that we become limited people rather than disciples who enjoy the freedom that Christ has won for us and for our world. Like the Corinthians, like the first disciples at the Sea of Galilee, we must all leave something behind and freely follow Christ's call. Our response to this freedom will be definitively, cosmically revealed at the Second Coming.

Whether it is Jonah, the Corinthian church, the first disciples, or we ourselves whom God calls, it is God who will show us the way in which to walk in truth and justice. And so with the responsorial Psalm 25 we pray: "Make me to know (Teach me) your ways, O Lord . . ." God's unfathomable love has been shown to us, above all in Jesus. How will we respond?

Fourth Sunday in Ordinary Time

• Deut 18:15-20 • Ps 95:1-2, 6-9 • 1 Cor 7:32-35 • Mark 1:21-28

With his first disciples, Jesus comes to the synagogue at Capernaum on the Sabbath and, as any male Jew could be, he is invited to offer words of teaching, presumably after one of the scribes has also commented on the readings. There seems to be a vitality, a new credibility and authority in Jesus' words that invite the synagogue's assembly to compare Jesus favorably with the scribes. As so often in Mark's gospel, miracles of bringing peace to the cosmos (4:38), of raising the dead (5:35), of feeding the hungry (6:34), of healing the tortured bodies and psyches of men and women (9:17) are, as in this first of Jesus' works of power, the work of the one is addressed as "Teacher." Jesus teaches so authoritatively by his words and works that the people are amazed.

In the synagogue there is a man possessed by a demon. Such a person should not have been there, and the aim of the synagogue authorities would have been to get rid of him as soon as possible. But Jesus' concern is not to evict the tormented man, but to exorcise the cause of his torment. Jesus has come to proclaim the reigning presence of God, has called his first disciples to be his companions in this mission, and now he enters into combat for the first time with the "kingdom" of Satan over which he established his authority in the wilderness temptation. What Mark has revealed to us in the preceding verses of his first chapter—that Jesus is the strong One possessed by the Spirit of God, that he is the holy and beloved Son of the Father—is shouted by the demon. But a demon speaking the truth is still a demon who can twist what seems the right words for a demonic end. Sadly, it will not be until Jesus hangs tortured and dead on a cross that the first human being—a Gentile centurion—will proclaim Jesus' true identity as "Truly, this man was God's Son!" (Mark 15:39). Contrary to the ancient belief that to know the name of someone gave one power over that person, the demon has no power over Jesus. "Keep quiet! Come out of him," is Jesus' response; his is the voice that his followers are to listen to, not the demon's. No details are given about the man's reaction; the healed man simply fades out of the narrative in the light of the important focus: the people's recognition that in their midst, in Jesus, is a new authority. And so Jesus' fame is talked about and spreads throughout Galilee. The true answers to "What is this?" and what the authority of Jesus will demand of his followers beyond his reputation as an exorcist, are the challenges not only to the Galilee of Jesus' time, nor to Mark's community who were suffering from the demonic persecution by the Roman authorities. They are also our challenges to resist the seduction of our contemporary demons of hedonistic pleasure, addictions, violence, consumerism, and all the other tempting voices, both within us and outside us, that need to be muzzled so that we can hear the authoritative voice of Jesus in the Scriptures, in prayer, in liturgy, and in the witness of our sisters and brothers.

The reading from the Book of Deuteronomy comes from a section of that book that deals with the authorization of leadership roles: royal, juridical, priestly, and prophetic. It is the last mentioned that is the concern of today's reading. The biblical author, although writing many centuries after Moses, uses the authority of his name for a "seconding" or affirmation of Moses' teaching. To be an authoritative voice in the community is the role of God's prophet, but in every age there is need for discernment that recognizes that, although the right words are announced as with the demon in the gospel, the motivation is not of God. The community of Israel is given criteria that will help their discernment, criteria useful not only to Israel, but to future religious communities.

A community has to beware of the self-accredited prophet. A true prophet will be raised up by God, "a prophet like me," says Moses (Deut 18:15). The prophet will be called from the community in whose religious traditions he or she is steeped. It is God's words that are put in the prophet's mouth. This does not mean that the prophet is comfortably compliant with and uncritical of the tradition, but rather that the prophet is a mediator between the people and God, constantly calling the people back to the truth that may have become obscured or distorted. The true prophets are humbly reliant on God, not on themselves, and even if the community disowns them—which it frequently does—they do not disown the community, because without a community there is no prophet. Down through the centuries, Israel's hopes led them to wonder if various individuals might be this promised messianic prophet of the end time (cf. Mal 4:5), and the crowds sometime voice the same wonderment and hopes about Jesus (e.g., John 6:14-15; Luke 24:19-21). With so many voices bombarding us today, from megachurches to megamedia—and sometimes the combination of both—we need to pray the responsorial Psalm 95 with great sincerity: to listen to God's word and harden not our hearts. The Deuteronomic criteria for the discerning of a true prophet are also valid today but, above all, it is when we open the ears of our heart to listen to "what the

Spirit is saying to the churches" (Rev 3:6), to the words of Jesus in our *lectio*, our liturgy, and in the witness of our brothers and sisters, that we hear the authoritative, selfless voice of the Prophet who has been sent to us to help us in our weakness and our struggles with our personal and social demons.

Paul is well aware of the unavoidable struggles and anxieties of his Corinthian community, and he wishes them to be free of these as much as possible lest they sap their energies for the following of Christ. What may at first hearing seem to be a negative attitude to marriage is, in fact, a beautifully nuanced pastoral affirmation of both the married and single life, and the male and female roles in achieving this. All lifestyles have their preoccupations, their competing loyalties, and their challenges, but the Christians should, above all, be preoccupied in their following of Christ within their particular way of life. Paul does not want to put any restraining noose (*bróchos*) on disciples that would cause disunity and anxiety, but only one that would protect them from being dragged away from fidelity to their chosen lifestyle and commitment to Christ.

Fifth Sunday in Ordinary Time

• Job 7:1-4, 6-7 • Ps 147:1-6 • 1 Cor 9:16-19, 22-23 • Mark 1:29-39

In the first reading, Job complains of the sores of humanity in general and then of his own condition in particular. Sitting with his three companions on the dung heap, listening to their unhelpful words, in the text we hear today Job breaks his silence. He is struggling to find meaning in life, comparing it with hard military service, with the drudgery of a hired day laborer, or even a slave. It is hard, humbling, and finite. Days and nights pass restlessly, weaving the pattern of our days. But Job does not compare human life to the productivity and creativity of a piece of woven cloth; rather, he likens it to the mechanical, repetitive movement of the shuttle. And when the thread runs out, life is over. Yet then Job's faith struggles through his anger and despair, and he addresses God, asking for remembrance in the concrete realities of his tormented life. The passionate poetry of this book denies any resigned shallowness in Job; it serves to tear apart conventional religious language— as the psalmists so often do, as the whole Book of Lamentations does—and allows us to glimpse a human cry for divine help with which we can identify. It tells us that lamentation can be right and proper before God and as part of our struggle to find God.

Perhaps our communal prayer needs to make more room for services of lamentation, services where the parish gathers with those who, for example, have suffered domestic violence, divorce and separation, abuse, retrenchment, or unemployment. Rituals can help a faith community, especially a parish, to "sit with" and support those who lament, not as Job's unhelpful or judgmental companions, but as people who are in prayerful solidarity with those who are suffering, who recognize human pain and hold it before God, asking: "Remember . . ."[10]

With the words of Psalm 146 we praise the Lord who numbers and names the stars, but this is not a remote God of the cosmos. This is the same God who knows and cares for the exiles and the brokenhearted and heals their wounds, a God concerned with those whom he raises from the dust so that they can again glimpse the stars.

In the gospel, God's remembrance of and compassion for suffering humanity comes most tangibly and radically in the healing presence of Jesus. From the religious service in the synagogue Jesus moves immediately into the house of Simon and Andrew, accompanied by James and John, disciples who are having a busy apprenticeship. In the healing of Simon's mother-in-law we have a vignette of the mission of Jesus, the free man, who cares nothing for taboos that prohibited the touching of a woman not one's wife, and especially on the Sabbath. Jesus has healed the tormented man in the synagogue, and he will make no discrimination between male and female, even though to hold the hand of the sick woman could earn him the accusation of ritual uncleanness. Compassion has a more urgent hold on Jesus, and his raising of her is by the same power that God will manifest in raising Jesus from the dead. The response of Simon's mother-in-law to her healing is to serve Jesus and his companions. The last use of this word in Mark's gospel is in Mark 15:41, and here it is again with reference to women who followed and served him, so framing the mission of Jesus from its beginning to his death with the service of women. It is a reminder, too, that all who have experienced the healing power of Jesus, in the flesh and in the Spirit, should respond with service of others.

Even though Jesus did not subject himself to Sabbath restraints, the crowds wait until "after sunset" when the Sabbath was over to bring those who are sick in body and mind to him. Jesus responds to the universal longing for wholeness and healing, vanquishing the reign of evil, yet commanding the evil spirits not to speak of him because not until his death will his true messianic identity be revealed. Before that, such a revelation, especially by the proclamation of the formerly possessed, could be manipulated by Jesus' enemies into false charges of his being on the side of the kingdom of evil (see Mark 3:22-27).

The one to whom Jesus is first accountable, however, is not the sick or possessed person, not Simon or his companions. Jesus' life is above all directed to God who is acting in him and through him, so early the next morning he seeks a place where he can be alone with God in prayer. Simon and some of his companions are described not as Jesus' "followers," but as those who "track down" Jesus. There is a note of accusation and misunderstanding in Simon's words: "Everyone is searching for you" (including us!). There is no appreciation of Jesus' own need to search for his God in prayer. What Jesus has heard in his prayer is the call to proclaim the reigning presence of God in other towns, to move on from the enthusiastic reception of yesterday, because that is why he came. How often are we tempted to stay with the "yesterdays" of success and acclamation and hesitate to go forward to the largely unknown "tomorrows" to which God is calling us? And how important is prayer in our discernment of God's call?

Like Jesus, Paul also hears the urgent call to preach the Gospel. He has proclaimed his freedom in Christ to the Corinthians (1 Cor 9:1), but then he startles his readers by a seeming contradiction. This freedom enables him to become a "slave," bound to service of all people. Paul has been freed of his "demons" as a former persecutor of the Christians. Now he adapts his preaching, but without compromise, to the various life situations of his audiences, appreciating their weaknesses so that he might win more of them to Christ. In the household of the church Paul has no concern for any payment except that of earning the blessings of the Gospel. To preach without receiving financial support releases Paul from any subtle pressure to please his audience or be subservient to his sponsors. Christ is his only sponsor, and Paul's versatility is obedient to the new realities that begin with Christ. The challenge to remain free of social restraints and ecclesial expectations that inhibit our proclamation of Christ's Good News; the balancing of financial survival and prophetic, often unpaid ministry, still confront the church today and demand our ongoing discernment and prioritizing.

Sixth Sunday in Ordinary Time

• Lev 13:1-2, 44-46 • Ps 32:1-2, 5, 11 • 1 Cor 10:31–11:1 • Mark 1:40-45

The leprosy about which the first reading and the gospel speak today is not to be confused with contemporary Hansen's disease, medically identified only in 1868 by the Norwegian scientist Gerhard Hansen. A number of conditions, especially those with the signs of scaly skin, swellings, and exuding bodily fluids, are described as "leprosy" in this Sunday's first reading from the Book of Leviticus. Skin that flaked off, fluids that were unnaturally exuded from the body, were considered to be conditions that violated religious-cultural boundaries connected with the integrity, and therefore holiness, of the human body, and so were considered to diminish the worth of the person. People with such conditions were banished from the community, compelled to cry "Unclean!" and make themselves obviously disheveled so that others would avoid them. To be "unclean" was also regarded as a moral failing and therefore sinful. The person who came into contact with such an afflicted one was regarded as contaminated and as ritually unclean and as adding to the moral pollution of the very gregarious Middle Eastern society. Leprosaria and Hansen's disease still exist in some parts of the world, but social and religious alienation because of other causes is sadly much more familiar. Who are today's "lepers," people whom some consider as "polluting" the homogeneous and often exclusive society by their differences in race, culture, social mores, or physical and intellectual disabilities? The attitudes of the Nazis to the Jews, the Hutus to the Tutsis, the second people to the first and indigenous people of a land, are bred by a "leper" mindset. What are our attitudes to those we might consider as weakening the moral fiber of society—the drug addicts, the HIV/AIDS sufferers, those in prison? Are we on the side of harsh, punitive justice or compassionate restorative justice? And do we consider that the pollution of our planet, by us, can be sinful?

The responsorial Psalm 32, one of the seven psalms called the "penitential psalms," offers a double beatitude, or "happiness" to the person who has a true sense of sin, confesses this, and receives God's pardon. The integrity with which the psalm is concerned is not bodily integrity, but the integrity of the spirit of repentance that is never self-congratulatory. A delightful anecdote was once recounted by Metropolitan Anthony Bloom, the late Orthodox archbishop of Sourozh and the UK. One of his admirers followed him slavishly to liturgies and functions, and after each one she would approach him with details of her spiritual progress and the sins she had overcome. One day she told him triumphantly: "Your Excellency, I now only have one sin left to conquer." Wearily the Metropolitan replied, "My good woman, hang on to it!"

In the gospel, Jesus is approached by a leper. After the reading from Leviticus it is easy to see how those suffering from this disease were regarded as the "living dead," social and religious "corpses" that haunted the fringes of towns, alienated even from their families, and hoping for alms or some meager kindness. Mark describes the leper as coming to Jesus and kneeling before him. This action and his profession of faith that Jesus can make him clean suggest that the leper senses in Jesus some holy power, for his disease was regarded as so devastating that rabbinical commentaries compared the cure of leprosy to raising from the dead, a divine prerogative. In the Old Testament accounts of the healing of Miriam when she is struck by leprosy

(Num 12:10-16) and Naaman (2 Kgs 5:1-19), these are clearly recognized as acts of God.

Jesus makes no attempt to move away from the leper. What he is moved by is compassion, the deep gut-wrenching response that identifies with the suffering of another, and his hand stretches out to touch the man and affirm his choice to heal him. How long had it been since the leper had felt the touch of another human being on his diseased flesh, had heard words of affirmation rather than insult? We should be more enlightened about the importance of touch—the holding of the hand of the seriously ill or dying person, the silent embrace of the bereaved. Yet for some people there is the almost hysterical avoidance of touching the HIV/AIDS sufferer, or of drinking from the Communion chalice lest, contrary to all medical opinion, one might be infected by this. Jesus' compassion and humanity bridge the gap between the holy and the unclean, freedom and taboos, sickness and health. And by this touching Jesus himself can be regarded as infected, as ritually unclean. The healed man is told forcibly by Jesus to say nothing to anyone about his healing, an injunction that "is the worst-kept secret in the history of secrecy!"[11] Jesus wants to emphasize that miracles are not an end in themselves, and for him to be known only as a miracle worker belies his true identity. It is the paradoxical publicity of his crucifixion that will be the scenario for the first faith-filled acclamation of Jesus as truly the Son of God, and this on the lips of the Gentile centurion (Mark 15:39).

Jesus tells the man to observe the Mosaic Law by showing himself to a priest for the confirmation of his healing, and to offer a public sacrifice, an act of worship from which his leprosy had excluded him. By this instruction Jesus shows that he respects the Mosaic teaching, even though he will soon clash with some of the scribes' interpretation of this. Ironically, the man now goes around publicly and freely, while Jesus must leave the town and go into the country to escape his unwanted publicity. Because he has touched the leper, according to the Law Jesus is also regarded as unclean and excluded. He has taken upon himself another's infirmity; in his passion and death he will be the Suffering Servant who bears all our infirmities and transgressions for the sale of our salvation (cf. Isa 53:4-5). Yet people still come to him, caring nothing for his "infection" and everything for his miraculous power. As those who come to Jesus, what are we seeking from him? Do we want to be infected with his compassion or with the miraculous? How does Jesus touch us—and how do we touch others?

Traditions that influence eating and drinking customs are common in many religions. Judaism and those of the Greco-Roman world of Paul were no exception. For Paul, the criteria by which Christians were to judge such customs are twofold: could a custom be observed without eroding faith in Christ, and does it demonstrate a sensitive regard for the consciences of others? For Jewish Christians, the Jewish dietary laws had always been a significant aspect of their identity as the people of God, and Paul does not demand that they disregard these customs but only that they do not impose them on their Gentile sisters and brothers who may have other traditions. To do all for the glory of God, even in the most ordinary but essential aspects of life such as eating and drinking, is what is important. Paul wants to be an example to the Corinthians of such commitment, trying to avoid giving offence to anyone and trying to please everyone—not for the sake of self-serving popularity and advantage, but so that his personal acceptance will make more possible the acceptance of the gospel of salvation that he proclaims. Just as in the gospel we see how Christ accepted the need of the leper to observe the Jewish rituals that would confirm his healing, so Paul adapts himself to the needs of his brothers and sisters, but without compromise of his radical faith in Christ. To walk the tightrope between cultural and religious adaptation and such faith is both necessary and daring. Vatican II spoke of the bountiful treasure that God has distributed to all the nations of the earth, and the mission of the church to try "to illumine these treasures with the light of the gospel, to set them free, and to bring them under the dominion of God their Saviour."[12] And within the church itself there is to be recognition of lawful diversity, which the council expressed as "unity in what is necessary, freedom in what is unsettled, and charity in any case."[13] This would be a program for communion and community that Paul would approve in any age.

Seventh Sunday in Ordinary Time

• Isa 43:18-19, 21-22, 24b-25 • Ps 41:2-5, 13-14 • 2 Cor 1:18-22 • Mark 2:1-12

Today's gospel is about a dramatic break-in—and breakthrough! Jesus has returned to a house, probably Simon Peter's in Capernaum, and the crowds are jamming every available space. Four men arrive carrying a paralyzed man and are unable to get anywhere near Jesus. No one is going to budge, to surrender their place to the less able person. But faith needs to be imaginative, and often is disruptive, so the faith-filled friends of the paralytic decide that it will be easier to unroof the clay and daub roof than move the determined people whose own priorities are an impenetrable barrier. In the household of today's church the selfish resistance to those with great needs may differ in quality, but it can still create a psychological or physical barrier that makes it difficult for people to come to Jesus or feel welcome in his church.

The man is lowered by his four friends into the room, and Jesus' attention is described as first focusing on their faith rather than on the paralytic who has just cascaded into the assembly. It is a wonderfully vivid narrative. With the friends no doubt gaping through the hole in the roof, Jesus then turns to the man who has been let down into his presence. No longer on the fringes, he is now right in the middle of the assembly, and this is where Mark wants his community to situate the sick and marginalized. "Seeing their faith . . . ," the faith of the four friends, Jesus now speaks to the paralytic with words of forgiveness. Jesus is not speaking about the origin of the man's physical disability, not connecting sin and sickness. (After all, the paralytic does not jump up off his mat when his sins are forgiven!) What Jesus is doing is offering God's healing of the man's sinfulness, a condition common to all humanity, even the scribes who sit judgmentally in the center of the crowd. We might imagine the scribes fastidiously dusting themselves down after the arrival of the stretcher-bound man and the accompanying roof debris. They murmur silently to themselves about what they consider as almost amounting to blasphemy: that Jesus is forgiving sins and so is doing what is considered to be God's prerogative (cf. Exod 34:6-7a; Isa 43:25). Jesus sees that it is not just their clothes that are in a mess, but also their hearts, and so he gives a verifiable witness to his healing power. As the Son of Man, the human one in whom the power of God is so radically present, he tells the paralytic to rise, take up his mat, and go home. This is a "resurrection" moment for the man, and he stands, picks up his mat, and walks through the crowd to the chorus of praise recognizing that what they have just seen is a work of God.

The repeated mention of the man's mat or stretcher that he drags out with him might make us wonder. Did he keep it at home as a reminder of this extraordinary meeting with Jesus? Or might he have used it to befriend others, as he was befriended, and carry others into the healing presence of Jesus? Mark surely intended this vividly described incident to witness also to the faith and practical action that should sustain others at times when they are spiritually, physically, or emotionally helpless and in need of friends.

We have to ask ourselves the same questions as those with which Mark faced his community in his gospel: How instrumental are we in bringing others to the saving power of God? Or how judgmental are we of our sisters and brothers—and even of God when he seems to be on the side of those whom we would rather crowd out of the household of the church? With the verses of the responsorial Psalm 41 we sing of the happiness of the person who does care for the poor and abandoned and who is therefore blessed with God's provident protection. This is what God is like, and this is what God's people should be like; this is what the Gospel has shown us in Jesus.

The reading from Second Isaiah is presented as God's address to the exiles who are returning from Babylon. Through the words of the prophet, God urges the people to be aware of the "new thing," the active intervention of God in bringing them out of Babylon. Their exile is to be transformed into a homecoming; God's judgment of his people's sinfulness becomes a promise of a wonderful future; their recent living death is replaced by hope. God's generous graciousness will banish the past and open the way to their future. God does remember the past infidelities of his people, but God forgives, while at the same time daring them to imagine and commit themselves to new, redeemed possibilities. An inordinate attachment to the past, a nostalgic refusal to move forward, is different from a faithful reverence for tradition. The latter affirms identity and fidelity; the former makes the people of Israel of the sixth century B.C.E., or the church of today, complacent and blind to the wonder of the new things God can do. The prophet uses lyrical imagery to describe such newness: an easy-to-travel road will be cut in the wilderness so that God's praiseful people may sing their way home to their forgiving God. This is the God who comes among us doing new things in Christ. As the healed paralytic cuts his way through the crowds and walks home with his mat, the crowds proclaim at the end of today's gospel: "We have never seen anything like this!"

For the next eight weeks the second reading is from the Second Letter of Paul to the Corinthians. In the verse before today's portion (2 Cor 1:17) we read that Paul is facing painful opposition within the Corinthian church from those who accuse him of vacillating and acting according to human standards, and so as a person who cannot be relied on to keep his promises or follow through his plans. This upsets Paul, and he responds with an emphatic self-defense.

It is a defense grounded in the fidelity and reliability of God who is the Promise Keeper from the time of Abraham. What Paul and his companions Silvanus and Timothy proclaim, they proclaim in the power of this God who speaks through them. God's promise has been most clearly and unambiguously kept in Christ, and in him God has established them as apostles. In Christ there is no wavering between "yes" or "no"; everything in him is a "Yes" to God, and it is this holy decisiveness, this "Amen," in which Paul shares.

For some of our contemporaries, especially young people, to have designer clothes with brand name prominently displayed seals one's fashion reputation. Paul reminds the Corinthians that they have been "branded" with the Holy Spirit as a pledge of God's faithfulness. This sealing is a first installment of and a down payment on the full payment that will come when, we hope, God speaks a final "Yes" to us at the end of our own lives and the world's history.

The presence of evil in the world, failures in social and ecclesial leadership, disillusionment with ourselves and others, may sometimes make us wonder if God is still keeping the divine promises. But, despite tensions and failures, the Gospel of Jesus Christ, the presence to us of the Christian community, and the experience of the Spirit in the depths of our hearts should ground us, too, in the fidelity of God.

Eighth Sunday in Ordinary Time

• Hos 2:16b, 17b, 21-22 • Ps 103:1-4, 8, 10, 12-13 • 2 Cor 3:1b-6 • Mark 2:18-22

The tragic marriage of Hosea to his promiscuous wife, Gomer, is used as a metaphor of God's relationship with Israel. Even though it may be difficult, especially for some women, to see beyond the imagery that is patriarchal and consonant with the Middle Eastern mores of the eighth to the seventh centuries B.C.E., as a man of his own time the prophet can speak in no other way. The poetry and passion of this reading should help us penetrate to the metaphorical level of its message. Ruth Padel comments that: "Greek roads used to be full of little three-wheeled vans with METAPHOR written, in Greek, on their front. I once asked a driver of one what his work was. 'Taking something,' he said, 'from one place to another.'"[14] Hosea takes marriage from its familiar "home" of human experience, and travels with it into the depths of a new relationship, that between God and Israel.

God is like the bridegroom who discovers the infidelities of his wife, Israel, and begs her to remember the earlier days of their wilderness relationship, the time of their intimate covenant making. God is ready to start again with Israel-bride, to pay another bride price for her, to ignore the shame of her dishonoring their relationship. Verses 19 and 20 (that for some reason are unfortunately omitted from the Lectionary) are like new wedding vows: "And I will take you for my wife forever; I will take you for my wife in righteousness and justice, in steadfast love, and in mercy." Because of God's passionate love for Israel, their reunion is described in the marital terms of "knowing" one another with interpersonal and experiential intimacy. The God of Hosea is a God who takes risks for love. The prophet assures us that God is always ready for new expressions of love that can bridge the divide of our infidelities and enable alienation to become reconciliation—if we are ready to surrender to the love of the Bridegroom.

Like the psalmist we can join with a mindful self-address of the blessings that God has shown us, despite our sinfulness. God is "a God of steadfast love and compassion." This is the holy name, God's deep personal reality revealed to Moses in the wilderness after God's people committed the sin of making and worshiping the golden calf (Exod 34:6-7). This is the God of the prophet Hosea, and our God, ready to put our sins at an unimaginable distance, "as far as the east is from the west," so that his children may know that the divine love is as constant and forgiving as the womb love of a parent.

In today's gospel some unidentified people approach Jesus and question him about the way his disciples behaved in regard to their neglect of fasting. Since a teacher was responsible for the behavior of his disciples, this is an implicit and indirect challenge to Jesus' own behavior, unfavorably comparing the fasting practices of his disciples with those of John the Baptist and the Pharisees. The only obligatory annual and national fast day was the Day of Atonement (Yom Kippur), but the Pharisees also fasted twice a week, some from the dubious motives of public parade of their piety (cf. Luke 18:12). In Mark's gospel, John the Baptist is already imprisoned, but his followers were imitating him "who came neither eating nor drinking" (Matt 11:18) while, in contrast, Jesus is accused of being a glutton and a drunkard.

The first reading has already introduced us to the metaphor of God as bridegroom in the Old Testament, and this same imagery is used in the New Testament to speak of the relationship of Christ and the church (e.g., Matt 25:1-13; 2 Cor 11:2; Rev 19:7, 9). In the gospel, Jesus responds to the question about fasting by comparing his "now" presence to that of a bridegroom at a wedding feast. If the guests at a wedding feast fasted, it would be an insult to the bridegroom. There is a proper time for everything, and Jesus then speaks about the days when the bridegroom will be taken away from his guests; that will be the time when feasting gives way to fasting. That the bridegroom is "taken away," and does not just leave of his own accord, strikes an ominous note, perhaps in tune with the verse that describes the fate of the Suffering Servant of whom Isaiah writes (according to the Septuagint translation): "His life will be taken from the earth and he will be led away to death" (Isa 53:8). Mark may also be reflecting the custom of his community to fast on certain days in memory of Jesus' death. There are "seasons of the soul" and seasons in the liturgical year when physically refraining from food reminds us of the spiritual hunger for God and the wedding feast of the kingdom, and our longing to be invited to it by Christ the Bridegroom.

Jesus then speaks with two homely mini-parables about his messianic mission, comparing it to old clothes and new patches, and old and new wineskins. If a new, unshrunken cloth patch is sown onto an old garment, the patch will shrink and rip the garment, and the damage to it will be even greater than when it was unpatched. In the case of new wine poured into old wineskins, the subsequent fermentation will split the wineskins and the new wine will be lost. Jesus is not rejecting the "old" cloth or the "old" wineskins of Judaism, but in his mission there is something radically new, a new event in the relationship between God and humanity that cannot be contained within the old structures of Judaism. There is concern, however, for both the old of Judaism and the new of the Christian community, as Fred B. Craddock comments:

> It is important to notice that in these verses Mark is not attacking the old. There is concern expressed about the loss of the old garment and the old wineskin just as there is about the loss of the new. Each has its integrity, and it would be a violation of both to treat the Christian faith as a compromise of the old and new, a synthesis of the two at the level of the lowest common denominator.[15]

For the followers of Jesus, this integrity demands the faithful cry: "New wine, new wineskins!"

Our discipleship, therefore, cannot be just a patch-up affair, with a few rituals and prayers sewn onto the fabric of our daily lives. Nor can we just pour a bit of the new wine of the Spirit into the well-worn wineskins of our everyday routines. Our baptism calls us to be people who are continually and radically transformed by the gift of God's love in and through Christ, and committed to witness to this in all the seasons of our lives, in the good times and the bad. We also need places and situations where Christians can search and speak without fear and prejudice, sometimes with anger, but always with opportunity for reconciliation as we try to respond to Jesus' call for "New wine! New wineskins!" Such was the hope behind initiatives such as the late Cardinal Joseph Bernardin's Common Ground or the meeting of a younger generation of Catholic moral theologians in the University of Notre Dame's New Wineskins conferences.

The story is told of the Rabbi of Kobryn who asked a follower of the Baal Shem Tov (the Besht), the famous eighteenth-century rabbi, whether any of the Besht's generation had left writings of his teaching as a heritage. "Oh, yes," replied the Besht's follower. "Are they printed, or are they still in manuscript form?" asked the Rabbi of Kobryn. "Neither," came the reply. "They are inscribed in the hearts of his disciples." In today's second reading we hear how, centuries earlier, another Jewish teacher had answered his critics in the same way.

Paul is experiencing some bad days within his Corinthian church. His opponents are accusing him of indulging in self-commendation, of preaching himself rather than Jesus Christ, something that is unthinkable for Paul who had introduced himself to the Corinthians as one who came among them knowing nothing except Jesus Christ, and him crucified (1 Cor 2:2). Paul has no intention of allowing a few negative but articulate voices to dominate, and he expands on what he had said earlier about the Corinthians: that they themselves are "the seal of his apostleship in the Lord" (1 Cor 9:2). He has no need, therefore, for letters of recommendation from patrons to enhance his status as an apostle and, quite likely, to expect favors in return for their endorsement. The Corinthians are his letters of recommendation because their commitment to Christ, that Paul has preached among them, is written by the Spirit of the living God on their hearts (cf. Jer 31:33), and not on tablets of stone. It is God, through Christ and in the power of the Spirit, who has made a new covenant with his people, and Paul or any missionary who proclaims this truth is only an administrator and enabler of this grace.

How do people read us? Can they see written in our lives the compassion and forgiveness that might attract them to Christ? Are we people who know the right time to rejoice or weep with others and for others? Are we so obviously in love with and transformed by our faith that others want to ask why, and who is the source of our transformation?

Ninth Sunday in Ordinary Time

• Deut 5:12-15 • Ps 81:3-8, 10-11 • 2 Cor 4:6-11 • Mark 2:23-28

Every Sunday the liturgy of the word brings the story of God's saving work to mind, and challenges us to live the implications of that memory in our own time and place. The first reading from the Book of Deuteronomy is very much about time, about the Sabbath, the seventh day to which, in the Jewish weekly liturgical calendar, all other days flow. The Sabbath is the only holy day included in the Ten Commandments (the Decalogue) in either today's version or in that of Exodus 20:1-17. In the Deuteronomic reading, the Sabbath is emphasized as a commandment of God that demands obedience for the sake of human equality and social justice. It is to be a memory that blows away the tyranny of the marketplace and economic endeavor, the divisions between rich and poor, slave and free, and is a reminder that the use or abuse of time is a constant challenge. A modern Jew writing of the Sabbath commented that: "We share time, we own space. Through my ownership of space, I am a rival of all other beings; through my living in time, I am a contemporary of all other beings."[16] For six days human work is affirmed, and the Sabbath is built on this regard for the dignity of labor, but the Sabbath is the institution that was intended to prevent dignity from deteriorating into idolatry and physical and psychological enslavement. This was the condition of Israel in Egypt, and the Sabbath is the subversive day when masters and slaves are equal, when the earth is free from exploitation, when servants and working animals are free of servitude, when workers are liberated from work.

Over the centuries, this law that was intended to enable freedom had been burdened with minutiae of observances that obscured its God-given intention, as today's gospel witnesses. For observant Jews, the Sabbath is the institution that does so much to remind them of their responsibility for social justice. Now that Sunday is often blurred into just another day, not very distinguishably different from the other six days of the week, do we Gentiles unconsciously recognize and long for the originating wisdom of the Sabbath? Many husbands or wives complain that work demands never allow them time for one another; employees say that intensive work hours can cast a shadow over their psychological and physical health; employers feel the pressure of needing to have 24/7 availability to remain competitive. Do we ever wish that just one-seventh of our lives could be freer for loving and humanizing relationships with one another and with God? Is our attendance at this weekly Eucharist caught up into such an experience?

With the words of Psalm 81, we sing our praises of the people's freedom when they were brought forth from the slavery of Egypt. But there is also a warning against the temptation to burden ourselves with the worship of new idols and alien gods. How do we name these today?

Last Sunday the gospel proclaimed that in the person of Jesus, and his words and deeds, there was an event so radically new that it could not be contained in old traditions, even though these were respected; an established order that could not cut Jesus down to its religious pattern. So it is with Sabbath observance; Jesus will authoritatively reread his Jewish tradition about the Sabbath, and consequently meet with increasing hostility from those who want to maintain the religious status quo. Jesus and his disciples are making their way through a cornfield on the Sabbath and his disciples pluck some of the ears of corn. The Pharisees blame Jesus for the conduct of his disciples, taking an extremely conservative stance and maintaining that this is forbidden on the Sabbath. But the Sabbath law as prescribed in Deuteronomy 23:25 did not forbid meager plucking, but only the more extensive and intensive work of reaping with the sickle. There is something more behind this first direct conflict between Jesus and the Pharisees and Jesus' reference to the occasion when David asked the priest for loaves of bread to sustain himself and his followers. The only bread available in the Temple was the holy bread of the presence, the twelve loaves placed freshly each Sabbath on the table in the sanctuary as an offering to God (1 Sam 21:2-6). If human need had taken precedence over religious law at the request of an authoritative person like David, Jesus implies that it should do so even more now because of his authority as "lord of the Sabbath." It is the claim to such authority over the Sabbath that lay at the heart of Jewish religious observance, rather than the plucking of the grain, that the Pharisees see as a threat to the religious identity of faithful Jews.

Jesus' authority continues to be revealed when he proceeds into the synagogue on that same Sabbath. Once again he is being watched. Seeing a man with a withered hand, Jesus calls on him to stand up. Immediately the man becomes the center of attention, and Jesus challenges his critics: "Is it against the law to do good on the Sabbath or to do evil; to save a life or to kill?" According to the Sabbath interpretation that had developed, only illness that was considered to be the cause of imminent death could be healed on the Sabbath. Other illnesses could wait until the Sabbath was over. But from Jesus' point of view, there is never a wrong day or time on which to do good, and to exercise authority over the sickness that cripples human life is an act of compassion and a law of love to which Jesus gives priority—and, indeed, a "Sabbath" priority of justice. Jesus tells the man to stretch out his hand, and with no words or touch the withered limb is healed. What is withered now are the hearts of the Pharisees, to such an extent that they go out of the synagogue to join forces with the Herodians, with whom they usually differed. So an unusual and expedient alliance of religion and politics is formed for the purpose of destroying Jesus. The shadow of the cross falls across Mark's gospel, a shadow that will become increasingly dark and lowering as Jesus continues his mission.

Does the church sufficiently respect this priority of human need in its law making, in its judgments about the pastoral involvement of clergy and laity, or about the teaching and writing of theologians? And are we ready for the conflicts that may overshadow our lives because we follow Jesus?

Paul could certainly answer "Yes" to this last question. His life as an apostle has been darkened by suffering—by difficulties, disappointment, persecution—but into this darkness God has shone his creative word, made flesh in Jesus Christ. As the cosmos became radiant with the creation of light, so Paul's ministry has been enlightened by Christ. He is the unveiled presence of God to humanity, and Paul again remembers the tradition that described how Moses' face so reflected the glory of God revealed to him on Mount Sinai at the making of the covenant that when he came down to the people he veiled his face lest the people should be afraid to approach him (Exod 34:29-35; 2 Cor 3:7-13). With Jesus there is no fear, no veil.

Paul is very aware that he and all Christians carry the light of Christ in the fragile vessels of their humanity. But just as a cheap lamp can carry oil and give as strong a flame as an expensive one, so God's gracious power can be given and held in our vulnerable clay, and yet burn brightly for the enlightenment of the world. In the kiln of Jesus' passion and death, his human clay was fired to become a vessel of imperishable life and beauty. So it will be with us; if we share the daily and mortal firing of suffering and death with Jesus, we will also share in and witness to the hope of his immortal, indestructible life.

Tenth Sunday in Ordinary Time

• Gen 3:9-15 • Ps 130:1-8 • 2 Cor 4:13–5:1 • Mark 3:20-35

"The call to grandeur and the depths of misery are both a part of human experience," declared Vatican II.[17] We cannot deny that life is filled with ambiguities, that we feel a split within ourselves, a sense of the loss of harmony and integrity; that both individually and collectively we recognize a struggle within us between good and evil, light and darkness. We may interpret and name this struggle in different ways; the Jewish-Christian tradition names it sin, and today's first reading is a grappling with its painful effects that are mirrored in our own human lives. A mythic story is the vehicle for the truths that are carried to us. "Myth" should not be equated in any way with "untrue," for in fact a myth is a story that, especially through the use of symbol, conveys deep and complex truths in a more accessible and memorable way.

The part of the narrative we read today describes the consequences of the disobedience of the man and woman in relationship to their Creating God. They have an insatiable desire to be gods themselves, to know everything about good and evil, and mistrust God and the word of God. In so doing they overreach and disown the gift of their humanity. In the earlier verses, the serpent is described as the craftiest of the animals; there is no naming of it as the devil or Satan. The serpent is introduced into the story as a metaphor that represents anything that may slither into the lives of human beings and offer shrewd options that can seduce us away from God. The sin of wanting to be like God that the man and woman had committed in common is now the cause of their estrangement. Joyful and uninhibited or "naked" presence to each (Gen 2:25), to the rest of creation, and to God has now become vulnerable "exposure." Neither can handle the consequences of the knowledge they have acquired. They have fallen out of their previous relationships with one another and with God, and yet God does not desert his sinful humanity. In anthropomorphic terms that are used to emphasize God's continuing closeness to the man and woman, God is described as walking in the Garden and searching for them as they hide in fear of the consequences of their disobedience. God must also confront them with their disobedience, question them so that they confess their guilt. We can surely recognize ourselves in their response. Both the man and the woman have been seduced, both blame each other for the knowledge their sin offers them, both try to rationalize their fault, and the man even implies that it is God's fault for giving him the gift of the woman! God then pronounces judgment on the serpent. Again what is first pronounced is the serpent's estrangement—alienation from the community of animals. From being craftier, it is now more cursed; its belly-crawling will be a sign of humiliation, its eating of dust implies degradation. It is a symbolic reminder of the subtleties of temptation that can insinuate themselves into our lives, and the deep conflicts and dehumanizing effects when we surrender to such temptation. Between the offspring of the woman and the temptations that are the progeny of evil, there will be a continuing enmity. Our very familiar statues of the Immaculate Conception depicting Mary with her heel on the head of a fang-bared snake are a popular misinterpretation (and mistranslation) of this Genesis verse. It is the *offspring* of the woman, not woman herself, who will crush the serpent's head. All those who resist the subtleties of temptations, who triumph over the humiliating and alienating conflicts and consequences of sin, will be heel-crushers of evil. Obviously, the Christ "born of a woman" (Gal 4:4) is the ultimate crusher.

Psalm 130, with which we respond to this reading, is a prayerful and faithful echo of the human predicament. As individuals and communities, we can be submerged in the depths of sinfulness and its consequences and so, like the psalmist, we wait for and hope in God to draw us out of the flood of evil, out of all those situations where death, not life, prevails. And just as God did not desert the man and the woman but continued to seek them and walk with them in the Garden, so we sing our belief that the God of steadfast love will hear our cries for forgiveness and redeem us from all our iniquities.

From his words to the Corinthians, it is obvious that Paul is also experiencing the depths of suffering, both physical and spiritual—the afflictions, persecutions, perplexities, and attacks about which we heard last week (2 Cor 4:8-11). But these do not overwhelm him; rather, they urge him to speak passionately to his communities about his faith, for what is believed must be proclaimed. There is both continuity with the faith that inspired the prophets and psalmists, "that is in accordance with scripture" (of the Old Testament), and also discontinuity that comes with the Good News of Jesus Christ. Paul and his Corinthians must be united in their faith in God who raised Jesus from the depths of the grave, and so will raise Paul and all who are sons and daughters in the Son.

This faith is transforming, even though we are not able to see the transformation. Paul contrasts the outer self with the inner self, the transitory with the eternal, the earthly with the heavenly. Over one, diminishment and death reign; over the other, life and resurrection will triumph. In this life, we will experience something of both death and resurrection, but in a transitory way, and so Paul compares our human existence in this world to living in a tent. Tents are temporary dwellings, pitched for a time and then folded up when we strike camp and move on. When in death we finally "fold up" our earthly existence and "move on," God has prepared for us a house that is "eternal in the heavens." This is the goal and hope of our journey. Are we, like Paul, urged to move from faith to speech, and bear witness to our faith in Christ, not only with our words but also with our lives? How concerned are we that more and more people in our world of family, workplace, community, and church may be drawn by such witness and come to share thankfully in this faith—to the glory of God, not our glory, as Paul encourages his Corinthians?

Between the two accounts of "family" incidents, Mark "sandwiches" a story of the mounting conflict between Jesus and the scribes, and there is in the narrative a bitter taste of the misunderstanding of Jesus by all those involved. From a human point of view, his family thinks he is out of his mind, and for his own sake they want to restrain him and rescue him from the crowds, not so much because Jesus and his disciples have no time even to eat a bit of bread, but because it seems that what they consider Jesus' insane behavior is shaming them! At this moment, both physically and symbolically, Jesus' family members are not related to him as "insiders," but as "outsiders," not only because they are standing outside the house where Jesus is, but also because they are far removed from understanding him. Jesus is "out of his mind," but in a different sense. He has no mind for the established socioreligious expectations that oppress and dehumanize people. He is willing to associate with them, offer his compassionate healing to their tortured bodies and minds—and be regarded by the purist elite as contaminated by them.

Now comes the "filling in the sandwich," the more significant encounter between Jesus and the Jerusalem scribes. These are the official religious teachers of the people, another group of accredited "insiders" who will show themselves to be radical "outsiders" in their relationship and attitude to Jesus. They have witnessed his power over evil, but now announce that this comes from Beelzebub, the prince of demons, who possesses Jesus. Not ignoring the scribes but calling them to him, Jesus responds with two parables. The first one, the "Parable of the Divided House," makes the logical point that if a kingdom or a household is divided it destroys itself. In the same way, if Satan drives out Satan (as the scribes accuse Jesus of doing), it will mean self-destruction for Satan. In the next, the "Parable of the Strong Man," Jesus is the stronger one (see Mark 1:7) who is in conflict, not collusion, with the strong power of evil, binding it up and plundering those imprisoned in physical and mental pain, and liberating them from possession by the structures that are the work of the less strong Satan.

Finally, Mark proclaims a christological truth. From the beginning of this gospel, Jesus has been possessed by the Spirit who descended on him at his baptism and drove him into the intimate wilderness encounter with God and his own God-given identity. For Jesus' opponents to convert this Holy Spirit into a Satanic spirit, is a malicious, vindictive, and pervasively evil accusation. The scribes see goodness as evil and accuse Jesus of blasphemy, a charge punishable by death (Lev 24:16). When brought against Jesus during his passion, it will be proximate reason for his condemnation and death (Mark 14:61-64). Such an accusation erects an impenetrable barrier between the scribes and their forgiving God. A similar stance finds contemporary expression in statements where God is named as a delusion and religion as a virus that takes people back to the plague-ridden Middle Ages or infects people with a range of modern maladies from child abuse to suicide.[18] In his more gentle, but sad and well-known comment on the judgmental attitude of some Christians, Hélder Câmara remarked: "When I give the poor food, they call me a saint. When I ask why the poor have no food, they call me a communist."

The gospel narrative then returns to the family of Jesus, including his mother. They are still outsiders, and must send a message in to Jesus. They would like him to come out to them, away from his new household, back into the circle of conventional and predictable relationships. But Jesus' creative, reflective, focused gaze travels around the circle of those in his company, and names as his brother and sister and mother those who do the will of God that they recognize in Jesus himself. Mary is mentioned only here and in one other place in Mark's gospel (Mark 6:3), perhaps a poignant insight into the truth that Mary, too, had to suffer the replacement of family ties by the bonds that created and sustained the new family and household of believers. And it is Mary, as the first among disciples, who did this most perfectly as she made a painful journey of faith through doubts, misperceptions, and dispossessions. This is a Mary whom we can surely identify with and admire, and thank God for her companionship on our pilgrimage of faith. For all humanity the primeval hostility between good and evil endures. Evil rears its head in different ways in different times and places; we need to see it with the eyes of Jesus, name it, and crush it with the power of God that is always available to us.

Eleventh Sunday in Ordinary Time

• Ezek 17:22-24 • Ps 92:2-3, 13-16 • 2 Cor 5:6-10 • Mark 4:26-34

Jesus' parables are not nice entertaining little stories. As John R. Donahue writes, they enable us "to be in contact with his imagination as it brings to expression his self-understanding of his mission and his struggle with the mystery of his Father's will."[19] As Jesus proclaims in the first words he speaks according to Mark (Mark 1:14-15), his mission is to announce the Good News of the kingdom, the reigning and transforming presence of God in his person and words, and call the people to faith and repentance. Like all the parables, the two parables of green and growing things we hear today are words of Jesus that tease us into contemplating our own lives and our response to the kingdom.

In the first parable, "The Seed Growing Secretly," Jesus compares the growth of the kingdom to the seed that is planted by the farmer who then retires from the scene into the rhythm of his everyday life. Day and night he wakes and sleeps, while the seed, once sown, has its own potential for growth independent of the farmer. The mystery of growth belongs to the seed and the soil, to the gradual "dispossession" of the hard little seed to the nourishing earth, and its consequent unhurried and gradual growth: first the stalk, then the head, then the full grain. The only activity required of the farmer is vigilant patience. In the dispossession that is his incarnation, even Jesus had to accept some unknowing, some surrender of events into his Father's hands (Mark 13:32).

Perhaps we have had the experience with children who have planted their seeds in the garden and, excited about the possibilities of the flowers or vegetables to come, must be dissuaded from regular and disastrous digging down into the earth to see how the growth is proceeding! The farmer must wait confidently on God's good time and providence, and eventually the time of growth and the time of harvesting will intersect. Once we have received the seed of God's word in the soil of our hearts, we must be ready for the dispossession, the gradual unfolding of the seed's potential that will push into our consciousness and transform our lives, making us a plentiful harvest and enabling us to become nourishment for others. Because the growth of the seed is God's secret, it can often happen in what, to our limited human perspective, are the most unlikely places: in the lives of the poor, the despised, the persecuted. This was surely a great consolation to Mark's community, for this was the reality of their lives. It should give the same hope and confidence to Christians today in our personal, communal, or national situations. What seems humanly insignificant, and even a failure, is transformed by God's power, just as the seed of Jesus' life fell into the ground of death to be transformed by his resurrection (cf. John 12:24). This is the great encouragement for disciples as we live between the planting and harvesting into the kingdom of God.

The "Parable of the Mustard Seed" and its surprising growth is also one of encouragement for struggling communities frustrated or despondent because of what seems the small and insignificant growth of the kingdom of God and its impact on the world around them. Jesus makes use of legitimate poetic license in exaggerating the size of the mustard seed ("the smallest of all seeds on earth") and the bush that grows from it ("the greatest of all shrubs"), in order to stress the extravagant and disproportionate growth of the kingdom. That God is in all our beginnings and endings is the great and faithful hope of Jesus' disciples. The mustard bush, we are reminded, does not exist only for itself, but it offers a welcoming refuge for the birds of the air who nest in its shade. So the Christian community should spread out its branches in welcome to others, especially to those who are enduring the heat of suffering, who are searching either physically or spiritually for some "shade" or sanctuary.

We often find it hard to be at home and comfortable with mystery; there is still the primeval temptation "to be gods," to know everything, to overreach our God-given humanity. That we have Jesus' word to "explain" to us the deeper meaning of God's action in our lives and our world, is the privilege of Jesus' disciples.

The reading from the prophet Ezekiel is also about growth. The prophet uses allegory, a narrative that enables new and hidden meanings to be discovered under the literal events and characters described. Ezekiel speaks of the relationship of God to the people of Israel who had been taken into Babylonian captivity in the sixth century B.C.E., constantly assuring them of God's abiding presence among them and to them, despite all appearances to the contrary. The God of this reading is an Eagle Wings God whom the prophet depicts as talking directly to the people. This God will pluck a tender shoot from the crown of a mighty cedar, the royal line of the house of David, and plant this fragile sprig on Mount Zion, reversing the failures of the kings of David's house and their reliance on political alliances. It will be cared for and cultivated by God until it grows into another strong cedar and can offer welcoming shelter to other creatures. God is a generous, loving, and promise-keeping God, proclaimed in both the Old and New Testaments as a God who raises up the humble and humbles the mighty, a God who will one day bring forth from the cedar stock of David the crowning shoot who will be the royal Prince of Peace, the Messiah, not only for remnant Israel but for all the nations. As with the seed and mustard plant, this will be the hidden work of God's grace in Christ, and a power that reverses all human expectations.

The responsorial Psalm 92 is one of the few psalms in the Psalter that is headed with a description of when it should be used. It is described as "A song for the Sabbath," and on our Sabbath we give thanks for God's steadfast love that plants us in this house of worship, waters us with the Word, and nourishes us with the Eucharist. By this tending we are enabled to grow into strong and committed people of God in whom the sap of God's grace will continue to rise so that we may be growing and green fruit bearers, even into old age.

In his words to his Corinthian church, Paul is an example of seeding, fruiting faith. "We walk by faith and not by sight," he writes. While we are at home in this life in our human bodies, we are away from being fully at home with the unseen presence of the Lord, so Paul feels a tension within himself. He would prefer to be "away from" suffering and opposition (and he is enduring plenty of this from within the Corinthian communities) and "at home" with the Lord, but he will stay the course with his church. Paul knows that the way we respond now to the everyday demands of faith, and the confidence we have now in the power of God working in unseen ways in us and among us despite opposition and failure, is preparing us for that not-yet final judgment of Christ when we hope to be fully at home with him.

Twelfth Sunday in Ordinary Time

• Job 38:1, 8-11 • Ps 107:23-26, 28-31 • 2 Cor 5:14-17 • Mark 4:35-41

This Sunday's gospel comes at the end of a day when Jesus has been teaching on the edge of the lake, the "boundary" between land and sea where he called his first disciples (Mark 1:16). It is a very human picture of Jesus who, after giving himself to the crowd, takes the initiative in telling the disciples that they are to go across to the other side of the lake. So the disciples take Jesus with them in the boat "just as he was," as a wisdom teacher and sower of the word, exhausted after a demanding day. Other boats are also mentioned in passing, to show how Jesus is gathering followers, but no more attention is given to them in the narrative. This is the first of six crossings that Mark describes, and they are much more than geographical excursions. Jesus has been teaching on the Jewish side of the Sea of Galilee; on the other side is the Decapolis, predominately Gentile territory, where the first person they will meet is the deranged and naked man who has been stripped of human dignity and now lives among the tombs. This nighttime boat trip is going to cross much more than water; it will be a boundary crossing into the new and unknown deep of Jesus' mission to the Gentiles. But before the pagan shore is reached there is also the boundary between fear and faith to be crossed, a boundary that is a challenge to disciples of all times—and this is often a rough crossing.

Mark is writing his gospel for a community suffering persecution, Christians who feared that any day they might be overwhelmed by either the waves of their own cowardice and infidelity to Christ, or blown off their Christian course by the fear of imprisonment and death. They could be tempted to believe that Jesus is "asleep" and cares nothing for them. In different contexts, we too are familiar with the storms that can brew in our own hearts. In this night seascape, Jesus is overwhelmed by sleep and lies calmly on a cushion in the stern of the boat. As still happens, storms can blow up quickly and suddenly on the Sea of Galilee, sweeping down from the Golan Heights. This night the wind and water are no more hospitable to the boat than Jesus' own family and the scribes have been to him (Mark 3:21-27), but Jesus models the faith that the psalmist expressed: "I will lie down in peace and sleep comes at once, for you alone, Lord, make me dwell in safety" (Ps 4:9). The struggle between fear and faith is a constant theme in Mark's gospel, continuing until the very last verse (Mark 16:8), but that we have a Gospel according to Mark witnesses to the final triumph of faith. Among these disciples are men who know this sea well, and for them to be afraid shows that their fear was humanly well founded. Although they have seen Jesus' power over the chaos that overwhelms people's bodies and minds, this crossing had been Jesus' idea, and their cries to him sound more like accusations of his lack of care for them than proclamations of their faith in him.

In the image of Jesus peacefully asleep in the storm-tossed boat there may be the memory of Jonah fast asleep in the bowels of the ship while God hurled great winds and waves at the vessel carrying the disobedient prophet away from his calling to the conversion of Nineveh (Jonah 1:4-15). Jonah has to resort to the much more dramatic and drastic solution of allowing himself to be tossed overboard before God will calm the storm. In contrast, Jesus rises from sleep, and the brief and powerful words of this most obedient prophet of God are enough to restore order out of chaos. Jesus rebukes the wind and the sea in the same way as he had "muzzled" or exorcised the unclean spirits and healed the tortured psyche of the man in the synagogue in Mark's account of Jesus' first miracles (Mark 1:23-27). And there comes a great calm.

Jesus' authority over the natural world confronts our faith in an unsettling way. As Michael Casey writes:

We do not mind a man forgiving sins (Mark 2:10) because the supposed effect is invisible and beyond proof—even if it is associated with a miraculous cure (Mark 2:12). Cures can be dismissed as merely "psychological." Our weak faith can dodge the question if there is some possibility of a "rational" explanation. The nature miracles are different. They confront our faith directly.[20]

Jesus' authority over the storm reveals him as Lord of Creation, and recalls the divine authority over the chaotic waters "in the beginning" (Gen 1:2) and when God divided the waters to allow the people to pass through from slavery into freedom (Exod 14–15). This divine prerogative is also praised in a number of the psalms, including Psalm 107 which is today's responsorial psalm. But the disciples are looking and not perceiving, listening and not understanding, despite the privileged instruction Jesus has given them (cf. Mark 4:10-12). Jesus' command of peace and stillness over the wind and waves assures the disciples' safe crossing, but their crossing from fear to faith is at a perilous beginning point. At least Jesus seems to suggest that the journey is possible. "Have you *still* no faith?" But the disciples turn to one another, not to Jesus, with their questions about his identity.

The Jesus who has risen from the sleep of death is the faithful hope of every disciple and post-resurrection community. Often the storms sweep down on us as suddenly as the wind and waves on the Sea of Galilee, and we find ourselves unprepared for sickness, for a terminal diagnosis for ourselves or a loved one, for the upheaval of personal relations, the painful work retrenchment. The mass media brings tragedies into our homes, and we may find ourselves saying: "Teacher, do you not care that we are perishing?" Yet Jesus is present in the storms, and will bring us to the shore of new beginnings and new initiatives. When the World Council of Churches was formed during the storms of the Second World War, it chose the logo that is still used today: a small boat with a cross for a mast, riding on the waves. Jesus crucified, but awakened from death in his resurrection, still travels in the boat of the churches.

The reading from the Book of Job is a beautiful companion for the gospel. It does what poetry is meant to do: give us surprising, even shocking juxtapositions of images that jolt us into new understandings. After thirty-seven chapters of Job's struggle with God and with his unhelpful friends, God answers Job out of the whirlwind with God's own questions and challenges that we might summarize as: "What do you know about how to run the world?!" And yet the image of creative power that God presents to Job in the portion read today is not of a mythological fierce battle but of the caring work of a midwife. The awesome, cosmic forces of the sea that threaten to engulf everything are taken by the Holy One and treated like a small baby brought forth from the womb of creation, swaddled in blankets of cloud, and laid down in darkness that quietens and calms it. Job realizes that order is born out of chaos, that God is in charge of the cosmos, and its forces have boundaries set for them by God. This is a God he can trust. We respond with verses from Psalm 107, a thanksgiving psalm for those who are like seafarers crying to God for their safety, and who are brought by God's loving-kindness through the storm to reach a safe port.

Like the disciples, Paul too has experienced the overwhelming power that is the love of Christ and his care for his people. But unlike the doubting disciples in the gospel, Paul now looks and sees Christ not only as a human being. He realizes that Christ is the one who brings life out of death for all humanity, and so in him all humanity is a new creation. Blown by the "whirlwind" of his Damascus conversion, Paul's faith and love of Christ enable him to cross the boundaries about which he writes to the Corinthians. In Christ we are all called to be boundary crossers: to cross from death to life; from selfish living only for ourselves to living for Christ; from human judgment of our sisters and brothers to seeing them as those for whom Christ lived, died, and was raised to life; from this passing world to the age to come when all will be brought to fulfillment and God's reigning presence will fill the whole of creation. Paul's witness is credible, because he can write like this even though he himself and the Corinthian church are "storm-tossed": by attacks on Paul's apostolic authority, by problems involving moral compromise and sexual deviance, and by some of the Corinthians' lack of practical concern for one another. We who have also experienced the loving-kindness of God in Christ are called, therefore, to be participants in his mystery, not just his admiring audience. The love of Christ should urge us, as it did Paul, to name and act against both the obvious and the more subtle storms and modern upheavals that threaten the lives of our sisters and brothers.

Thirteenth Sunday in Ordinary Time

• Wis 1:13-15; 2:23-24 • Ps 30:2, 4-6, 11-13 • 2 Cor 8:7, 9, 13-15 • Mark 5:21-43

It is to be hoped that the whole of this gospel is proclaimed today, as the option for the shorter version cuts out the portrait of the woman with a hemorrhage that is framed by the two-part narrative of Jairus's daughter. Mark deliberately structures his narrative so that the two stories relate to one another by contrasts and by similarities: contrasts between a young woman with some status (as the daughter of a synagogue official) and a marginalized woman; between a public healing and a private domestic event; between the responses of faith and disbelief of the onlookers. As for the similarities: faith in Jesus is professed by both a man and a woman; both women are anonymous, the one known only as the daughter of her father, the other as "nobody's" daughter; in both incidents, touch is important—the woman touches Jesus and he touches the dead girl. And in both miracles, "twelve years" is mentioned.

Jairus is a synagogue official, responsible for its good order. Jesus has already stirred controversy among some sections of the synagogue assemblies (cf. Mark 3:6); yet, with desperate courage and wild hope, and his status notwithstanding, Jairus violates all this good order with which he is charged. He appeals not to the synagogue but to Jesus for the healing of his daughter. In the dust at the feet of Jesus, Jairus begs him to come down to his house and lay hands on her. Jairus knows that he is asking Jesus to break the laws of ritual purity that forbids a man from touching a woman not his wife, and especially one who might well be dead by the time Jesus arrives (cf. Num 19:11-13). As we will hear later, the "little girl" was twelve years old, and therefore a young woman of marriageable age. Perhaps we might also be allowed to hear an "off-stage" voice of a wife and mother who urges her husband to "Get Jesus!"

As Jesus and Jairus are on the way to his house, they are followed by a great crowd, and also Jesus' disciples, no doubt eager for some movement up the social ladder and away from raging Gentile demoniacs, one of whom Jesus has just healed (Mark 5:1-20). But the straight-line journey to Jairus's house is interrupted. A woman who is hemorrhaging, probably from a gynecological cause, worms her way through the crowd and touches his clothes. According to the precept of Leviticus 15:19-20, she is regarded as ritually "unclean." A terrible legalistic burden on women had developed from what may have begun as a protection of the rhythms of feminine sexuality and an attitude of awe before the mystery of the flow of menstrual blood that was seen as both sustaining and draining the life of the community. In first-century Palestine, a menstruating woman was excluded from relationships with her husband, family, friends, and worshiping assembly. Anyone or anything with which she came into contact during those days was also regarded as unclean. For twelve years, Mark tells us, the desperate woman had wasted money on physicians, and becoming even worse she had endured a living death of alienation. Regarded as a "contaminant," she should not even have been out in a pressing crowd; but although she had probably become an expert in strategies of invisibility, she is ready now to risk being identified in the desperate hope that if she could only touch Jesus' garment she would be made well. (In Greek, "well" is also the word used for "saved.")

As she touches Jesus, the woman knows immediately that she is healed. In the depths of her body there is a sigh of relief and joy. In the midst of many people who are no doubt touching and hustling him, Jesus is concerned with only *one* woman, turning round to ask: "Who touched my clothes?" The disciples regard this as an incredible and unwanted interruption. Like us, they are ready to complain about anything they regard as delays to the "real" work—until we come to the realization that the interruptions *are* our work, especially when they involve responding with compassion to the needs of others.

The woman comes forward, and the crowd melts out of the narrative except as a witness to her brave truth-telling. She falls down "in fear and trembling," but caring nothing now about who hears her story. Then from being "nobody's daughter," disowned as wife, or mother, or sister, or friend, she hears herself named by Jesus as "Daughter." Jesus sends her away in peace, for her faith in him has brought not only physical healing that allows her to return after twelve years to her normal everyday relationships, but also establishes a new relationship as a member of the family of faith.

And so as Jesus continues to Jairus's house, continues moreover as someone who has violated taboos and been "contaminated" with ritual uncleanness by the woman, word comes that the girl has died and so there is no need to trouble Jesus anymore. But Jesus encourages Jairus to have the same faith as the woman. "Do not fear, only believe." When they reach the house, Jesus faces ridicule, scorn, and the ultimate enemy—death. But the gospel professes that in the presence of Jesus all death is only a sleep. This miracle is to be away from the crowd and professional mourners. With only Peter, James, and John, the privileged inner core of disciples, and with the girl's parents clinging desperately to the last thread of hope, Jesus takes the girl by the hand and tells her to "rise up." That Mark has retained in this narrative the mother tongue of Jesus and those with him, adds to the precious intimacy of the miracle. After her rising from the dead, she begins to walk around, and Jesus tells the young woman's parents to give her something to eat—a sequence of events that parallels the resurrection appearances of Jesus himself to his disciples, and has eucharistic memories for Christian communities gathered as we are today for a meal of thanksgiving and nourishing.

The young woman is, says Mark, twelve years old. Blood now courses again through her body and, at about the age of beginning menstruation, she now has a future and a marriageable hope. The woman who had hemorrhaged for twelve years, whose menstruation was her shame, is also healed and whole. Both women can now go and live their womanhood in peace and wholeness, for God's reigning presence has touched and restored their lives through Jesus who cares nothing for the barriers of cultic and ritual observance when these block the way to compassion. These women announce to us the situation of women throughout the world who, for whatever reason, are still conditioned or condemned to insignificance or abuse; all those women who are still marginalized by society, yet who grasp bravely at other possibilities. Nor can the church opt out of its responsibility. The church's teaching about nondiscrimination needs to be applied to its own affairs. It must refer constantly back to Jesus and his way of relating to women and men in the Scriptures.

The portion from the Book of Wisdom is also concerned with death and life. It emphasizes the "wholesomeness" or "integrity" of creation, of all that comes from the hand of God and is, therefore, to be recognized as "very good" (Gen 1:31). Both humanity and the cosmos delight in this relationship, refuting any concept of a malign influence that lurks in some cosmic force. There is now universal scientific agreement that dangerous climate change is largely human-induced. Our failures in stewarding God's gift of creation and our blatant abuse of it are sinful and contribute to the destruction of life, not its endurance. The author of the Book of Solomon had no access to faith in the privileged transformation of creation through the life, death, and resurrection of Christ as we pray in the Second Eucharistic Prayer: "He is the Word through whom you made the universe, the Savior you sent to redeem us." Every Eucharist is a thanksgiving memorial for God who is at work in creation as well as redemption. When we come to the Eucharist we lift creation up to God; we remember Christ's healing of creation, as in the bodies of the women in today's gospel; we offer for healing the vulnerable state of the community of life on our planet Earth. Our ecological imagination and our eucharistic faith meet in the transformation of the "fruits of the earth and the work of human hands" into the sacramental Body and Blood of Christ. To live eucharistically, therefore, we must live in daily love and respect for all human and planetary life.

Paul has very much in mind the responsibility that Christians have for one another. As a good psychologist, he first affirms the Corinthians in the rich gifts of grace they have received, and their admirable response to these ("sometimes" is best left unspoken!). He then reminds them of the love of Christ who became incarnate in the poverty of our humanity so that we might become rich in his promise of eternal life. Paul appeals to the Corinthians to remember this and be motivated by Christ's infinite generosity to do something to help the poor Christians of Jerusalem. In practical terms, he encourages them to contribute to the collection for them, recalling also the experience of Exodus 16:18 and the collection of the manna: "The one who had much did not have too much, and the one who had little did not have too little." Paul does not want to impose any economic burden on the Corinthian church, but encourages them to a balanced generosity that would also strengthen the bonds between Jewish and Gentile Christians. Poverty is never to be idealized, but the church's preferential option for the poor makes us servants of the poor Christ for the sake of greater equality and human dignity.

Fourteenth Sunday in Ordinary Time

• Ezek 2:2-5 • Ps 123:1-4 • 2 Cor 12:7-10 • Mark 6:1-6

Viktor Frankl, the Austrian Jewish psychotherapist who endured four years in Nazi death camps, knew by bitter experience that what gives light must endure burning. He remembered the light that radiated from those who remained decent human beings in the midst of the darkness of suffering and dehumanizing conditions, even though death from the fires of the crematoria overshadowed them and often claimed many of them.[21] Each reading this Sunday is about those who were singed by failure and vulnerability, but who continue to be a guiding light to their communities. Ezekiel is sent by God to the people named as rebels, who are obstinate, defiant, and deaf to God's word. Paul finds himself facing opposition both from those who regard themselves as "super apostles" and who tout around the word of God for their own reputation, and also from the members of the Corinthian church who have fallen under their influence. And Jesus is found to be unacceptable and offensive in his own hometown of Nazareth.

In the first reading we see Ezekiel prostrate before the overwhelming glory of God, and then raised by the Spirit to stand before God's presence to hear God's word. He is called to uproot himself, go to his people in exile, and speak to them God's word. Ezekiel was a priest, exiled with other upper-class compatriots to Babylon in the first wave of exile in 597 B.C.E., and as a sadly perennial attempt at a brain drain that conquerors impose to reinforce and subjugate the conquered. Ninety-three times in this prophetic book, Ezekiel is referred to as *ben adam* ("son of man"), often translated as "mortal" or "human one" to emphasize the contrast between the human messenger and the God who sends him to speak the prophetic word of God. Ezekiel is given no encouraging job description, no assurance of human success. To the contrary, he is told that his audience will be unresponsive and hostile. His assurance of success does not lie in the responsiveness or obedience of those to whom he proclaims the word, but in the prophet's unflinching and passionate obedience to the proclamation. It is the word of God that appoints him, anoints him, and transforms him, even though so often it will not be the word that the exiles want to hear. The prophet must accept the human limitations of his divine calling, must accept a persisting failure of human insight—that a prophet is often not recognized or honored by those closest to him or her. Neither God nor his prophet is responsible for people's obtuseness. In his very calling, God prepares Ezekiel for human failure and we, who may also experience so much failure, respond to the reading with Psalm 123. It is a cry from a people who have suffered the humiliation of exile. Once again, they can sing this song of ascent as they go up to Jerusalem, praising God for the graciousness of his mercy in bringing them home, and now making a pilgrimage of thanksgiving for their deliverance from the contempt of their oppression, and continuing to look to the One who is always a Master or Mistress who cares for their servants.

In the second reading, Paul proclaims that the authentication of his apostleship does not lie in the revelation of God's glory in some mystical experience he had (2 Cor 12:1-7), but is revealed in his weakness, in his failures and suffering. There has been much speculation about the meaning of Paul's "thorn in the flesh," and the exact meaning of this we will never know, but surely the opposition he has met from the "super apostles" (2 Cor 11:5) and those under their influence in his own community are a significant aspect of the evil that attacked and undermined him not only physically but also in his personal integrity. Paul does not suffer complacently or delight in his victimhood; three times he pleads with God to relieve him of this suffering, not so much for himself but because he saw it as an impediment to his already threatened ministry among the Corinthians. But then comes what Paul recognizes as the most precious revelation from the Lord: that his weaknesses and failures are what hollow out his personal depths, emptying him of any illusions of his own success, and so creating a space in which the power of the crucified and risen Christ can dwell and work in and through him. It is only when we humbly perceive our own weaknesses that we can glimpse God's glory, and be ready like both Ezekiel and Paul to stand up and hold to the ground of our faith.

Some cultures speak of the "tall poppy syndrome," the delight that some people have in cutting people down to size—usually a bit smaller than *their* size—by belittling them through subtle innuendo, and disguising resentment of another person's achievements by damning with faint praise. When Jesus is invited to teach in the Nazareth synagogue on the Sabbath, he fails to live up to the expectations of his hometown. What Jesus spoke to the synagogue assembly we are not told, but they were the authoritative words of the one who has exorcised, healed, raised from the dead, and proclaimed the Good

News of the kingdom. But in some way the listeners consider that Jesus' words go against their own comfortable interpretation of family customs or established religion traditions. Here is the Nazareth version of the "tall poppy," so Jesus has to be cut down to the hometown size expected by those who think they know everything about him and his family, and recognize him as a local craftsman. Jesus embodies the "scandal" of the ordinary, and familiarity breeds contempt in the assembly whose perceptions are limited to the domestic and parochial. They are closed to any surprising presence and action of God that would violate their own expectations and insight, and consider their own wisdom to be superior to that of Jesus. They ask the right questions, but their prejudgment supplies them with the wrong answers, and amazement deteriorates into offense and rejection. It is another example of misunderstanding about which we have heard on the last Sundays: of the religious and civil authorities who are conspiring about Jesus' destruction; of his family who wanted to bring him outside the house where he was teaching and back into their traditional embrace; of his terrified disciples in the storm; of the scornful mourners at Jairus's house. Jesus summarizes his sorrow in his words: "Prophets are not without honor, except in their own hometown, and among their own kin, and in their own house." If the synagogue assembly is amazed at Jesus and has no faith in him, Mark comments ironically that Jesus is amazed at their lack of faith that leads to Jesus' powerlessness, because for his deeds of power to be effective they must be worked in the context of faith. Jesus has failed to call forth faith where he might have most expected to find it.

That the "Word was made failure and died among us," is the source of our hope, not despair, for as Maria Boulding, o.s.b., writes:

> If you have ever been sickened by the failure of some enterprise into which you put your best efforts and the love of your heart, you are caught up into the fellowship of Christ's death and resurrection, whether or not you thought of your experience in that way. God had dealt with our failure by himself becoming a failure and so healing it from the inside. This is why we can meet him in our failure; it is a sure place for finding him, since he has claimed it. So central is failure to the Easter mystery that a person who has never grappled with it could scarcely claim to be Christ's friend and follower.[22]

We may still be more inclined to listen to those who appear to be prophets on the celebrity circuit rather than those with whom we rub shoulders daily. "Who do they think they are?!" may not be unfamiliar words on our lips or in our hearts. We need humble ongoing and Gospel-based discernment of the authenticity of prophets. Continued success is a dangerous criterion.

Fifteenth Sunday in Ordinary Time

• Amos 7:12-15 • Ps 85:9-14 • Eph 1:3-14 • Mark 6:7-13

Jesus has not been deterred by his rejection at Nazareth and continues to teach among the surrounding villages, but now it is time to send the Twelve to do what he has been doing.

When Jesus called these disciples, Mark described them as "those whom he wanted, and they came to him" to be "with him" and "be sent to proclaim the message, and to have authority to cast out demons" (Mark 3:13-15). We might be excused for wondering if they really are ready, for although they have been with Jesus as he taught, exorcised, and healed, and had experienced his rejection by his hometown synagogue, their main recorded response to him has been the accusation of not caring much about them in the middle of the storm, and impatience with him over the "interruption" of the hemorrhaging woman! But, for our consolation, Jesus is willing to work with flawed disciples, and still dares today to send out men and women like ourselves to be instruments of the healing power and authority of God. What we hear in this gospel is both challenge and consolation to Mark's Christian community and every community that, through baptism, is called and sent on Jesus' own mission.

Now the "see, judge, and act" apprenticeship of the Twelve is to be tested in their first mission. Equipped only with the authority of Jesus' word and the memory of his example, the Twelve are sent out like their ancestors, with exodus urgency—with their walking staffs and sandals, for they are on a new and urgent journey to free enslaved bodies, hearts, and psyches as Jesus has done. They are to travel in pairs, with respect for the Jewish tradition that required that the validity of witness must be verified by at least two people (Deut 17:6; 19:15). There is to be no dallying or packing bags with things that are not really needed and will only become an intolerable burden along the way. Their missionary survival kit consists of the authority of Jesus and his word, the providence of God, and the hospitality of those who will open their hearts and homes to the Twelve. The one tunic they are allowed may also be symbolic of the single-mindedness that Jesus expects of those who, as Paul wrote to the Galatians, "have clothed yourselves with Christ" through baptism (Gal 3:27). No matter what the quality of the hospitality offered to them, the disciples are to accept this and stay put. Searching for more congenial accommodation or company is not to be part of their journey. For people to welcome the Twelve, knowing that they have associated with the taboo, marginalized people, will spread the kingdom of compassion, and offer the possibilities of a welcoming reentry into religious and social relationships for the outcasts and shunned who have been healed.

If they are not well received, the disciples are to leave, not responding with any harsh words, but merely with the Jewish symbolic gesture of shaking off from their feet the dust of the unwelcoming place, as Jews did when returning to Israel from foreign soil. All that the inhospitable household was left with was insubstantial dust, rather than the word of God. We all need to be honestly and humbly discerning about when to stay and when to leave a particular mission, "And take upon's the mystery of things, / As if we were God's spies," said King Lear.[23] In the Christian sense, we are to be "God's spies," reconnoitering the possibilities for announcing the reigning presence of God in human lives in our own situations. And we must be prepared to fail, as Jesus and his followers failed, but without turning such failure into a career of self-pity.

In the eighth century B.C.E., Amos is called by God and sent on a mission with nothing but the prophetic authority of God. From his home in the southern kingdom of Judah, Amos is plucked from his work as a herdsman and fig tree dresser, one who punctured the fruit and removed the insects that would destroy it. He is sent as an unlikely prophet to prune God's people in northern Israel with his cutting words and draw out from them the evils, especially of injustice, that were corrupting them. His is a voice of alternative imagination, associated neither with any shrine nor court, as some prophets were, nor with any particular school of prophets. He is simply God's prophet, called by God's free choice. Bethel was an important shrine in the northern kingdom, and its priest, Amaziah, tells him that he is not welcome there. His words to Amos are not necessarily hostile, but this is Amaziah's territory and a royal sanctuary, and the presence of someone with no allegiance to the northern kingdom or the way in which prophesying might be expected to accommodate the wishes of its king, could be dangerous for the northern nation, for Amaziah, and for Amos himself. Much better that Amos should get back to his home territory and do his work, "earn his bread" there. Amos's response is both direct and simple: He had not chosen to be a prophet in Israel; God had chosen him, and that is what he will be, welcome or not. This is enough for Amos; this is enough for the missionary Twelve; and this is to be enough for us, especially when we need to disturb or be disturbed for the sake of justice. Psalm 85 is therefore a fitting response. When faithfulness, justice, and peace are active in and through a community, this is evidence of God's presence. It is as though God and his people meet and "kiss" each other in love.

The Letter to the Ephesians, from which we read for the next seven weeks, is held by most scholars to have been written by someone other than Paul, who was a close disciple of Paul, and wanted to encourage the Ephesians by collecting, editing, and circulating aspects of Paul's thoughts. When speaking of the author, therefore, "Paul" will be used in this sense.[24] Ephesians is cosmic in its scope, praising the plan of God to unite all things, in heaven and on earth. This is a timeless and limitless blessing bestowed on those who have been chosen by Christ, and perhaps the best way to listen to this reading is not to try to analyze every word or phrase, but surrender thankfully to "the praise of his glorious grace which he freely bestowed on us in the Beloved." Redemption and forgiveness, wisdom and faith, and the adoption into the family of God are the free gifts of God who makes us sons and daughters through the Blood of the Christ who is God's only true Son from the beginning and until the ages run their course. Ephesians reminds us that we are called and chosen by God not because we are holy, but so that we might become holy, in Christ. Warmed and softened by his love, we take the impression of the Holy Spirit who is both the "seal" that is a claim of God's ownership, and the "pledge" of our inheritance to come. The whole reading begins and ends in praise.

Sixteenth Sunday in Ordinary Time

• Jer 23:1-6 • Ps 23:1-6 • Eph 2:13-18 • Mark 6:30-34

Between today's and last Sunday's gospel, Mark sandwiches the narrative of the martyrdom of John the Baptist, which the Roman Catholic Lectionary reads on 29 August, the feast of his beheading. The position of that detailed narrative is significant, however, for our appreciation of this Sunday's gospel as it is both a flashback to and a forward glimpse of the consequences of preaching a gospel of repentance. The flow of Mark's narrative implies that as it was for the Baptist, so it will be for Jesus and those whom he sends on mission. Not only the calm waters and green pastures of missionary success lie ahead, but also the journey through the dark valleys of suffering and death. But for now, on the apostles' return from their first mission, Jesus listens to their accounts, which can hardly be thought of as an apostolic debriefing (Jesus who had sent them on *his* mission says nothing), but rather as an announcement of all that *they* had done. Jesus then invites them to: "Come away to a deserted place all by yourselves and rest a while." The place to which Jesus invites his apostles is described as a wilderness, and in this naming there is already a hint that Jesus is hosting them into more than a getaway holiday. The wilderness is where Jesus withdrew to prepare for his own mission; when he went out to pray, it was in lonely places; and in the wilderness sojourn their ancestors were taught, cared for, and fed by their provident God. This will be an opportunity for the apostles' new nurturing.

Their "rest" will not be just a cozy "Jesus and us" occasion, but rather a "Sabbath" rest of creative, renewing relationship and teaching. This is not to deny that there needs to be concern for our own rest and refreshment, a different tempo for our lives after a time of intense ministering to others, but very often we consider that this means an escape from the deepest source of our energy and nourishment, with the consequent temptation to no prayer, no worship, no attention to anyone but ourselves—days off from Jesus.

Jesus and the apostles step ashore and land in the midst of the enthusiastic crowds that had hurried to the same place on foot. One can imagine less enthusiasm among the disciples! Jesus sees the crowd as "like sheep without a shepherd," recalling a familiar image of God in both today's first reading and the responsorial Psalm 23. Jesus' first reaction is one of compassion, that gut-wrenching, womb love that acts for life in the midst of any interruption. It is not because of the people's enthusiasm for Jesus, which may arise from mixed motives, but because of their own suffering that arose largely from a desperate need for responsible leadership that Old Testament references to the shepherding image was often evoked (see Num 27:17; 1 Kgs 22:17; Ezek 34:5-6). Graciously, and with extraordinary availability, Jesus puts aside his own agenda for the greater need of the crowd, and begins to teach them and to nourish them with his word.

And how do our responses compare with those of Jesus? Do we often complain that we could be really good followers of Jesus if we were not so often interrupted in what we are doing by other people, or do we realize that if God is not in the interruptions, it may be very difficult to find him? How ready are we, with our own individual and communal gifts, to offer some direction to those hungering for truth? Can we recognize them and name them, try to serve and encourage them: by face-to-face contact, by advocacy, by Internet communication and support, by informed and responsible voting at election time—whenever and however we "step ashore" among them?

The compassion of Jesus for the crowds who were like a flock without a shepherd stands out brightly against the dark foil of Jeremiah's pronouncement of doom on the seventh-century B.C.E. monarchy of Judah. The political and religious leaders have failed to gather and shepherd the people of God entrusted to their leadership. Through the words of the prophet, God reproaches them for their irresponsibility, for offering no guidance or care to their people. God will take care of the people because of the neglect of their leaders. These leaders of God's people have become misleaders. They will be judged by the way they treated the most vulnerable members of the community: the economically oppressed, the powerless, the marginalized. Today's political and ecclesial leaders stand under the same judgment.

For his neglected people, God will show care in a very different way, gathering the remnant out of the lands where they have been scattered, and shepherding them back to their own homeland. Yet there is hope, God promises, of good shepherds, just leaders who will restore a rule of justice and love. Such hope converges to a God-given center that will hold, to the bright point of messianic promise. A royal shepherd and a righteous leader will branch from the stock of David, from the stump of the tree that has been hewn down by the injustice and unrighteousness of so many of its kings. This ideal leader will be the gift of God to the gathered and no longer scattered people, a human ruler rooted in the flesh and blood of his royal ancestors but, more importantly, one whose reign will be characterized by righteousness, by proper relationships between God, the people, and the king himself. In fact, as a reminder of the source of this hope, the one to come will be named "The Lord is our righteousness."

We respond to this reading with Psalm 23, probably the best-known and most-loved psalm in the Psalter, and often chosen when we are facing turmoil, such as the death of a loved one. It is a psalm of confidence and trust in the Lord who is "my" shepherd, and the psalm continues to be prayed in the intimacy of this first-person relationship. The psalmist is realistic; he knows there will be dark valleys as well as still waters and green pastures; that sometimes the shepherd may need to use his crook to prod the reluctant sheep as well as guide the willing. The Lord is also the host who prepares a table and nourishes us so that we have a serene strength in the face of our enemies. In the Lord, goodness and mercy accompany us all the days of our life, and are made flesh among us in the compassionate Shepherd of today's gospel. In the church today how much we need contemporary shepherds who will walk with us through the dark valleys of their people's lives, even though death may lurk there for themselves; who unite rather than scatter the so-called progressives and conservatives; who are moved with compassion for the crowds rather than with criticism.

The Gentiles of the early church had to walk through their own dark valleys as they met hostility from some Jewish Christians to their admission as full members of the Christian communities, and the Jewish Christians were alarmed at the disregard of the Gentiles for their holy traditions. Paul writes that with the ramrod of the cross Christ has broken down the dividing wall of hostility, and Christ has become the meeting place for divided humanity. Sadly, aspects of the Mosaic Law had become a symbol of resistance and exclusiveness to which the death of Christ puts an end. The "wall" is a provocative symbol for those of us who experienced or remember the pulling down of the Berlin Wall or the dismantling of the Iron Curtain, and the ongoing challenge to build peace and liberty in their stead. Tragically, there are still walls that divide: Palestinians from Jews, people and nations from one another. They may be made of concrete and barbed wire, but often that material barrier is only the external expression of centuries of hostility in human hearts.

Christ calls each one of his followers to the ministry of reconciliation and peacemaking. There is still much to be done if we are to overcome the divisions of race, gender, social status, the separation between our Christian churches, the many ingrained prejudices to other religions—and become a new humanity in Christ. Much religious and social division is due to igno-rance of one another, as Robert Frost reflected in his poem "Mending Wall." Fences and walls do not necessarily make good neighbors.

Seventeenth Sunday in Ordinary Time

• 2 Kgs 4:42-44 • Ps 145:10-11, 15-18 • Eph 4:1-6 • John 6:1-15

John's gospel is given a privileged place during Lent and Easter, but in the three-year cycle of the Lectionary we have no "Year of John." So that the significant John 6 is proclaimed at some time in the cycle, the reading from Mark's gospel is interrupted at the point where Mark is about to describe the feeding of the five thousand, and the "Bread of Life" chapter is inserted from this Sunday to the Twenty-first Sunday in Year B.

The first short reading is obviously chosen because its theme is related to the gospel: the miraculous feeding of a large number of people with a small amount of food. A great famine has afflicted the land, but it seems to be ending when a man arrives with food from a place that, by its name, Baal-Shalisha, may have been the site of a cult centered on the fertility god Baal. He does not offer the privileged firstfruits of the harvest to that god, but to "the man of God," Elisha, and his band of prophets. Surprisingly, Elisha tells him to give the twenty loaves of barley and the fresh ears of grain in his sack to the one hundred hungry people who are with Elisha. When Elisha's servant objects that this amount of food is obviously inadequate for the number of people, Elisha repeats his instruction and gives the reason for his certainty that there will be enough for everyone—"For thus says the Lord . . ."

We may be inclined to regard such stories as quaint anecdotes, but they witness to fundamental aspects of biblical faith: concern for the poor and needy and regard for their physical needs; the power of God's word, and the overwhelming generosity of God who blesses and multiplies the small offer-ing of human hands so that there is always more than enough for our needs. And so, gathered around the table that provides our eucharistic bread and wine, the firstfruits of Christ's sacrifice, we acknowledge God's goodness to us as we repeat after the verses of Psalm 145: "You open your hand, satisfying the desire of every living thing."

The account of the feeding of the five thousand is the only miracle recorded in each one of the four gospels. John's narrative is true to his portrait of a more self-sufficient Jesus who knows what is in everyone (cf. John 2:27-28). For John, miracles are "signs" that point to a reality beyond themselves, to the identity and truth of Jesus. It is Passover, but the disciples and the crowds that follow Jesus to a mountain by the side of the Sea of Galilee are a long way from where the religious leaders would expect them to be for this festival, namely, in Jerusalem. John's account is concerned with how people respond to Jesus. The crowd is enthusiastic about his healing of the sick and they hope that they will get something out of their following of this miracle worker. Although he knows what he will do, Jesus asks Phillip what they should do about buying bread for the people, and Phillip's response is logical: it would cost more than half the annual wage of a laborer to give this number even a few crumbs, and Jesus and his disciples don't have that kind of money! Andrew's response is pragmatic, producing one small boy with five coarse barley loaves and two dried fish, a typical and minimal meal for two poor people, not five thousand! All these responses are inadequate, then as now, for what is most important is not utilitarian satisfaction, not logic or reason, not even the miracle that Jesus will work. The gospel concern is that people see what happens as a "sign" that points to something more and beyond, to who Jesus really is, and how he will satisfy not only empty stomachs but also empty hearts.

Jesus takes the little that is offered to him, and in his hands it becomes an abundant meal. Jewish memories and Christian eucharistic themes (well established in the Johannine communities near the end of the first century) are woven together as Jesus takes the bread, gives thanks, and, unlike the Synoptic Gospel accounts, distributes both the bread and fish himself. John is not concerned with practical catering logistics, but with the theological emphasis that in this Passover feeding Jesus becomes a personally nourishing presence to each person. This food that he distributes is more precious than the manna, for the people were not to leave any manna until the next day (Exod 16:19-20) because it would decay. Whatever fragments (*ta klásmata*) are left over from the lakeside meal are not perishable; they are to be gathered up (*synágete*) and cared for by the disciples. In the early church, the eucharistic assembly was sometimes spoken of as the "gathering," and the eucharistic bread as the "fragments."[26]

The response of the crowd is to hail Jesus as a prophet, one like that promised in Deuteronomy 18:15, who would usher in the messianic era.

Knowing their intent to take him "by force," to manipulate him to their own political and material expectations of what the messiah should be and do, Jesus "withdraws" only to return later for a deeper engagement with the crowd, as we will hear in the continuation of the Bread of Life discourse on the following Sundays.

We bring to this Eucharist the little that we have, all the fragments of our inadequacies, our successes and failures, our hopes and fears. We offer them to God with the fruits of the earth and the work of human hands, and these small gifts are transformed and offered back to us as the gift of Jesus' sacramental Body and Blood, into whose life we are gathered. This is not logic, pragmatism, or self-satisfaction; this is *eucharistía*, thanksgiving for God's abundant and eternal generosity.

Those to whom the Letter to the Ephesians is written are implored to live a life worthy of their Christian calling. A "prisoner of the Lord" may refer to physical imprisonment, or it may refer to the love of Christ that has captured Paul, but either explanation gives a strong, personal witness and encouragement to the Ephesians themselves to continue to walk in fidelity to the call of Christ. The word for "walk" is often translated as "lead," yet the more literal translation gives the sense of a public, visible way of life that is proud of its commitment. This commitment is to virtues that strengthen the unity of the community and define Christians, and those listed can provide us with a searching "review of life" with which to reflect on our own living as members of the Body of Christ. The love with which we should relate to one another is spelled out; it is not just a warm fuzzy feeling, but is expressed by humility that defuses competitiveness, and gentleness that is reverent and considerate of other people. To be patient is to suffer what we consider the shortcomings of others and to be tolerant rather than short-tempered. If as individuals we live in community in this way, we too will be bound together not by a prisoner's chains, but by the unity of the Spirit and the strong fetters of peace. For Christians in societies where individualism and competition are considered acceptable, even promoted norms, such a challenge is not easy. The sources of the unity of the Christian community that Paul emphasizes read like (and may have been) a liturgical hymn of belonging to the one Body of Christ, filled with the one Spirit, called in the one hope of salvation. This unity is expressed by fidelity to one Lord, commitment to one faith, and the lifelong celebration of one baptism that acknowledges the one God who is both transcendent and immanent in all creation, both cosmic and human. As we look around our eucharistic assembly, this is the hidden and huge mystery that binds us together.

Eighteenth Sunday in Ordinary Time

• Exod 16:2-4, 12-15 • Ps 78:3-4, 23-24, 25, 54 • Eph 4:17, 20-24 • John 6:24-35

In the reading from the Book of Exodus, we are in the midst of a grumbling community on the brink of rebellion against their God. Their petulant complaints contrast with God's loving care that has delivered them from slavery in Egypt into desert freedom. Their cries on account of their Egyptian taskmasters (Exod 3:7) have become self-centered mutters about Moses and Aaron whom they accuse of leading them into death, not life, and they are even beginning to regret God's choice of themselves for special attention! We know how easily our memories of the past can become selective and nostalgic in present difficulties, and this is what happens to the Hebrews. The diet of slaves is romanticized into eating to their hearts' content of the fleshpots of Egypt, and wilderness freedom is reduced to empty stomachs.

Yet God is patient with his people and promises to send them bread from heaven to satisfy their hunger so that they will remember the wilderness as a place of God-given life. This gift will also be a test of their obedience, as God gives Moses instructions about how and when the bread is to be gathered, and adds that the extra bonus of quails will fly over the camp to provide the people with meat. The Lectionary omits the very specific directives prohibiting gathering on the Sabbath but allowing a double portion of bread to be gathered the day before. The reason for such directives is to distinguish the Hebrews' action in the wilderness from that in Egypt; with God providing them with food as his free people, there is no need to hoard anxiously or barter like slaves, but only the need for trust in God. Walter Brueggemann comments that "the bread is given of God's providential ordering of creation."[27] Probably the "bread" was the secretion of the tamarisk tree that hardened into a flaky white substance when the morning dew evaporated but, unfamiliar with this, the people asked: "Man hu?" (Hebrew, "What is it?"). The final words of the reading that we hear today emphasize what the manna is all about: it is a sign of God's unfailing love for the chosen people, even when they are grumbling and rebellious. This should be an encouragement to us.

In the verses of the responsorial Psalm 78, history becomes poetry, memory becomes prayer, and to hand on the sacred traditions about Israel's relationship with their God from one generation to the next is seen as a sacred trust. God's steadfast loving-kindness for Israel is shown in the gift of the manna, here called "the bread of angels," and the gift of the Promised Land. The verses that recite the people's failures are omitted, a rather optimistic editing given our human inclination frequently to forget God's good gifts and concentrate more on grumbling than gratitude.

The gospel continues the narrative about the incomparable gift that Jesus is and offers. The crowd that we last saw wanting to make Jesus king has hustled into boats and chased after him, and their first question to him seems a trivial one about when Jesus got to Capernaum. Perhaps they are wondering if it is time for Jesus to serve the next meal! Jesus lets them know that he has no illusions about their motives and their search for him as the bountiful supplier of food for their stomachs rather than as the source of spiritual food that endures for eternal life. Just as an important person would put a seal on a document to indicate that the words come with the authority and authenticity intended by the sender, so God has put his seal on his Son, the Word of God, who carries his message with divine credentials. But the people would prefer to bypass Jesus as a messenger and mediator, and question him about what they themselves can do to perform the works of God. Jesus tells them that the work of God is to believe in the one God has sent, for faith is the true miracle. The people recognize he is speaking of himself, but their argumentative questions show that they want to be in charge, even of this faith! Give *us* a sign, and then *we* will judge whether we should believe in you or not. *We* have the manna tradition of our Moses and our ancestors, and if you conform to something like that *we* might consider the evidence for belief in you!

Jesus then reinterprets their biblical traditions for the people so that they might become less fixated on their material hunger and on the past—which their memories can also manipulate selectively. It was not Moses, says Jesus, who was responsible for the gift of the manna but, as we have heard in the first reading, that "bread from heaven" was the gift of his generous Father to a grumbling and rebellious people, and a test of their obedience. Jesus cannot be charged with spiritualizing away the human need to be fed—he has, after all, just fed five thousand—but his vision is of a larger nourishment and wisdom that reaches beyond stomachs to hearts, beyond Israel to the whole world, beyond earth to heaven, beyond time to eternity. Still wanting to be in control, the people ask Jesus to give them this bread always. The time has come for Jesus to speak directly: "I AM the bread of life," he replies. The memory of the manna, the nourishment of the Mosaic teaching/Torah, the continual search for wisdom (Sir 2:21): these gifts of God will not be dismissed by Jesus, but will be reinterpreted and transformed by him. It is through the gift of Jesus that these gifts reveal God. He promises that the nourishing of hunger and the quenching of thirst will be available not only to Israel, but to anyone who comes to him and believes in him. We are the inheritors of that promise—if we come to Jesus in faith, and if our hunger and thirst for him has not been blunted by stuffing ourselves with materialism or simply boredom, by addiction to what can be death-dealing, not only medically but also spiritually, or by the allure of the latest newly advertised diet of spirituality.

The Letter to the Ephesians also emphasizes the new, but this is the wisdom that comes when the Ephesians "learned Christ." It is not a case of learning *about* Christ, but learning *him*, his way and truth, and stripping oneself of anything that would distract from that. The memory of their baptism, of becoming a new person in Christ, is recalled by the image of "putting on Christ." Clothing is an indicator of personality, of social status and belonging (ask any adolescent!), and a reflection of the wearer's culture—in other words, it can be a metaphor for identity. At baptism we were clothed with a white garment as a sign of our new personhood in Christ, and the prayer of the rite acknowledges this garment as an outward sign of the Christian dignity that has been bestowed through the sacrament. The prayer continues with the hope that, with the help of family and friends, that baptismal dignity will be carried unstained by sin into the everlasting life of heaven. We all grow out of the material garment, but the continuing challenge is to grow into what it symbolizes: the new self created in God's love and holy truth for the new age and the new creation. Such a radical transformation is our possibility, as it was for the Ephesians.

Nineteenth Sunday in Ordinary Time

• 1 Kgs 19:4-8 • Ps 34:2-9 • Eph 4:30–5:2 • John 6:41-51

At times it may all seem too hard. God seems to be asking too much of us in our faith and our work. What we do, even (especially?) for God, isn't appreciated; our family and friends take us for granted or even exploit us; the church seems to lack compassion and relevance. And so we are quite ready to join Elijah in his "situational depression" of the first reading! Today we hear about an Elijah who is no longer the boisterous and self-confident prophet who triumphed over the false prophets of Baal in the big burn-up of Elijah's sacrifice and the watery failure of theirs on Mount Carmel (1 Kgs 18:20-40). Now Elijah faces personal burnout. Was he too theatrical, too committed to a one-man show, too sure that he alone would root out false prophecy from Israel (forget about the hundred prophets hidden by Obadiah in the caves in 1 Kings 18:4), too vicious in his slaughtering of the prophets of Baal? It seems so. Jezebel is after him, and it's all too much for Elijah. He escapes into the wilderness and sits down under a solitary broom tree, a fragile flowering plant that, despite its frailty, can survive in the desert. Elijah doubts that he can. His self-confidence has withered and his self-pity is in full bloom. But then his heartache, his death wish becomes a painful prayer. He hangs onto a wisp of belief that there is a God out there, somewhere, whom he can at least ask "to take away my life, for I am no better than my ancestors." The lines of relationship and communication are opened, even if it is by angry faith—and God responds. God, too, is after Elijah.

God's plan of action for Elijah is first to give him the gift of sleep for his physical well-being. Then an angel, a messenger of God, touches him and encourages him to get up and eat the hot scones and drink the water that has been provided. Elijah begins to realize that he is not alone, but neither is he ready to move away from his broom tree, so back he goes to sleep. And back comes the messenger of God for another feeding episode. Again the angel touches Elijah, tells him to get up and eat, adding that he needs this strength for his journey. Then with his stomach filled and his spirit touched, Elijah is ready to move on through the wilderness, and we learn where he is now heading: to Mount Horeb (the northern name for Mount Sinai). After a journey of forty days and forty nights, Elijah reaches the place of the sacred revelation to his ancestors, the mountain where God revealed himself to Moses and gave him the wisdom of the Torah with which to nourish Israel.

So often we need the touch of another "angel" in our wilderness moments: those times of grief, of real or perceived misunderstanding by our brothers and sisters, or those tragic days of disillusionment with ourselves and our world when it seems preferable to lie down and sleep, even the desperate self-inflicted sleep of death. The phone call, the visit, the letter, the invitation to a meal, even a cup of coffee—are simple "touches" and eating experiences that can help us rise and continue on our life's journey. And our sharing of memories of our ancestors in the faith who survived difficulties and tragedies may also encourage us on the way. The Word of God shared in such circumstances is a powerful support, as revealed by a story told by the late Francis Xavier Nguyen Van Thuan, once archbishop of Ho Chi Minh City, then president of the Vatican's Council for Justice and Peace. For thirteen years he was imprisoned in North Vietnam, nine of those in solitary confinement. On one occasion a copy of the New Testament was smuggled into the prison for the Catholic prisoners. So that they could all share it, they ripped it into little sheets that were then distributed and memorized, truly "by heart." Every sunset, the prisoners took it in turn to recite aloud the part they knew. It was so moving, said Van Thuan, to hear the Word of God in the silence and darkness, recited with such strength of faith that no one could doubt the presence of God in the Word.

In the continuation of the reading from John 6 there is movement to another level of understanding of what Jesus means by "bread": from material bread, to the bread that is the work of faith, and now to the bread that is Jesus himself. We should not be too eager to hurry on to eucharistic references—not yet.[28] The challenge to the people is to recognize Jesus as the revelation of God's word. When they come to him and accept to be taught his wisdom, his words become a source of life. In his person and words, Jesus sets before the people a feast that will be nourishment for eternal life.

The religious leaders (named as "the Jews," the fourth evangelist's selective terminology for those who oppose Jesus) are foolishly certain that they know all about him because they know his parentage. They have closed the ears of their hearts to anything Jesus has said about "my Father" and the unique relationship of this Father and Son. They are not ready for a surprising God, for a God who can be present in the prosaic and ordinary, present in this man who claims to have been sent by God, to speak the words of God, to have seen God, and who has the temerity to endorse himself by the teaching of the prophets (e.g., Isa 54:13) and compare himself more favorably with some of the wonderful events of Israel's past, such as the feeding with the manna that was God's gift from heaven. From speaking of "this bread" of his teaching, Jesus now unambiguously points to himself: "I AM the living bread that came down from heaven," says Jesus. The manna was sustenance for a time but Jesus' revelation will nourish for eternity; the manna fell from heaven but, as John proclaimed at the beginning of his gospel, Jesus is the Word who was with God and was God from the beginning, and who came from the place close to the Father's heart to make God known in our human flesh (John 1:1, 14, 18).

Today's gospel concludes with Jesus speaking of the bread he will give for the life of the world as "my flesh." There may be some eucharistic hints here, but the word "flesh" (*sarx*) refers first of all to Jesus' humanity, his way of being in the world and his self-gift to the world. This is his mission, a consequence of the Father's love for the world (John 3:16), that will lead him into his death and resurrection for the life of the world. How this relates to the Eucharist will be further revealed as we listen to the Bread of Life Discourse on the following two Sundays.

There are always options available to us in our journey of faith. Like Elijah, we may feel it would be easier to opt out, perhaps with a struggle, perhaps with a whimper, and often because there is no "angel" around to help us. Or we may join the ranks of the murmurers, resistant to new ideas, new wisdom, new interpretations, even if from the highest teaching authority in the church—an ecumenical council such as Vatican II. Or we may continue to do the hard work of faith and come to Jesus to feed on his word and wisdom, given to us especially in the Scriptures, in the eucharistic Liturgy of the Word, and in our personal *lectio divina*.

The Letter to the Ephesians reminds us of the practical, everyday demands of the hard work of faith, especially in community relationships. There is nothing very distinctive or surprising about this list of ethical behavior—except the motivation. The Ephesians are called to such behavior so that they will not grieve the Holy Spirit of God with which they have been sealed. The seal of baptism identifies Christians as the sons and daughters of God, and is a pledge of the fulfillment of their freedom and redemption. Since they have been transformed by the Spirit, anything that threatens the bonds of love in the community is to be avoided. Our own experience can witness to the truth of the undermining of relationships in a family, parish, or any other close-knit community when resentment is cherished, and being a victim develops its own misconstrued status. The violent outbursts of anger, the shouting that often accompanies this, the pervasive negativity that can make a quarrel out of anything, the slander of people behind their backs, and the undercurrent of malice that seeps into thought and action—all this is to be put away and replaced by mutual kindness, tenderheartedness, and forgiveness. By the end of the reading, the trinitarian motivation for conduct is proclaimed: God has loved us and forgiven us in Christ, and the fragrance of his sacrifice permeates the church, the Christian community that lives according to the Spirit. Once again, we have a challenging "review of life" for our personal and communal reflection.

Twentieth Sunday in Ordinary Time

• Prov 9:1-6 • Ps 34:2-7 • Eph 5:15-20 • John 6:51-58

In the reading from the Book of Proverbs the wisdom of God is imaged as feminine, as Lady Wisdom or Sophia. Any masculine imagery is completely absent; even her staff are servant girls. Wisdom's creativity has built the house of the cosmos, and she now wants to share with her guests the lavish menu of creation. She does not demand attendance at her banquet, but sends her servant girls to persuade "the simple" and "those without sense." This does not mean that her guests are to be stupid, but rather that they are those who have a simplicity that recognizes they are not self-sufficient, that they have more to learn about the way of wisdom, and so will respond to the invitation to: "Lay aside immaturity and live, and walk in the way of insight." To enter into Sophia's house is, therefore, more than entering into a one-off feast; it is to accept the invitation to a way of life in which God's generosity is experienced "now," but "not yet" in the time ahead that will offer even more bountiful feasting on her bread and wine.

As humble people who trust in and are dependent on the generosity of God, the verses of the responsorial Psalm 34 give us the words to express our thankful praise. In the antiphon we are urged to "taste and see that the Lord is good," in other words, to try out living in the way of wisdom: a way of reverence for God, a way of peacemaking and peace-seeking. Hopefully, this will result in a lasting "taste" for such life.

Then in the gospel we see Jesus, the Wisdom of God, and the most generous host who offers his word and his person for our feasting. This Sunday's reading from the Bread of Life Discourse may represent a more radical rethinking of last week's gospel, perhaps composed at a later stage of Johannine preaching and inserted into the final editing of the Gospel as a witness to the community's developing eucharistic faith. To underline its significance, the first verse of the reading repeats the last verse that we heard last week: "I AM the living bread that came down from heaven. Whoever eats of this bread will live forever, and the bread that I will give is my flesh for the life of the world." Some would even see here the Johannine equivalent of the words of institution that the Synoptic writers insert into their Last Supper accounts.

"How can this man give us his flesh to eat?" is the horrified response of "the Jews." Perhaps we, also, can be too caught up in the question of *how does Jesus become "present"* in the bread and wine? The more important gospel question may be *how we, as believers, become present* to the mystery of the risen Christ, alive in the church. One clear answer is: through eating the flesh and drinking the Blood of Christ. The meaning of this phrase spirals through several meanings. Literally, "flesh and blood" means the whole human person. Applied to Jesus, it is also a proclamation of faith in the Incarnation when "the Word became flesh and dwelt among us" (John 1:14). On a third level, it calls to mind the truth that Jesus gave his entire life, his crucified flesh and his shed blood, for the sake of the world when he was lifted up in his crucifixion and glorified in his resurrection. Eating and drinking constitute a powerful reality and symbol of shared life. What we are offered by Jesus in the Eucharist is not a comfortable "Jesus and me" hospitality, but a personal, communal, and cosmic intimacy in and with his full reality, his risen glory as the firstborn of all creation. It is a mutual indwelling, a continual abiding in the source of life that Jesus shares with the one whom he calls Father. Those who ate the manna in the desert died, but those who feed on the sacramental bread of life, on his flesh and blood, will live forever.

This is the mystery of faith to which we respond at every Eucharist. It is also our mystery and the mystery of all the members of the Body of Christ. As St. Augustine told his people:

> If, therefore, you are the Body of Christ and his members, your mystery is present at the table of the Lord; you receive your mystery. To that which you are, you answer "Amen!"; and by answering you subscribe to it. For you hear: "The Body of Christ!" and you answer: "Amen!" Be a member of Christ's Body so that your "Amen!" may be true.[29]

In Jesus is not only the hunger of his Father for the world's salvation, but also all our hungers that he gathers up for safekeeping in his love. So we are in communion with Jesus and his whole kingdom project, especially his concern for the poor, the sick, the hungry, the disadvantaged, the sinners, and the searchers. The hospitality of God in Christ to the dregs of society who were so often at table with him during his life must now be the practical concern of each one of us, the members of his Body. Without such concern, are we really being a eucharistic people?

To escape the 1848 famine, a poor Irish family decided to emigrate to America. On the lowest and most crowded deck, the father warned them all to keep to themselves. Food was doled out of their closely guarded hoard, but their six-year-old "explorer" was a constant worry. Only a few days out from the port of their arrival, the boy begged his father for a few pennies with which to buy some more food. In response to his mother's pleading, the boy was given two precious pennies and went off. After an hour, the frantic parents went looking for him, and found him in a large dining room, eating everything in sight. His father seized him, yelling angrily that they could never pay for all this! But the child looked up and said with his mouth full, "Da, you don't understand. The food's free. It all comes with the price of the ticket!" If only the family had reached out to others, and not been so self-contained and protective of their own small resources, they would have known this. Baptism is our "ticket" that gives us entry into the Body of Christ where the food is free and the sharing so lavish that there are always leftovers, as we heard in John 6:12. And all is paid for by the life and love, the death and resurrection of Jesus.

The Letter to the Ephesians reminds Christians that they need to be discerning and reflective about the various invitations to "feasting" that society offers. In the world in which Christians live, drunkenness (and other addictions) can drug one's judgment. What should intoxicate us is being filled with the Spirit of Jesus, and an awareness of what this means for our everyday living. Special mention is made of the presence of the Spirit in communal prayer and in the singing of the psalms, for in this worship all are united heart to heart in thanksgiving to God, not just as individuals who are "doing their own thing" side by side. When the time of worship is over, the song of thanksgiving to the Father should continue to be echoed in people's hearts "at all times and for everything," as the Holy Spirit plucks the chords of our human experience, now transposed to a higher key in and through Christ.

Twenty-first Sunday in Ordinary Time

• Josh 24:1-2a, 15-17, 18b • Ps 34:2-3, 16-21 • Eph 5:21-32 • John 6:60-69

This is a Sunday of challenging vocational choices. In the first reading, Joshua, the successor of Moses, gathers the people at the shrine at Shechem in the land that will later be known as Samaria. Joshua realizes that the generations born after the Sinai experience are in danger of failing in their covenant commitment to God who gave them the Promised Land in which they are now becoming a nation and so, gathered "before God" (probably before the ark of the covenant), he gives the people three options. They can just look to the past and their ancestral gods; they can surrender to the present attraction of worshiping the fertility gods of the land in which they are now living; or they can live as people of integrity and faithfulness who keep covenant with their one God who has been unfailingly faithful to them. Joshua unhesitatingly witnesses to his and all his household's choice: "We will serve the Lord."

Probably a covenant renewal was a regularly repeated liturgical event in which the people affirmed their fidelity not only to God but to one another, and at which new members may have been incorporated into the larger household of Israelite faith. It would be a reminder that God is not tied to any one geographical land, but inhabits the landscape of the heart of those who walk in integrity and continue faithful to their faithful God.

In very different contexts, these options still have relevance for us. We can choose to live with what we might perceive as the securities of the past, to succumb to the temptations of the sociocultural present, or to go forward trusting in the God who continues to bring us out of slavery into freedom.

The responsorial Psalm 34 is the same as last Sunday, but with some different verses that highlight the possibility and implications of choosing either the way of the wicked or the way of the just. To be just does not ensure a distress-free life, but there is the assurance that God will hear the cries of the brokenhearted and be present to them. Once again, the antiphon encourages us to "taste" this truth, to discover it by our experience of life and of faith.

The time of decision-making has also come for those listening to Jesus'
Bread of Life Discourse. It is not only his opponents, but his followers, his
own disciples, who are scandalized by his words. They complain that it is
an intolerable teaching, too hard, too offensive to accept. They have been
nourished at the table of Torah wisdom and are not prepared to accept any
new spiritual food. Surprisingly, after all the talk about "flesh," Jesus now
says that it has nothing to offer. But here Jesus is saying that from a purely
human point of view (especially one's own) what he has been saying makes
no sense. He will not conform to the expectations of those who want to
judge him according to their own superficial experiences. Jesus descended
from heaven to speak the words of spirit and life in a way no one else can
(cf. John 3:31-36), but some of those listening to him would like to see him
ascend to heaven as the Jewish tradition held that their revelatory ancestor
Moses had ascended. Jesus leaves his followers free, neither asking them to
stay nor giving them permission to go. Their choice, this crisis moment, is
personally theirs . . . and ours.

Then Jesus asks those who are still with him one of the most moving
of gospel questions: "Do you also wish to go away?" It is Simon Peter who
answers, and for the first time in John's Gospel someone explicitly accepts
Jesus for the most foundational and significant of reasons: because he is the
Holy One of God who offers them the words of eternal life. Today's Lectionary portion finishes here, no doubt to conclude the Bread of Life Discourse
on a positive note, but we also need to hear the last two verses, to realize
that even at the moment of this profession of profound faith (John 6:71-72),
the church is haunted by the reality of betrayal that lurks in the background
and is always a tragic possibility for any of Jesus' disciples. One night Peter
will huddle in the dark corner of denial, and Judas will betray his master.
To continue with Jesus is an ongoing struggle with the possibility of right or
wrong decisions for or against him. There are times when we, too, may have
felt like walking away from the Eucharist: tired of words about it that seem
empty of spirit and life, bored with poor celebrations of it, some of us leaving
because change is too slow, others because it is too fast. Basically, we are like
the people listening to Jesus in this gospel, and like the community for whom
John wrote his gospel: we can be tempted to want Jesus to conform to our
expectations of how he should be present in and to his church in word and
sacrament; we are intolerant of his willingness to be present in the poverty
of so many eucharistic liturgies—which is not to say that we do not do all
we can to have good liturgies. But perhaps our greatest betrayal is our failure
to realize that when we are not in communion with our sisters and brothers
we fail to be in communion with the Body of Christ. Peter's response: "Lord,

to whom shall we go?" faces us with the memory of the Servant Jesus who went to death, who gave his full human reality, his body and blood, for us, so that we might share in his eternal risen life.

Today we also conclude our readings from the Letter to the Ephesians. The text begins by reminding the church that its members owe reverence to one another, and then continues to speak of the relationships of husbands and wives in marriage. We have to accept that it is the traditional patriarchal marriage of the time and place about which the author is writing, and this presents difficulties for receiving this passage in a sociocultural context that is very different from that of first-century Ephesus. Rather than focus on problems, it will be more profitable to concentrate on aspects that have continuing validity. Margaret Y. MacDonald gives a succinct summary of these as:

> . . . the transformative power of love, the importance of using one's relationship with the Lord as a means of discerning how to treat others, and the value assigned to marriage in general (sometimes forgotten in a church eager to encourage celibacy). In addition, the author of Ephesians clearly understands household relations as having been transformed in Christ.[30]

The marriage of Christians is more than a contract; it is a covenant of love, and this text sees it as a metaphor of the self-giving relationship between Christ and his church. A man's authority or a woman's subordination is not the issue. Indeed, if men were to love their wives with the sacrificial love of Christ, the patriarchal structure and privileges would be no more. The love of husbands and wives is to be a love of equal intimacy that joins them as one flesh (Gen 2:24). Another subversive note to the patriarchal structure is the willingness of the man to leave his own home of origin for the sake of his wife, rather than his wife leave her home. Just as marriage is a mystery of love, so is the love of Christ for the church.

Twenty-second Sunday in Ordinary Time

• Deut 4:1-2, 6-8 • Ps 15:2-5 • Jas 1:17-18, 21b-22, 27 • Mark 7:1-8, 14-15, 21-23

Today's gospel proclaims an encounter of Jesus with some of his opponents named as "Pharisees and some of the scribes who had come from Jerusalem." Jerusalem was the center of formal opposition to Jesus by those who were fearful of the loss of personal power, overly concerned with the externals of religious appearances, or devoted to censorious inquiry into minor deviations from the established way of doing things religious while ignoring more serious matters. In this sense, every religious group, in the present as well as the past, has those who "come from Jerusalem"—self-appointed custodians of the faith with, for example, their checklists for liturgical "irregularities," and their floods of negative letters to bishops. What sparks this Markan controversy is concerned with eating, and today we hear these words as we are gathered as a listening and eating people.

Traditions are necessary for the identity of any group, both secular (think of sports teams!) and religious. As Eugene LaVerdiere writes:

> Traditions are pervasive, tenacious, and very important, but they are not absolute, and their value can be questioned. Traditions spring from a particular history and shaped by common beliefs. They nourish a community's ideals, and they in turn are nourished by those ideals.
>
> When a life context that inspired a set of traditions dies or is drastically altered, traditions it once sustained become lifeless and meaningless. That does not mean they are immediately abandoned.[31]

The life context of the early Markan church was being drastically altered by the numbers of Gentiles who were entering into the Christian community. Tension inevitably arose between these new converts and the Christians whose faith had been nourished in the rich soil of Judaism. Many of the latter felt that the traditions they held dear, and that were reconcilable with following Jesus, had been carelessly trampled down or uprooted by the Gentile Christians to whom such traditions meant little or nothing. On the other hand, the Gentile Christians felt coerced by what, to them, were meaningless laws and rituals. To reconcile both groups in baptismal freedom and love was an ongoing challenge for community leaders. The "traditions of the elders," rightly understood, were not an attempt to bury the commands of God under suffocating trivia, but rather to aerate the whole of Jewish life with mindfulness of the people's identity and responsibilities as God's people. For the sake of the non-Jewish readers, Mark enumerates some of the traditional rituals of washing that are observed. These had not originally been binding on anyone but the priests who were required to wash their hands before offering sacrifices (Exod 30:18-21; 40:31-32), but the Pharisees, according to their traditions, have extended these requirements to the Jewish laity because of their vision of every Jew as priestly and every home as a domestic temple.

Jesus responds to the Pharisees' challenge about the behavior of his disciples (for which their master was always held responsible) with a quotation from the prophet Isaiah, addressing them as "hypocrites." Out of the strong Jewish prophetic tradition of self-criticism, Isaiah spoke of religious practices that were on the lips but not in the heart as a superficial and external "playacting" at true religion. The Pharisees have fallen into the same religious trap of absolutizing their own human traditions of outward observance, not the commands of God. What should be washed is not so much pots and pans and hands, but their own hearts. External rituals have value only insofar as they encourage or express the dedication of our hearts. Before we eat as a eucharistic community, are our hearts clean?

Finally, Jesus tells his disciples that what truly defiles a person does not come from without, from the food that we take into our bodies; what defiles a person is the moral impurity and ethical evil that is first savored in the heart, not in the mouth. As if to emphasize that he is not setting aside God's tradition, Jesus enumerates a catalogue of vices, all of which are either directly proscribed in the Ten Commandments or indirectly related to them. Nineteen centuries later, another Jew would make a choice against "defilement" and for purity of heart in the tradition of true religion. Etty Hillesum, a young Jewish Dutch woman living in Nazi-occupied Amsterdam, and soon to die in Auschwitz at the age of twenty-nine, wrote in her extraordinary diary: "Every atom of hate we add to this world makes it more inhospitable . . . and every act of loving perfects it."[32]

Although written many centuries after the death of Moses, in order to emphasize the "seconding" or affirmation of the Mosaic teaching/Torah, the speech from which we read today is ascribed to Moses as the ideal human leader and close friend of God who speaks directly to the people to urge them to fidelity. The law is much more than a human invention; it is God's gift to the people, and so it is not something to be tampered with. Whereas the laws of other nations in the ancient world around Israel were usually designed to win the favor of the gods, Israel's law was a favor of God, a divine initiative offered to the people with whom God has a special loving and close relationship. This respect for the teaching does not exclude the ongoing interpretation of the Torah that is evident in the Book of Deuteronomy itself, and for which the Book of Deuteronomy was so important to both Jews and Christians.

As the definitive interpreter of the law, Jesus stresses in the gospel that it is the interiority of the people's obedience that is essential. They are urged to give a deep, not surface assent to the law: to listen to the teachings, to do them, to observe them diligently. This obedience will have positive effects as a witness to other nations of the wisdom and discernment of Israel and the closeness of their God to whom they must cling in good times and bad.

Our response to this reading with Psalm 15 is significant. Probably originating as part of an entrance rite conducted by the priest as pilgrims prepared to enter the Jerusalem Temple, it makes no mention of ritual or sacrificial requirements. What does gain a person access to the holy place is obedience from the heart expressed in integrity, honesty, and love of one's neighbor. It is a reminder to us, also, not to become obsessed with liturgical minutiae that may deafen us to the cries for steadfast love of God and our sisters and brothers.

As we begin to read the Letter of James, he too reminds us that God is the source of every good gift, including our own Christian birthright. God's goodness does not wax and wane or fade like the lights of heaven; as "the Father of lights," God is our constant enlightening and guiding presence. This Father is also responsible for our re-creation, for the salvation that is offered those who are born again of the truth of God's word. As in the other readings for this Sunday, the interiority and intimacy of God's word is emphasized in the beautiful image of a word planted deep within us that will grow and transform us if we humbly make our hearts the welcoming and good soil for it. To provide such soil, we must weed our hearts of the suffocating growth of wickedness about which we can so often deceive ourselves or fail to notice. Religious defilement is a matter of the heart, and James grounds his words in practical love, in the integrity of hearing and doing that results in the care of vulnerable people such as needy widows and orphans, those without any legal status in society. Whom would we name as needing such care today; and as we leave this eucharistic assembly, is there at least a tiny shoot of determined action on their behalf that springs up from the Word that has been implanted in our hearts?

Twenty-third Sunday in Ordinary Time

• Isa 35:4-7a • Ps 146:7-10 • Jas 2:1-5 • Mark 7:31-37

Every generation should be aware of the persistent realities that can make a wilderness of our human existence: the exile from their homelands of millions of wandering refugees; the captivity in modern slavery and trafficking, especially of women and children; the suffering from physical, intellectual, and psychological disabilities. In the reading from Isaiah we hear a poem of praise to the good news of God's recreating love, and the faithful hope that sometime, somehow, God will transform a disordered world.

In the cultural and religious context of Isaiah's world, deprivation of life-giving rains and deprivation of physical abilities such as sight, hearing, or mobility, were all considered disorders of creation. Since all came from the creativity of God, only God could transform and heal these disorders. How and when this will happen the prophet cannot say, but he can encourage the people to trust in the future reigning presence of God when their redemption, both spiritual and physical, will be realized. In this hope the people, always and everywhere, must persist even in the midst of suffering.

In the gospel, Jesus seems to make an involved and impractical journey into the Decapolis ("ten cities") that were previously under Jewish control but had become Gentile territory. Mark, however, is not concerned with geography but with announcing the boundary-breaking mission of Jesus, the Messiah for all nations. "They," the anonymous crowds that we can presume are Gentiles, bring to Jesus a man who is deaf and has an impediment in his speech, two obviously related disabilities. First-century Decapolis was not a world of computerized hearing aids or bionic ears, and in its predominately aural–oral culture a deaf person was at a severe disadvantage. So significant is hearing and speech to human relationships that, as we have heard in the first reading, the unsealing of the ears and the loosening of the tongue were considered by the prophets to be signs of the new, joyful, and healed creation that the messiah would herald. When Moses tries to wriggle out of his calling by God to be the liberator of his people, his excuse (quite ironically articulate!) is that he is slow of speech and tongue. To this God replies: "Who gives speech to mortals? Who makes them mute or deaf, seeing or blind? Is it not I, the Lord? Now go, and I will be with your mouth and teach you what you are to speak" (Exod 4:11-12). In the Scriptures, therefore, deafness and speech impediments are not just of physical concern. They are also symbolic of disciples in any age or situation who are deaf to the word of God and mute or incoherent in their response to and proclamation of it.

Very likely, the man in Mark's gospel had been the butt of jokes and unsympathetic mimicry as he stuttered his life away in his small, isolated world. Yet some of his acquaintances are compassionate enough to bring him to Jesus, begging Jesus to speak to the man in the only language he can understand—the language of touch. Jesus takes him away from the crowd, and even from his helpful companions. Perhaps this is because of Jesus' delicate consideration for the man, lest the amazed babble of the crowd at his cure is too overwhelming as his first hearing experience; or perhaps it is to ensure that the first words the man hears are the words of the Word.

The actions of Jesus are unusual, and described in detail. Instead of the simple taking by the hand or laying on of hands in the miracles he worked in Jewish territory, there are fingers in the man's ears, touching of the man's tongue with Jesus' spittle, looking up to heaven, and sighing. Such folkloric actions resemble those of first-century faith healers, and seem to be an "inculturation" of Jesus' miracle working in non-Jewish territory, a considerate translation into gestures that would have been familiar to a Gentile. Then Jesus speaks a single word: "Ephphatha!" and speaks it in his Aramaic mother tongue. Mark courteously translates it for us: "Be opened!" but the fact that he retained the Aramaic adds a note of privilege and respect to the human words of Jesus. It would not have been such an unintelligible word or a magical incantation in the Decapolis where many spoke a kind of Aramaic dialect. But it is more important that not only the deaf man hears this word, but that all who come to Jesus recognize this as the command to us of the most open One—open to God's will, open to healing of the suffering of our brothers and sisters.

What happens next is a new creation, such as that hoped for by Isaiah in the first reading. With open ears and unshackled tongue, the man speaks plainly—to Jesus, for they are on their own. Here is a model of discipleship that is recalled in the baptismal rite of every Christian. As the child's or adult's ears and mouth are touched by the minister of the sacrament, these words accompany the action in what is still called the *Ephphatha* rite: "The Lord Jesus made the deaf to hear and the dumb to speak. May he (soon) touch your ears to receive his word, and your mouth to proclaim his faith, to the praise and glory of God the Father." Throughout our lives we need to come to Jesus, or be brought to him by the compassion of others, for the healing of whatever is an impediment to our baptismal commitment.

After his healing Jesus gives the man no orders; he simply lets him go to be his free, healed self. But to the crowd he says not to tell anyone about the miracle, for even though their response is in superlatives—"He has done everything well; he even makes the deaf to hear and the mute to speak"—the truth of Jesus is much more than that of a miracle worker. Mark salvages the disobedience of the crowd by making them a symbolic chorus in which believers can hear an echo of the creating God whose work was "very good" (Gen 1:31).

In the second reading, James begs his community to be open to the poor, and make no distinctions based on class and money. A beautiful example of Christian obedience to this is illustrated by an incident in inner Sydney where a homeless man, Karl Kulper, known to all as "the old gentleman," had lived for twenty-five years in a bus stop outside the large St. Vincent's Public Hospital. Despite offers of other accommodation, Karl preferred his bus stop and his daily routine of going from local café to café, eating his favorite egg-and-bacon sandwiches. Also part of his daily routine was acting as escort to the St. Vincent's nurses when they finished their late-night shifts. Karl would meet them outside the hospital and make sure they boarded their buses safely. He showed kindness to everyone, and no one questioned or judged him. A year after his quiet death, which was mourned by the hospital staff and many of the local workers and residents, the Sisters of Charity, administrators of the hospital, and the State Transit Authority ensured that Karl's memory lives on. A plaque celebrating his life has been fixed to the bus shed over the place where his ashes have been built into the wall. It reads: "A resident of St. Vincent's bus stop for 25 years. Karl, in your bus stop in heaven may you rest in peace." James would applaud these words with his own: "Listen, my brothers and sisters. Has God not chosen the poor in the world to be rich in faith and be heirs of the kingdom that he has promised to all who love him?"

With what integrity can we, as disciples, pray today's responsorial Psalm 146 with its praise of God who cares for the disadvantaged of our world? Can we praise such a God and remain deaf to their cries and mute in our advocacy for them?

Twenty-fourth Sunday in Ordinary Time

• Isa 50:4c-9a • Ps 116:1-6, 8-9 • Jas 2:14-18 • Mark 8:27-35

Like last Sunday, the Lectionary selections stress the importance of openness to the word of God. As the Babylonian exile is coming to an end (ca. 539 B.C.E.), the Isaian Servant has such an "ear," a personal availability to whatever God asks. His calling is not only to endure with profound faith in the midst of his own vulnerability and suffering, but also to use this experience to offer comforting words to those who are in similar circumstances. It seems that, for unspecified reasons, the Servant's actions were regarded as subversive and inflammatory. Perhaps his encouragement caused the exiles to be more aware of their own identity as God's people rather than submit to the authority of their captors. The Servant, however, willingly suffers beatings and insults, refusing to allow himself to take the role of either victim or rebel. As though involved in a court trial, the Servant is a determined and defiant witness to his faith in God's protection and vindication. This is the greatest comfort in the Servant's and our own suffering: that such suffering is not a sign of alienation from God but rather of the presence of God to the faithful witness.

With the responsorial Psalm 115 we express our faith in God who is the One with the most open ear to our cries for help and who saves us when we ourselves are helpless. What the Servant hoped for has become a reality to be praised. That the psalmist does not record any specifics of the suffering except that it could be death-dealing, makes it easy for us to own and pray the psalm in any particular and painful experience.

The gospel of this Sunday has often been called the "hinge" of Mark's gospel because it swings open to the reader the way of suffering, death, and resurrection that the Servant Jesus will follow. That Jesus and his disciples are "on the way" to this future is repeated many times in the second half of Mark's gospel, and especially in the three passion predictions and the consequent instructions on discipleship, the first of which we hear today. Jesus takes his disciples to the area around Caesarea Philippi, in the foothills of Mount Hermon and near the headwaters of the Jordan. Herod the Great had built a temple there in honor of Caesar Augustus and, after Herod's death, his son Philip renamed the place for Caesar Augustus and himself. B(P)anias was the name given to Caesarea Philippi by the Greeks because of a huge cave sanctuary dedicated to the nature god Pan. Near this monument to pagan gods, to past military power and worldly wealth, and to often ruthless political leadership and domination, Jesus begins to teach his disciples the difference between a triumphant and a suffering messiah.

The disciples are relieved by Jesus' first question: "Who do people say that I am?" This is a safe question that can be promptly answered with the impersonal: "They say . . ." So the disciples comfortably suggest John the Baptist or Elijah or one of the prophets. But then the conversation becomes personal, and Jesus asks the hard and direct question that every one of his followers must answer: "But who do *you* say that I am?" The disciples fade away into silence until, as usual, Peter manages to summon his faith resources and declare that: "You are the Christ (Messiah)." Peter has the right words, but as the following dialogue will show, he speaks out of his own partial faith and preconceived ideas about the messiah. The shadow of the Cross has already fallen over Mark's gospel (Mark 3:6), apparently unnoticed by the disciples, who are much more aware of his miracles. Jesus offers Peter no word of affirmation or congratulation, but imposes silence on him and the disciples until they have come to grips with the truth that it is a suffering and risen Jesus whom they are following.

Jesus then begins to teach them that his way will lead to suffering, rejection, death, and resurrection. About the last mentioned, Peter tunes out; it's too difficult, and anyway all he can focus on is that things seem to be turning out badly, and this wasn't at all what he meant by acclaiming Jesus as the Christ! Peter does not just correct Jesus or offer another opinion; he *rebukes* him. "Rebuke" is the same word that has been used since the first chapter of Mark's gospel to describe the action of an exorcism, so Peter is presuming to "exorcise" Jesus! Jesus responds with his own exorcism of Peter, calling him "Satan," or "stumbling block," and commanding him to get behind him and not dare to try to trip him up on the way of salvation that leads through suffering to the cross and risen glory.

Peter is silenced, and Jesus then speaks to the crowd as well as to the disciples. This is not just a crowd at Caesarea Philippi that seems to materialize out of nowhere. Mark wants to locate his first-century community, and all future Christian communities, in this scenario of where Jesus' words erect a greater memorial to the Gospel paradox: that it is by taking up our cross, losing our lives, and following Jesus that we save our lives for eternal life. In our contemporary "pain-killer culture,"[33] many of us struggle, even more than previous generations, to trust Jesus' words that there is a place for suffering in God's plan of salvation. Jesus was a compassionate healer; he sent out his disciples to heal, and the church calls and supports the many women and men, at home and abroad, who either work face-to-face with those who are suffering or advocate for them. In the fields of medicine and bioethics that aim to cure disease and improve the quality of life, the church is also present both personally and financially—but never at the cost of regarding suffering as incompatible with human dignity. Like Peter, are we much readier to accept Jesus the miracle worker rather than Jesus who is both Messiah and Suffering Servant?

Faith, says James, must be translated into action. Discipleship is not about finding a comfortable place of refuge with a compassionate God who has a preferential option for the poor but makes no demands on us to do likewise. Every Sunday we gather "in the name of Jesus" and, theoretically, not one of us would disagree with what James says about our brothers and sisters who are both physically and spiritually hungry, naked, cold. Practically, however, does our liturgy rehearse justice? Do the fervent proclamation of creedal formulas, our affirmation of the Word of God, our prayers of intercession, our partaking of the sacramental body that is broken for a broken people and our drinking of the cup that Christ drank to the dregs for a suffering world, impel us to do compassion and justice beyond the liturgy? Do we enflesh, with our own service of the poor of our world, the Word that came among us in Jesus the Christ?

Twenty-fifth Sunday in Ordinary Time

• Wis 2:12, 17-20 • Ps 54:3-8 • Jas 3:16–4:3 • Mark 9:30-37

On one occasion after the composer Robert Schumann had played a very difficult étude, one of his listeners asked him to explain the piece. Schumann replied by sitting down at the piano and playing the same étude a second time. This Sunday's gospel may seem to be like Schumann's reply—a repeat performance for disciples who appear not to have heard much of what Jesus told them in his first passion prediction. But Mark also plays some significant variations on the theme of the gospel we heard last Sunday. The crowds have gone, and Jesus is journeying with his disciples, focusing his full attention on them—and they need it! In the verses immediately before this reading they have rather accusingly asked Jesus why *they* could not cure the epileptic boy, to which Jesus' response implies that it was because of their lack of prayer and faith (see Mark 9:18-19).

Jesus again names himself as the Son of Man, with memories of the Daniel figure (Dan 7:13-14) who comes to announce the end of one age and the beginning of another. Jesus looks beyond his earlier reference to rejection by the elders, the chief priests, and the scribes, and says that he will be handed over into "human hands" to be put to death, and in three days will rise again. Silence, dense and dumb, descends on the disciples. This time not even Peter summons up an argument. They don't understand what Jesus is saying and, what is worse, they are afraid to ask and learn what Jesus means—and what might be the implications for them if they keep on following a master who seems headed for suffering. We too know the temptation in difficult times to stop questioning and questing, and hope that the disturbing problems will go away and leave us to a complacent life in our comfort zones.

Jesus will not allow this, so when they are alone together, "in the house," he questions the Twelve who, "on the way" of increasingly obtuse discipleship, have miraculously found their tongues in order to argue with one another about which one of them is the greatest! The silence thickens. It is as though the disciples have been deaf to everything that Jesus has said about his vulnerability and powerlessness in "human hands." So Jesus sits down, taking up the position of a rabbinical teacher, and calls the Twelve to himself just as he had done initially (Mark 3:13). They need to be shocked out of their competitiveness and power-seeking, not by reprimand but by reversal, by action that will proclaim that, in the reign of God, to be first is to be last of all and servant of all. Gloomy silence gives way to astonishment when Jesus does what would be almost inconceivable in first-century Palestinian culture, where children, along with women and slaves, had almost no social status. In front of his twelve adult male disciples, Jesus wraps his arms around a disregarded child. Only one other time in the New Testament is such an intimate gesture mentioned—in the father's welcoming embrace of the returning Prodigal Son (Luke 15:20). Here "in the house," a symbol of the domestic church, is a parable in action which teaches that what should characterize the ecclesial household is inclusion and equality, not exclusion and superiority. In Jesus' day to extend hospitality to such little ones would be considered ridiculous because, although hospitality was such a significant Middle Eastern virtue, so was the return of hospitality. What could a child offer in return? But Jesus is teaching his disciples that these are the very "little ones" who are to be welcomed down through the ages: the ones who have no social status, no vote value, those whose human dignity is ignored or violated. To welcome them is to forge a link in the chain of what binds together those who offer such hospitality with Jesus and his Father.

The reading from the Book of Wisdom offers us an insight into the psychology of the violent and unjust. The gentle and just person becomes such a silent reproach to the wicked that they intend to "ambush" the just one, which conjures up the image of a pack of wild animals lying in wait for their solitary prey (cf. Ps 17:11-12; 59:3-4; 64:2-5). The resentful wicked will attack the good person whom they regard as an implicit criticism of their own behavior, their disobedience to the law, and their upbringing. The dynamic of violence gathers momentum—from annoyance, to cruelty, and finally to threats of death that test not only the resolve of the just but also God's fidelity to the persecuted one. How many personal, domestic, and national disasters have been sucked into such a destructive vortex? It was such violence that struck down the crucified Christ, but it was also God's fidelity that raised him to glory. In this faith and memory we pray the responsorial Psalm 54, praising God who upholds the lives of the just ones against the proud and the ruthless.

James also contrasts two kinds of people. First, there are the jealous and ambitious who have a wisdom, a perception of reality that is "from below," that is earthbound and arrogantly concerned with self-aggrandizement. The lives of such people are oriented to ambition and competitiveness that cause disharmony in their relationships. The other kind of people are those who follow the path of wisdom "from above," who see life in terms of doing compassion and making peace. They act out of integrity, not hypocrisy. We may be horrified by the tragedies of global violence and the atrocities of war, but James' words remind us that these large social diseases are spread by what is endemic in "unwise" human hearts like our own, hearts that can only be healed by turning to God in a radical conversion of our way of life to the way of holy wisdom.

Twenty-sixth Sunday in Ordinary Time

• Num 11:25-29 • Ps 19:8, 10, 12-14 • Jas 5:1-6 • Mark 9:38-43, 45, 47-48

"But they're not one of us!" is an exclusive catch-cry that can be raised in many contexts, from the bullying on the school playground to that in the much more serious social, political, and religious arenas. Just consider, say these cryers: migrants will take our jobs, asylum seekers will threaten our security, community housing in our street for people with disabilities will lower our property values, ecumenism and contact with other religions will dilute our faith! And those who hold these views consider that they have a monopoly on wisdom and insight!

In the gospel proclaimed today we hear exclusion spoken from the midst of the Twelve. John is their indignant spokesman, informing Jesus that a man "who is not following us," is "exorcising in your name." The real issue from John's point of view is not that this man is *not following Jesus*—after all, he is doing his healing acts in Jesus' name, which implies some faith in Jesus; the problem is that he is *not following the Twelve*! They tried to stop him, apparently unsuccessfully, since they make an implicit appeal to Jesus to do something about it. Jesus responds to John's indignation by telling him that they should see such a person not as a competitor but as a companion along the way, even if he is not physically traveling with the Twelve, because "Whoever is not against us is for us." Work for the kingdom is not to be the jealously guarded preserve only of the disciples who are physically accompanying him.

Jesus expands on what being "with" him means. In a land where the availability of water can mean the difference between life and death, offering someone a cup of water symbolizes the simple but generous hospitality that should characterize a Christian disciple, for doing this to another is doing it to Christ. Those who are aiming to be "the biggest and the best," even religiously, can too easily overlook or disparage the service of the "little ones" of great faith: the behind-the-scenes workers in a parish; those who seem to have the gift of a spontaneously positive response to everyday relationships and crises; the people who welcome demands on their time without fuss and with unfailing generosity. "Little ones" may also refer to those who are young in faith, new members of the Christian community. As a parish, how hospitable have we continued to be toward those who were baptized at Easter, or have we forgotten them and the drama of the Great Night? How inclusive are our attitudes to people who are entering from surprising—and even from what some "established" Christians might consider unwelcome and scandalous—quarters or lifestyles?

Strong feelings evoke strong language, and the Markan Jesus uses vivid images to heighten the impact of his words about the sin and scandal of those who are a stumbling block to the faith of others. Rather than concentrate on criticizing those whom we consider "outsiders," disciples need to be self-critical. The harsh words about self-mutilation are to be taken figuratively, not literally. It would be better, says Jesus, to go through life physically handicapped than to give scandal by our sinfulness and so become spiritually maimed and unfit for the kingdom of God. The final image of "hell" or "Gehenna" refers to what was a valley just outside the city of Jerusalem, and once the site of Canaanite human sacrifice. The Israelites had converted this into a garbage dump where the stench of the burning refuse became a constant reminder of corruption and a symbol of punishment. The alternative is the life of the new heavens and the new earth, the Isaian memory that probably lies behind this verse (see Isa 66:22-24). As we have prayed in the responsorial Psalm 19, it is only by trusting in God's guidance as do the simple, those who are wise enough to know their own frailty, that we can live wisely, truthfully, and reverently.

The incident described in the Book of Numbers is also about inclusion and exclusion. Joshua's complaint to Moses is a version of "but they're not one of us!" He is referring to the two men, Eldad and Medad, who had remained behind while the seventy elders assembled with Moses at the Tent of Meeting. There God had gifted the seventy with a share of the prophetic spirit already bestowed upon Moses so that they might share in his authority and help him bear the burdens that come with such responsibility. Joshua is distressed when he is told that the two "outside" the Tent of Meeting and back in the camp are also prophesying. Even though it seems that they were numbered in the seventy, Joshua is a stickler for details; Eldad and Medad did not come to the Tent of Meeting and so seem to him to be flaunting the authority of Moses. Joshua is not ready to allow for the surprising action of God's spirit outside established structures, but Moses corrects Joshua. The jealousy that Joshua professes for Moses' authority—and we may also suspect for his own—is misguided. Moses welcomes and encourages the work of God's Spirit wherever and however it is manifest. The Spirit is not exclusively possessed and controlled by a community's leaders. Then, as now, theirs is a particular charism, but Moses' wish is always valid: "Would that all the Lord's people were prophets . . ." and would that hierarchical leadership today recognize this as the great Pentecostal gift to the Christian community (cf. Acts 2:17-18). What is needed is the enabling of this gift.

James' words are fierce and passionate in their denunciation of the rich who have acquired their wealth through unjust means and who use it unjustly. He does not condemn wealth as such, but rather the unscrupulous and inhumane attitudes found among some rich people. For them life is defined in terms of having, not being, and so they arrogantly consider that they can use any means to increase their wealth. This warped attitude of heart spills over into social distortion: into the exploitation of workers, into widening the gap between the extravagant lifestyle of the rich and the subsistence struggles of the poor. It is time, says James, for the self-satisfaction of the rich to turn to lamentation, to recognize that material possessions will corrode, and that if this is all our life is about, we will disintegrate with our possessions. God will hear the cries of the exploited and oppressed, and will judge those who are deaf to them. We may feel that we can do little to bridge such a social divide, but we can challenge it—with the witness of our own just living, with prayer, with our advocacy for the poor, and with the power of the ballot box.

Twenty-seventh Sunday in Ordinary Time

• Gen 2:18-24 • Ps 128:1-6 • Heb 2:9-11 • Mark 10:2-16

In no generation and in no culture has there ever been a "golden age" when all marriages have been perfect, but the longing for this is also universal. In the reading from Genesis we have the beautiful story of God's plan for the creative relationship of man and woman and their unity in diversity as "one flesh."

The highly symbolic narrative is told in such a way that, as hearers, we are allowed to listen in to God's reflection. All that God has made is "good," but what is not good is that man, the human person (*adam*) should be alone. So God delegates authority to man and allows him some decision-making about whom he will choose for a "helpmate." The Hebrew word that is used here is '*ezer*, a word also used to describe God (Exod 18:4; Ps 121:1-2), and so does not denote subservience or inequality but a partnership of blessing. Over the animals that come before him, man does have some authority, suggested by the fact that he names them; but none of them does he choose for a partner. So then God takes the initiative, casting a deep sleep on the man. What is happening is a profound mystery, a deliberate and unique act of God's creative love in which the man has no part. Man has been made from inanimate dust (Gen 2:7); "rib" is living, human material. What God "builds" from this is another human person who can relate in equality to the man. The author's concern is not with an accurate physiological or evolutionary account of the creation of the human couple, but with a symbolic description of the relationship between the man and his partner. Like a delighted matchmaker, God presents this new companion to the man, and the first words of humanity recorded in Genesis are a love song to the one who is the three-times repeated focus of companionship: "this one," who is hailed as "bone of my bone and flesh of my flesh." Again, this is no physical reference, but a traditional expression of a lasting relationship that occurs in the Old Testament, for example, between Laban and Jacob (Gen 29:14), and the tribes of Israel and David at Hebron (2 Sam 5:1; 19:12-13). In Hebrew there is word play and an accompanying entry of sexuality: the man is now called *ish* rather than *adam*, and the woman is *ishshah*. Later reflection threw back into the last verse of today's reading the comment that because of the depth of the relationship between man and woman, even in a patriarchal society, a man disengages himself from his family of origin to become "one flesh" with his wife. That the man and woman are "one flesh" does not refer only to sexual intimacy, but to the fact that:

> . . . man and woman constitute an indissoluble unit of humankind from *every* perspective. . . . In seeking to address these issues in a responsible manner, we must go beyond the text and draw insights from other parts of the Scriptures and from our own experience in and through which God continues to speak.[34]

The responsorial Psalm 128 rejoices in God's blessing on work that produces fruitful fields and relationships resulting in fruitful marriage. The joy of children assures the continuance of the family from generation to generation. This psalm is another song of ascents that pilgrims sang as they went up to Jerusalem and the Temple. On their pilgrimage to the place of the Presence, they brought with them the thanks and needs and hopes of their everyday lives in which their families were so important. As we pray this psalm today, we might remember not only the families for whom a happy dwelling place and peaceful relationships are a reality, but also those whose homes are overshadowed by domestic violence and abuse, and the families destroyed and scattered by war, famine, fire and flood, those for whom gathering happily around a family table seems an impossible dream. On them we pray peace.

Some Pharisees come to Jesus to confront him over his interpretation of Scripture and, specifically, how he understood the matter of divorce. Jesus throws the question back to them by asking what the Mosaic Law commanded. The Pharisees reply that a man is permitted to give his wife a bill of divorce and send her away. Jesus shifts the discussion away from this law (Deut 24:1-4), the interpretations of which could range from the permissive to the stringent. He goes beyond the question of "is it lawful?" and beyond legalistic arguments to the plan of God for relationships between men and women. The focus then becomes marriage, not divorce.

The prophet Malachi had denounced divorce, appealing to the creation story that we have heard in the first reading (Mal 2:13-17). Jesus also takes a prophetic, countercultural stance, and refers to this same Torah text. This encounter with the Pharisees comes in the section of Mark's gospel where the focus is on the cost of discipleship, as proclaimed the last three Sundays, and fidelity in marriage is never a cheap grace. Jesus refers to Moses' concession about divorce as something that was allowed because of a "sickness" of the heart or "cardiosclerosis," to give a literal translation of "hardness of heart." The same words are used to describe their ancestors' wilderness rebellion in Psalm 95:8-9. In the divine plan for whole and healthy human relations in marriage, God did not intend divorce, says Jesus.

"In the house" with his disciples, Jesus expands his teaching, probably reflecting the Markan concern to strengthen the marriage commitment in the Christian communities in the Greco-Roman world where divorce was common, and women could also divorce their husbands. Jesus' message is not only uncompromising, it is also countercultural, passing a subtle judgment on the double standard that allows one course of action for men but denies the same for women. Not only does a woman who has been divorced by her husband and marries another man commit adultery; it also works the other way, says Jesus. That he should accuse of adultery a *man* who divorced his wife and marries another woman, offended patriarchal honor! But both the man and the woman have equal rights and responsibilities to God's plan for their unity in "one flesh."

Jesus' teaching on marriage and divorce flows directly into the description of his blessing of the young children, and once again we see the obtuseness of the disciples. Their selective memory has forgotten the words and action of Jesus when he placed and embraced a little child in their midst as a sign of their responsibility to and love of the insignificant and unimportant ones (Mark 9:36-37). They "rebuke" the people, presumably the children's parents, and most likely their mothers, just as Peter had "rebuked" Jesus, had tried to "exorcise" him of his ideas about suffering and death (Mark 8:32). Once again Jesus turns the rebuke back on the disciples in an attempt to rid them of their spirit of preoccupation with power and status. The disciples' stern, dismissive words to the people bringing the children to Jesus contrast with Jesus' words of gentle encouragement to those who want him to touch their children, to have contact with Jesus' own holy person and have him call down on them the blessing of God. Jesus again embraces the children, hugging to himself those who are helpless and dependent. We should not hear this gospel as a sentimental romanticizing or idealizing of children, but as an embrace of Jesus for all those who have no status, no claims to make, no power to wield, and so are receptive to the great gift that is offered—the kingdom of God. With what have we been touched: with the distorted hope of the disciples for power, or with willingness to be "little ones" who are open to and receptive of the reigning presence of God?

The Letter to the Hebrews reminds us that by his incarnation Jesus entered into full human solidarity with all men and women. Because of this, he accepted to have no divine privileges and had no shame in becoming, for a little while, "lower than the angels." But then, through his suffering and death, Jesus is crowned with glory and honor in his resurrection. To be in solidarity with us means to experience the suffering and death that is part of every human life. Jesus is the pioneer of our salvation, the one who makes the path for us by walking this right human way to the Father and enabling us to follow. Children of the one Father, we are all brothers and sisters of Jesus.

Twenty-eighth Sunday in Ordinary Time

• Wis 7:7-11 • Ps 90:12-17 • Heb 4:12-13 • Mark 10:17-30

Although referred to as the Book of the Wisdom of Solomon, this book was written sometime in the late first century B.C.E., perhaps at Alexandria where there were tensions between the Greeks and the Jews, who were denied Greek citizenship. While Hellenism has its influence on this book, it is the Hebrew Bible that is its dominant point of reference, although the book is not part of the Hebrew canon. The portion that is read today is a reinterpretation of the prayer of King Solomon for wisdom (1 Kgs 3:5-9), and its deliberate attribution to Solomon adds to it the authority of an ideal figure who both yearned for wisdom and knew his own limitations.

In Solomon's prayer, wisdom is personified as feminine, as the intimate companion of God in the creation of the world and the human heart. God answers Solomon's prayer with an abundance of wisdom that Solomon esteems more than power and wealth, precious gems or honors. Solomon is so captivated by wisdom that, as in a passionate love affair, everything but the beloved becomes comparatively worthless.

The responsorial Psalm 90 reminds us that all wisdom is the gift of God's faithful love. With the psalmist we pray that we may have discerning hearts to recognize the finitude of human life and make the most of our days by responding to God's love, looking beyond our own human limitations and mortality. Taught by holy wisdom, our days and years should be filled with neither shallow optimism nor cynical pessimism; nor should we live under "the tyranny of time" that can dominate our lives with exhausting activity and competitiveness in the workplace, and even in the family. What should dominate our lives is the love of God, and the love that we return to God is the wisdom that will transform our lives.

On the way to Jerusalem, Jesus continues to make radical demands of those who want to be his disciples. Last Sunday it was about marriage; today it is about money. We meet a man who has a sense of his own mortality and a hope for eternal life. He comes eagerly and respectfully to Jesus, running to him and kneeling before him to address him sincerely as "Good Teacher." Jesus reminds the man that it is God who is good, an important reminder for all disciples not to forget that Jesus' human presence and mission is to make present among us the abundant and unfathomable goodness of God. The eternal life that the man is seeking is the gift of God. Then Jesus places the man within his own faith tradition, quoting to him some of the "social commandments" of the Ten Commandments, with the Markan addition of "you shall not defraud." The man replies that all his life he has kept all these commandments.

Jesus gazes at the man and loves him so much that he gives him the radical answer that his radical question deserved. Jesus asks him to discard everything, to extend his love of God to the poor by selling all he owns and giving the money from this transaction to them, leaving himself dependent on nothing but treasure in heaven, and then come and follow Jesus. To stand bare and dispossessed before the God who is good, with radical trust in God's gifts, is the way to the eternal life for which the man had approached Jesus. But then a shadow falls over the bright landscape of this encounter of eager love. The man is shocked by Jesus' reply, and instead of following he goes away "grieving, for he had many possessions."

There is certainly much of which we can be possessive—ambitions, relationships, social status—but Mark does not want us to leave the question of wealth and material riches too quickly. It is surely significant, especially for disciples in affluent social situations, that this portion of the gospel continues with two more conversations: one with the disciples who are with Jesus and have witnessed his meeting with the rich man, and the other with Peter who wants to clarify the disciples' situation.

Just as Jesus had looked at the man, he now looks around at his disciples with the same look of penetrating love—and he looks at us, his church. He tells us that riches are a great obstacle to entering the kingdom of God, and calls us "children," reminding us that we must have a sense of our dependence on God for all good gifts. To drive his point home, Jesus makes an exaggerated and metaphorical comparison. For a rich person to enter heaven is as difficult as a camel getting through the eye of a needle! The disciples do not have the wisdom of the first reading, and are still caught in the convention that sees riches as a sign of God's blessing; so, more astonished than ever, they ask one another: "Then who can be saved?" But only Jesus can answer them. It may be humanly impossible, he says, but nothing is impossible to God. It may take a miracle for a rich person to be saved—but trust God to work this, because before God we are all beggars of love and salvation.

Then Peter, typically, asks his "What about us?" question. Peter and the disciples have left what they had to follow Jesus, but such dispossession is not a matter of just one leaving, as Mark's gospel will show. The disciples are finding it hard to leave their preconceptions about the messiah, about suffering, about who should be first and last; and in Gethsemane the disciples will leave everything not to follow Jesus, but to run away from him (Mark 14:50-53). Jesus assures Peter that those who do give up the "everything" of possessions and relationships for the sake of following him and the Gospel with which he identifies himself, will receive a hundredfold: new relationships in the new family of Jesus' followers, new possessions that are the fruit of doing and hearing the word of God and, the most cherished possession of all, the eternal life they had witnessed the man was seeking. But with all these benefits will come persecution, for no disciple can escape the Cross.

The word of God is like a sword, says the Letter to the Hebrews, that can slice with delicate surgical precision through our divided loyalties, the secret intentions of our heart, and our hidden thoughts, and expose them to God who knows us in our deepest truth. This will be painful, but God is not "a big brother watching" us; God is the One who gazes on us in Jesus with love and longing for our faithful discipleship.

Twenty-ninth Sunday in Ordinary Time

• Isa 53:10-11 • Ps 33:4-5, 18-20, 22 • Heb 4:14-16 • Mark 10:35-45

No one in Mark's gospel approaches Jesus as arrogantly as James and John in today's reading. But perhaps our criticism of these two disciples who, with Peter, comprise the most intimate core of the Twelve, needs to be modified if we are honest with ourselves. How often do we, too, approach Jesus with self-centered demands about our own plans rather than with deep faith in *his* plans for us?

It is as though James and John have not heard one word of what Jesus has told them about the suffering and death that await him in Jerusalem. All that they are concerned about is what Jesus can make happen for them when he comes into "his glory." What they want, they tell him, are the two best places next to him, on his right and on his left. Perhaps it is Jesus' deep sorrow at the obtuseness of the brothers' request that tempers his response to them. He answers with the images of "cup" and "baptism." In the Old Testament, the cup was a rich and ambivalent symbol. It could refer not only to overflowing joy and communion with God (Ps 23:5) and God's salvation (Ps 116:13), but also to the draining of the painful cup of punishment (Ps 11:6; Isa 51:17; Jer 49:12). In his passion Jesus will gulp down the sins of the world, drain the cup of suffering and wrath so that it may be refilled with the joy of salvation. Can the brothers drink this same cup? The baptism of which Jesus speaks is his total submersion in the flood of suffering and death. Can James and John go with him into these depths of his passion? Again, before we pass judgment on them, we need to ask ourselves if we accept the consequences of our sacramental baptism—a baptism into Christ's death so that we may rise with him in newness of life (cf. Rom 6:3-4). In the mention of the cup, do Christian communities hear and obey that echo of the Eucharist that also initiates us into participation into the self-giving of Jesus and a sharing in his thirst for justice? The paradox of Jesus' Good News must be constantly repeated: that there can be no glory without a share in his suffering.

The failure of his disciples to understand him, his mission, or his relationship to his Father, was an aspect of Jesus' suffering. Their desertion on the eve of his passion would add to the bitterness of the cup he would drink, would be another flood of pain sweeping over him. Power and triumphalism, the desire for first places in the kingdom, have nothing to do with Christian leadership, yet into the hands of these frail and failing human beings Jesus entrusts the Christian community that would, in the power of his love and forgiveness, struggle through to resurrection with him. This is both our challenge and our consolation.

The other ten disciples, who were so glum and dumb when confronted by Jesus' earlier prediction of his passion, regain their voices to argue and bicker among themselves, angry over James' and John's approach to Jesus. We might suspect that this reaction is not so much because of the inappropriateness of the brothers' approach, but more because these two had beaten the other ten to it! Knowing that earthly ambition (transferred to heaven!) and competitiveness were what the disciples had in their sights, Jesus calls them together to try to teach them, yet again, what is to be the foundation of their identity: the service of others that reflects the self-sacrificing service of Jesus. Kingdom greatness is the gift for those who make no claim to power and status. The demand of James and John: "Teacher, we want you to do for us whatever *we* ask of you," needs to be transformed for and by all disciples into: "Teacher, we want to do for you and for many whatever *you ask of us.*"

Isaiah proclaims the Servant who endures agony and absorbs suffering into his own person, offering this to God so that through him God may work salvation for many. When his sufferings are over, the innocent Servant will realize what he has accomplished by the power of God and will rest content. About how this will happen, or who the Isaian Servant is, the faith and poetry of the text is reticent. God's word will bring about what God intends (Isa 55:11), even though it takes centuries of waiting for its accomplishment in the Christ who came to serve and suffer, to die, and to save us for truly human as well as eternal life. As we pray, our trust is in God, but we have a more confident hope than was possible to either the psalmist or Isaiah, for we know God's love and mercy is upon us in Christ.

In the reading from the Letter to the Hebrews, the author describes Jesus as both the Son of God and the most authentic human being who carries all the members of the human family with him into the presence of God. Jesus knows our limitations because, in his humanity, he shared in them fully: the limitations of time and place, of ethnicity and culture, of temptation and suffering. Our ability to identify with him depends on such human limitations; our assurance of eternal mercy depends on his high and heavenly priesthood. Jesus is both high priest and sacrifice. It is his own blood that has been sprinkled for an eternal mercy offering; his own body has been ripped apart so that now there is no curtain separating the Holy of Holies from the people, and nothing can stop us from approaching God in and through the new Holy of Holies, the new Temple, which is the glorified body of the risen Christ. We can now come "boldly" to God, the throne of grace, not with the self-centered insolence of James and John, but with brave confidence in the One who has drunk the cup and undergone the baptism of suffering so that he might be the saving Servant of all humanity.

Thirtieth Sunday in Ordinary Time

• Jer 31:7-9 • Ps 126:1-6 • Heb 5:1-6 • Mark 10:46-52

The Jericho of the first century C.E. was a splendid oasis city of fine palaces, pools, baths, and public buildings in the Roman style. Herod the Great and his son, Archelaus, both lovers of things Roman, had embellished this ancient city, and with its temperate climate Jericho had become a favorite wintering place for Jerusalem's elite. Close to trade routes, with its own profitable crops, it was also a convenient gathering place for pilgrims preparing to go up to Jerusalem, a distance of about 30 km. For this steep and dangerous ascent it was much safer to travel in large groups, and Jericho was, therefore, a good place for beggars to sit by the wayside, hoping that the pilgrims' pious thoughts might prompt them to toss a few coins.

In this setting we meet the blind beggar, Bartimaeus, "son of Timaeus," as Mark thoughtfully translates for his Gentile Christians. Mark had placed the healing of a blind man before the first of Jesus' three passion predictions (Mark 8:22-26); now, after the third prediction we heard last week, he describes the healing of Bartimaeus. Both of these "seeing" narratives frame the "blindness" of the disciples. The restoration of Bartimaeus's sight is the last healing before Jesus' passion begins, and the disciples plunge deeper into spiritual blindness regarding the suffering Messiah. In contrast to such blindness, the healing of Bartimaeus is offered to us as a model of insight into the following of Jesus to Jerusalem and the scandal of the Cross.

Bartimaeus is sitting at the side of the road, not going anywhere, as Jesus and his disciples approach. They are going somewhere, on the way to Jerusalem. When he hears that Jesus of Nazareth is passing by, hope begins to germinate in the dust that is his own broken self as well as his sitting and begging place. Exiled into destitution by his blindness, probably fallen out of family favor ("Timaeus" means "respected one") because of the mistaken idea that physical disability was also indicative of a moral taint, Bartimaeus begs for more than alms. With the eyes of faith he shouts out to Jesus, using not only his everyday name but also a messianic title: "Son of David, Jesus, have mercy on me!" The crowd tosses Bartimaeus the rebuke and scorn that are so often earned by those who have the courage to profess their faith, especially if they are regarded as unimportant, marginalized people. The blind Bartimaeus cannot find his way to Jesus; only his longing again reaches out to him across the distance, begging Jesus to have mercy on him.

And even in the crowd Jesus is aware of the individual, of the tattered man who is eager for personal contact with him. For that, Jesus will take the time and interrupt his journey. Jesus' command to the crowd to "Call him here," combined with the persistence of Bartimaeus, seems to transform them from rebuking to encouraging Bartimaeus, and their voices become a kind of resurrection chorus that urges him to have courage, rise up, and answer Jesus' call. Bartimaeus's response is not only an exultant physical leap, but also a leap of faith. He throws away his cloak, his last poor shred of possessions that, for a beggar, served as coat, sleeping bag, and scrappy collecting rug for the few coins tossed his way. Nothing now matters to Bartimaeus, not even his dusty "bit of turf" that, like every beggar, he would have guarded so jealously. Bartimaeus is about to be newly clothed with the identity of a follower of Jesus, an eager beggar of the abundant riches that can be expected as a disciple.

Jesus asks this beggar "outsider" the identical question that we heard him ask the two privileged "insider" disciples in last Sunday's gospel: "What do you want me to do for you?" The contrast of Bartimaeus's response with theirs is both poignant and prophetic. Blinded by self-aggrandizement to the demands of following a suffering and servant Messiah, the disciples had asked for the best places in the kingdom. Ambition and possessiveness will soon cause them to leave everything to run away from Jesus, but Bartimaeus, aware of his poverty and disability, asks for nothing but that he may see, addressing Jesus reverently as "Rabbouni," "My master." This address is only used one other time in the New Testament—when Mary Magdalene recognizes her risen Lord (John 20:16). Jesus knows that the blind man already has the seeing eyes of faith, and he tells Bartimaeus that it is this faith that now restores his physical sight. "Go; your faith has saved you," says Jesus. No longer confined to groping his blind way around the place, Bartimaeus can "go" wherever he wants to, but his choice is to follow Jesus "on the way," the way that leads to Jerusalem, the city of passion, death, and resurrection.

Are we aware of our own blindness, of our inability to recognize Jesus who is passing through our everyday lives? From the depths of our spiritual poverty and disabilities, do we urgently ask for insightful faith so that we recognize who Jesus really is? Or are we reluctant to leave even the small, secure territory of our reputation or material comfort that we have staked out for ourselves and push forward to Jesus, ready to enter with him into whatever "Jerusalem" he will lead us into, with his promise of a share in his passion, death . . . and resurrection?

The first reading from the prophet Jeremiah and the responsorial Psalm 126 are also professions of joy as the blind, the lame, the pregnant women, and those with children—the needy and exiled remnant of Israel who have difficulty in traveling on the way to Jerusalem—now shout and sing their way back home. In these verses from Jeremiah's sixth-century B.C.E. "Book of Consolation" (Jer 30–31) we can hear a distant echo of Bartimaeus's joy. God will lead back a community of the weak, not an army of the strong, to repossess their land. It will not be an easy way, but Jeremiah announces that this vulnerable, dependent people will be brought back, gathered and led by a Shepherd Savior. With another gentle and loving image, the prophet assures the people that God is like a father caring for his firstborn, carrying the poor and weak safely home.

Psalm 126 is often interpreted as a song of the returning Babylonian exiles, as the verses describing the joyful fulfillment of the dream of returning home to Zion (Jerusalem) would suggest. But it could well be a prayer on any occasion when the nation was threatened and the people's urgent, hopeful cries are carried to God by the memory of past salvation that has turned wilderness into fruitfulness, tears into shouts of joy, dreams into realities. How many of today's exiles—from their homelands, from their families, from the church, from their own true selves—might own the words of this ancient prayer, or might be remembered by us as we pray it today "at home" in our faith community?

The Letter to the Hebrews describes the Levitical high priest as called by God and appointed to be a mediator between humans and God, without arrogance and with humility. As a human being, the high priest was also vulnerable, not immune to sinfulness. In describing the function of the high priest it was stressed that, as well as offering sacrifices in atonement for the people's sins, he must also offer them for his own sins (Lev 9:7; 16:6, 15-16). The recognition of his sinfulness should make him sympathetic to sinners, not high-handed in his dealings with them, especially if they acted more out of ignorance than deliberate malice. Christ, too, did not take the calling of High Priest on himself, but was called and anointed by God as the priestly and royal Son. By his incarnation, "in the days of his flesh," he belonged to the people, as did the Levitical priesthood descended from Aaron; by quoting Psalm 110:4, the author of Hebrews also identifies Christ as a priest-king in the lineage of Melchizedek, the mysterious priest of the encounter with Abraham (Gen 14:18-20) about whom no human origins are mentioned. Throughout his life, and in the offering of the supreme sacrifice of his death, Christ deals with humanity with the humility and gentleness that make him the unique mediator between God and humanity. And his vulnerability, not any impassive superiority, was the source of his ability to recognize and empathize with human limitations, especially with those like the marginalized who are so much the focus of this Sunday's Lectionary, and with us when we also are literally and symbolically begging in the dust.

Thirty-first Sunday in Ordinary Time

• Deut 6:2-6 • Ps 18:2-4, 47, 51 • Heb 7:23-28 • Mark 12:28b-34

The conclusion to the Pontifical Biblical Commission's 2002 document, *The Jewish People and Their Sacred Scriptures in the Christian Bible*, states: "Without the Old Testament, the New Testament would be an incomprehensible book, a plant deprived of its roots and destined to dry up and wither."[35] This Sunday's gospel bears witness to Jesus' deep insertion into the traditions of his Jewish people and the intrinsic relationship of the two Testaments.

Although written long after Moses, to give it significant authority the Book of Deuteronomy is presented almost entirely as farewell speeches of Moses to the assembled people of God, urging them to fidelity to the Mosaic teaching. In return for their obedience is the promise of prosperity, good land, and long life down through the generations. Then come the verses that are the great creedal proclamation become prayer, beginning with the word that calls Israel to the primary response to the word of God: "Hear/Listen . . . (*Shema*)." This is not just a call to attention, but a summons to active, undivided allegiance to the one God of Israel. These are words that are not just to be written on a scroll, but inscribed on the heart so that the one God may be the foundation of Israel's life and enable the people to resist all the corruptions of other gods. Every morning from the age of thirteen, observant Jewish men and boys (and some women in the Reform tradition) bind these words with leather straps (Gk., phylacteries or Hebrew, *tefillin*) to their forehead, to the biceps of their left arm, which is nearest to the heart, and extend the straps around their arm to their left hand. This is a ritual dramatization of what is prayed in the *Shema*, that loving commitment to God will involve the whole person: the thoughts of the mind, the emotions of the heart, the works of the hand. Down through the generations Jews continue to pray the *Shema* daily at home and in the synagogue; in the Nazi death camps these words had risen like a love poem through the cascade of gas and the smoke of funeral pyres; and on their more gentle deathbeds they have been whispered with the last breath.

The Austrian psychotherapist Viktor Frankl recalled what he said was perhaps the deepest experience he had in the Auschwitz concentration camp. On arrival, he was made to surrender the manuscript of his first book on psychotherapy. Stripped also of his own clothes, naked and shaved, he was handed the worn-out rags of an inmate who had already been sent to the gas chambers. Then he describes what happened next:

> Instead of the many pages of my manuscript, I found in a pocket of the newly acquired coat one single page torn out of a Hebrew prayer book, containing the main Jewish prayer, *Shema Yisrael*. How should I have interpreted such a "coincidence" other than as a challenge to *live* my thoughts instead of merely putting them onto paper?[36]

The repeated refrain to the responsorial Psalm 18 is an acclamation of God's love, love that is as abiding as a rock, as strong as a fortress, as protective as the shield bearer who walks in front of the anointed king.

In the verses immediately before today's gospel we learn that Jesus is in the Temple (cf. Mark 11:27), confronted by the heckling and casuistry of the leaders of the religious establishment. There is not much love around as they question his authority. One scribe, however, stands attentively on the margins, obedient to the primary command of Judaism to "Listen." In Jesus' words he hears truthfulness and integrity, and the ensuing encounter that the scribe initiates by coming up to Jesus is a model for searching faith. The scribe's question: "Which commandment is the first of all?" is not intended to provoke argument but is a sincere quest for truth, and dialogue, not debate, is the result. Jesus answers the scribe by quoting the verses of the *Shema* we have heard in the first reading, but then he adds to this Leviticus 19:18: "You shall love your neighbor as yourself." The scribe had asked Jesus for one "first of all" commandment; Jesus responds with two commandments that bind together love of God, of neighbor, and of self. Following Jesus' words there is a moment of rare intimacy, of agreement between him and the scribe, between the old law and the new. Then the scribe comments that the love of God and neighbor, which Jesus has joined, should take precedence over any sacrificial cult or ritual empty of such love. In the scribe's words are an echo of the prophetic words that cry out for justice: "I desire steadfast love and not sacrifice, the knowledge of God rather than burnt offerings" (cf. Hos 6:6; Amos 5:23-24; Mic 6:6-8). Jesus affirms his insight as one that brings him close to the reigning presence of God.

This meeting of Jesus and the scribe becomes an enactment of the great commandment of love. They treat each other as neighbors, transcending party politics and religious differences, crossing the dividing line between "you" and "us." In the sea of hostility that Mark describes in this chapter of his gospel, the mutual affirmation of Jesus and the scribe is like an island of reconciliation. It surely has much to say to us, as individuals or communities, about the course we should set in daily relationships or in ecumenical and interfaith dialogue, for "Law can lose its heart; ritual can lose its reason; a relationship can lose its love."[37] With Mark, we should know only too well that Judaism has no monopoly on such distortions of faith.

The Letter to the Hebrews exalts the priesthood of Jesus, but not at the expense of denigrating the Levitical priesthood of Judaism. The Levitical priests were, of course, subject to dying; their office would survive (until the destruction of the Temple in 70 C.E.), but it would be exercised by different persons, transmitted by heredity. In contrast, the high priesthood of Jesus "continues forever." Jesus is always "on call" as our mediator with God. Although he identifies with our human weaknesses and vulnerability, he is without sin and has no need to continually make sin offerings for himself as well as the people. The sacrifice of Christ's death was one, sufficient, and eternally lasting and efficacious for the salvation of the world. The installation of a Levitical priest required no oath taking, but the appointment of Christ as high priest was validated by the oath of God. It is this one-time, unique sacrifice of Christ, offered in perfect love of God and all humanity, that is infinitely better than any burnt offering. It is what gathers us today as "Eucharist," as thankful people around this altar; and it is what should send us out as eucharistic, priestly people to love and serve our sisters and brothers.

Thirty-second Sunday in Ordinary Time

• 1 Kgs 17:10-16 • Ps 146:7-10 • Heb 9:24-28 • Mark 12:38-44

Today we meet three generous givers: the Old Testament widow of Zarephath, the New Testament widow in the Jerusalem Temple, and the most generous giver of all—the Christ who sacrificed his life for us.

If the Lectionary portion had begun two verses earlier, we would realize the important fact that it is the word of God that, during a devastating drought, commands the prophet Elijah to go to a widow who is living in the city of Sidon. God tells Elijah that he "commanded" this widow, a non-Israelite, that she should feed the prophet when he comes, despite her own life and the life of her son being threatened by the drought. But the commanding word of God will come to the widow through the words of the prophet, and so for both Elijah and the widow it is obedience to the word of God that will save them. This Sunday's reading begins with the arrival of Elijah at Sidon as the widow is preparing her pitiful meal of flour and oil as a last supper for herself and her son before they die of hunger. As Jesus was later to remind his hometown synagogue assembly—to their great indignation—God is free to act beyond the borders of Israel, free to cross the boundaries of nationality and ethnicity, free to work in and through a woman who, in the land of the Canaanite Baal, speaks to Elijah of "*your* God." Elijah and the widow minister to one another. She shares the poor meal she has and, in return, while they are sharing food together, Elijah gives her God's assuring word: that she and her son will have sufficient oil and flour to survive the famine.

Elijah and the widow both trust in God's word, surprising as it might have been to both of them—to Elijah approaching a Canaanite woman, and to the woman being approached at such a desperate moment. How does our trust in the word of God measure up against theirs? And what is our hospitality to people of other religions, or none, especially in times of their great need? Drought and famine stalk our planet, and often because of the trail of destruction that our noncaring "ecological footprints" have trod. Have we a large vision of this and a willingness to take personal, communal action, and also advocate with our governments, especially through the ballot box?

The responsorial Psalm 146 calls us to praise our faithful God who cares for the oppressed. It is a wonderful checklist for our social justice toward those who are poor because of physical or social disadvantage and the structures that keep people imprisoned in poverty. It was through the words and approach of the prophet Elijah that the word of God and the providence of God came to the widow of Zarephath. How can we bring these same gifts by our human and prophetic approach to the poor?

The scribes about whom Jesus speaks in today's gospel are very different from the truth-seeking scribe of last week, and so a reminder to us not to be universally sweeping in our judgments of any group of people. The scribes about whom Jesus warns his disciples are probably the more significant Temple lawyers preoccupied with their own status and with being recognized publicly as people of moral substance. They paraded outwardly what they believed to be their religious superiority, expecting substantial honors and salutations while, in reality, their inner lives were insubstantial and hypocritical. Jesus has hard words for their failure in social justice toward widows for whom the scribes often acted as legal agents, managing their affairs to their own scribal advantage when these women had no husband or adult male relative to care for them. Widows bereft of family support were easy victims of such financial abuse that tragically compounded the physical and social abuse they could suffer. Instead of receiving the compassion commanded by the Mosaic teaching and the prophets (e.g., Exod 22:22; Deut 27:19; Isa 1:17; Zech 7:10), widows often found themselves destitute victims of fraud at the hands of the unscrupulous whom they may have trusted, scribes included.

Jesus is described as sitting "opposite the treasury," and so opting to teach in the Woman's Court of the Temple. In this area were thirteen trumpet-shaped receptacles to receive alms for the upkeep of the Temple. In the Temple, devoid of paper money, it was the large donations that reverberated loudly through the court to trumpet the generosity of the donor. But Jesus listens with the ear of his heart to the whisper of the two small coins dropped in by the poor widow. She gives two *lepta*, the least valuable coins in circulation at the time, and worth about one sixty-fourth of a *denarius* or "penny," the average daily wage of an unskilled laborer. And the widow gives *two* coins, not just one. The narrative seems to suggest that the widow is not bitter over her misfortune or her possible defrauding; for her, the upkeep of the Temple, the holy Place of the Presence, is her first priority.

Jesus' condemnation of the unscrupulous scribes is part of his public teaching, but then he calls his disciples to himself to impress on them the significance of the widow's action. We have already seen Jesus calling the attention of his disciples to children, defenseless "little ones" (Mark 9:36-37; 10:14-16); have heard how Bartimaeus tossed away everything to go to Jesus. Now Jesus solemnly points to the widow as one who gives God "all she had to live on," her whole livelihood.

We should not read into this gospel a romanticization of poverty nor a condemnation of large donations. It is the motivation behind gifts, large or small, that is important. To give out of our surplus may be useful for taxation purposes, or a generous donation may be great publicity for the corporate business image; contributing to costly buildings or supporting grandiose schemes may often have the aim of making a name for the donor, regardless of the consequences, especially for the poor. We may be able to think of times and places when the church is not exempt from such temptations. It is acting out of love, the motivation that is not economic, promotional, or ostentatious, that makes the difference in the eyes of God. We can surely look around our parishes and see the faithful, generous people who give out of their poverty and also out of their riches.

In both Testaments, the widow is an icon of what we call today the "feminization of poverty." Tragically, what imposes impoverished widowhood on millions of contemporary women is not the religious establishment but genocide, war, HIV/AIDS. Poor widowed grandmothers are caring for their grandchildren who have been orphaned by these scourges, and the United Nations Commission on the Status of Women states that the majority of the more than one billion people who live on a dollar a day or less are women.

Only one chapter later, Mark begins the narrative of Jesus' passion, when he will drop all that he has to live on, his very life, into the treasury of the grave, from which he will rise as the new and living Temple. The Letter to the Hebrews reminds us of Jesus' ultimate, once-and-for-all act of self-offering for the forgiveness of our sins. Now, as the eternal high priest, he continues to intercede for us in the sanctuary of heaven as we await his Second Coming in glory. In every memorial acclamation after the eucharistic consecration, we profess our faith in the mystery of Christ, and in our sacramental communion we become one with his loving generosity. . . . Or do we? When we examine our hearts, do we realize that we, too, can become somewhat hypocritical? We participate in the external rituals of worship, yet even as we do so is our concern more with self, with what we want and what others think of us, rather than our communion with Christ and his presence in our needy brothers and sisters?

Thirty-third Sunday in Ordinary Time

• Dan 12:1-3 • Ps 16:5, 8-11 • Heb 10:11-14, 18 • Mark 13:24-32

No one who has stood before the fresco of Michelangelo's *The Last Judgment* that covers the whole wall behind the altar of the Sistine Chapel, or gazed at a reproduction of it, takes it as a literal or "photographic" record of the future! It is, however, an imaginative and significant statement about the end time, even though Michelangelo was thwarted in some of his artistic statements. He had insisted, for example, on painting all the figures completely naked to emphasize their essential human equality and the justice and fairness of Christ's judgment, uninfluenced by any power or social status with which someone may have been clothed (metaphorically) during life. It was probably the Pope's Master of Ceremonies, Biagio de Cesena, whose face appears appropriately as Minos, the pagan judge of the underworld, who called in another artist to paint flowing garments on all the figures! Both the beginnings and the endings that we have not experienced can be spoken of only in the images and symbols of myths or apocalypse that "unveil" a glimpse of the more significant but hidden reality beyond that which is apparent. This is how Jesus speaks in today's gospel. His concern is with the end *for* the world, not *when* and *how* it will end—issues that have such recurring fascination for many fundamentalists.

To try to express the inexpressible and imagine the unimaginable, we need the language of poetry and imagery, but poetry and imagery that is not divorced from human experience. The Old Testament prophets had spoken in this way, using cosmic imagery about the "day of the Lord" when divine judgment would come upon Babylon and the other nations (e.g., Isa 13:1-22; 34:1-15), when they remembered the times of devastation of Israel and its people (Ezek 32:7-8), or when Israel herself would be the subject of both punishing plagues and God's saving presence (Joel 2:18–3:21).

In the language of apocalypse, the first reading from the Book of Daniel describes what has not yet taken place but is a revelation granted to Daniel: the struggle at the end of human history, and the judgment of both the virtuous and the wicked. Though projected back into times of Israel's earlier suffering, it is the general consensus of scholars that the Book of Daniel is a prophetic book written by a pious Jew in the second century B.C.E. to encourage his people who were suffering great tribulation under the Hellenist ruler Antiochus Epiphanes IV. In 167 B.C.E. he had captured and desecrated the Jerusalem Temple, and not until three years later would the Maccabean revolt succeed in reclaiming and rededicating this hub of Jewish life. Not only was military might a threat to Jewish life, but it was also threatened by the conflict between faith and culture, with some Jews deserting their ancient and holy traditions in favor of the new Hellenist customs and practices. The Book of Daniel urges them to stand firm and resist both the military might and the cultural temptations of Hellenism.

In the imagery of this portion, Michael (Micha-el, "who is like God"), the patron and defender of Israel and the messenger of God's will, is described as a warrior-judge who stands up for God's people in the time of distress, and checks those who are gathered before him for either reward or punishment. The great reward for those who have struggled is something new and unique in the Old Testament: the first unambiguous reference to the resurrection from the dead. This is the huge hope and confidence that, even when life in this world is ended, God never forgets those who have suffered and kept faith with the divine will. Resurrection will be part of the triumph of God's saving justice that will transform cosmic and human history. In Psalm 17 we pray with the psalmist that our memory of the steadfast loving-kindness of God may always be the center of such faithful hope and obedience. Although not professing life after death as does Daniel in the face of death, the psalmist is brimming with trust in God with heart, soul, and body. We are privileged to know that the confidence of the psalmist became a hope fulfilled in the resurrection of Jesus who shows us the path through death to eternal life.

Mark wrote his gospel a few years after the destruction of the Jerusalem Temple in 70 C.E. What the evangelist and his community had heard, and perhaps some of them experienced of that shattering end, is merged with the announcement of the end time in Mark 13. Like a kaleidoscope, other fragments of Markan memory also fall together in a pattern in this chapter (sometimes called Mark's "Little Apocalypse"): the chaos out of which God brings the order of the first creation; the Old Testament description of the tribulation, the "birth pangs of the messiah," from which would be born a new heaven and a new earth (Isa 65:17); the end time of Jesus' death with its cosmic darkness (Mark 15:33) that gives way to resurrection light and life.

Although this text is so rich in biblical allusions, Mark reaches beyond all precedents to what is radically new and unimaginably hopeful because the Second Coming of the Son of Man will not be one of fury and destruction, but of great power and glory. There is no emphasis on judgment, but rather on the gathering of a worldwide community of God's people. Apocalypse has often been called "the literature of the dispossessed," and just as the Book of Daniel tried to give hope to Jews who were facing great suffering, so Mark wants his Christians, and all who face persecution and suffering, to live their lives against a horizon of hope in Jesus, Son of Man and Messiah, especially when tragedies strike and it seems that everything is falling apart. It is Jesus who is the eternally holding center that will draw to himself, from the four corners of the world, the people from all nations to whom the Gospel has been preached (Mark 13:10) and who have lived faithfully through suffering.

Jesus then tells his disciples the mini-parable or "lesson" of the fig tree. Although many trees in Israel are not deciduous, the fig tree does go through an annual cycle of growing leaves, bearing fruit, and losing leaves. When the sap rises in the spring the branches become tender, leaves sprout, and one knows from reading these signs that the time of fruit bearing is coming. The tribulation of the end time is like God's rising sap that will make us supple and ready for new fruit bearing in a new season in a new age that the Second Coming of Jesus will inaugurate. But unlike the predictable ripening of figs, the end time is God's secret and surprise because it is God's plan for humanity and the cosmos. What we can be confident about is that the harvester Christ, at that future time, will be near "at the gates," holding them open for the entry of the faithful into the kingdom. We have the assurance of Jesus' abiding word that this will come to pass.

And so the implication of these last words from Mark's gospel for this liturgical year has the same urgency as those we heard at the beginning of this Year B (Mark 13:33-37): to be vigilant and prepared *now* for what is *not yet*. From that First Sunday of Advent to this Sunday, how have we measured up to this ongoing discernment and conversion?

The Letter to the Hebrews proclaims Jesus as the great High Priest who, by his once-and-for-all sacrifice, has opened heaven for those whom he sanctifies. He has accomplished what the sacrifices of the old law could not. The image of the Levitical priests standing as was customary to offer sacrifice day after day is taken as a symbol of impermanence, whereas Christ, after the offering of his sacrificial death, "sat down at the right hand of God," his work complete. Just as a ruler would have the names of those he conquered carved into his footstool as a sign of their subjugation "under his feet," so Christ is the victor over all sin. The author of the Letter to the Hebrews sees everything through the prism of the sacrificial death and resurrection of Christ that transforms, rather than denigrates, the holiness of the temple, the tabernacle, and the priesthood of Israel. This is our hope and our sanctification.

Thirty-fourth Sunday in Ordinary Time

The Solemnity of Our Lord Jesus Christ, Universal King

• Dan 7:13-14 • Ps 93:1-2, 5 • Rev 1:5-8 • John 18:33b-37

Is our God cozy or cosmic? That is the large and exciting question that challenges us on this last Sunday of the liturgical year as we celebrate the Solemnity of Christ the King. It is the celebration of the climax, not only of this year of grace, but also of the end, the omega point of the mystery toward which we orient our lives. As Vatican II teaches in the Pastoral Constitution on the Church in the Modern World: "The Lord is the goal of human history, the focal point of the longings of history and of civilization, the center of the human race, the joy of every heart, and the answer to all its yearnings" (art. 45).

In biblical tradition, dreams and visions were considered vehicles of divine revelation, and for persecuted people they were indicators not only of what could be, but what will be if informed by faith in God. In the first reading, Daniel has a visionary openness to the hopes and passions of the Jewish people who, as was mentioned last week, were suffering persecution in the second century B.C.E. Immediately before today's portion, a vision of the empires that would subjugate Israel has been described, but then Daniel gazes into his night dream and penetrates to the vision of one "like a human being" (or "Son of Man"). This figure comes on the clouds of heaven, a symbol often associated with the revelation of God (cf. Ps 18:10), and rides them as a royal chariot. The mysterious figure does not approach "the Ancient One" (or "the Ancient of Days") directly, but is presented according to royal etiquette. This title implies an enduring, everlasting presence—the presence of God. The one who comes into this presence is installed by God as the universal ruler who will govern with justice, not because of political conquests or alliances, but by the gracious will of God. The rise and fall of kingdoms that had been revealed to Daniel do not apply to this Son of Man, for his dominion will be an everlasting one. Although he has been commissioned in heaven to a reign of justice, although the kingdom is God's kingdom, the Son of Man's reign will be exercised on earth.

Our response to this reading with verses of Psalm 92 is a confident acclamation of God who is clothed with authority and dignity. In this Lord and king we have confidence whenever contemporary "beasts" or sufferings emerge to threaten with chaos the stability of our personal or more global worlds, for God's reign spans all time and eternity.

The Gospel proclaims that in Jesus the reigning presence of God comes among us in the flesh. Rather than Jesus being put on trial by Pilate, it is the Roman governor who is put on trial by the eloquent Word who stands before him bound as a prisoner. "Are you the king of the Jews?" asks Pilate, understanding kingship as political, with possibly religious implications, and therefore wary of any claim that could be a challenge to absolute Roman authority. Jesus replies with a question that seeks to confront Pilate with his own personal commitment as opposed to what "others" tell him about Jesus. The issue is no longer Jesus' guilt or innocence, but whether Pilate will respond to the truth of Jesus' kingship. Three times Jesus speaks of what his kingdom is not. It is not of this world in the sense that it neither takes its origin from here, nor is it an earthly kingdom that would be a rival to Caesar and Roman imperialism. But it does belong *in* this world and its followers do have a role to play in human affairs of justice. Like Jesus, his followers are not power brokers or mercenaries defending their own "kingdoms" of political or religious power; violence, exploitation, and opportunism have no part in the following of Jesus.

"So you are a king?" pushes Pilate, and Jesus responds to what Pilate has called him by speaking of what his power really is: the power of the truth John proclaimed in the Prologue: "The Word became flesh and lived among us, and we have seen his glory, the glory of a father's only son, full of grace and truth" (John 1:14). The life, death, and resurrection of Jesus testify to this truth, and all who listen to Jesus and commit themselves to his wisdom will belong to the truth and to his kingdom. Pilate can make no sense of this. His world is more concerned with illusions of grandeur than with truth.

On this day we all stand not before Pilate but with him, to be interrogated by Christ the King. What power do we seek and how would we like to get it? Do we excuse ourselves of manipulating and exploiting others for the sake of safeguarding our own status or progress? How often do we strike out with the violent word or the cutting silence? Timothy Radcliffe queries whether our fascination with the countless TV shows and books that are concerned with the "naked" something or other, with either self-revelation or the exposure of others, is an indicator of a frustrated hunger for truth? He goes on to comment that in Dante's *Inferno* "the icy heart of hell was kept for those who undermined the human community of truth: the liars, the fraudulent, the flatterers, the forgers, and worst of all the traitors."[38] Do we belong to the community of truth that listens to and follows Jesus?

With the reading from the Book of Revelation (the Apocalypse) it is not as though we are standing with Jesus before Pilate, but rather that we are standing under one of the magnificent domes of an ancient cathedral and gazing up at the golden glory of a painting or mosaic of Christ Pantocrator, a cosmic and glorified Christ who is "ruler of all." The verses read today are part of the letter or writings addressed to the seven (the number of symbolic fullness and universality) churches of Asia by John the seer, sometimes also referred to as John the elder to distinguish him from the writer of the Fourth Gospel. About it there is a sense of urgency, a call to fidelity because "the appointed time is near" (Rev 1:3) when something of world-shaking significance will be revealed. For the early church of the late first century there was the expectation that the Second Coming of Jesus and the end time of human and cosmic history was near at hand. Two millennia later, we are a generation that knows that was a mistaken view, but every generation must sustain the sense of urgency because our generation, like every generation, has only our own limited time in which to accomplish what we can of God's kingdom work.

Jesus Christ is given three titles that have depths of meaning for the Christian churches to whom the Book of Revelation is addressed, and to all future Christians, especially in times of suffering and persecution. He is "the faithful witness," "the firstborn from the dead," and "the ruler of the kings of the earth." Just as Jesus had stood as a faithful witness to his mission before Pilate, so must his followers stand before any authority that threatens their faith. Jesus is the "firstborn from the dead," the firstfruits of the resurrection that will be harvested by all who bear faithful witness, even unto death, and especially by martyrdom. As "ruler of the kings of the earth," a title given to the Roman emperor, it is Jesus—not any "Caesar" anywhere or at any time— who has universal, eternal, and cosmic authority. This authority is the power of redeeming love that consecrates the community as priestly and as sharing in the offering of glory and praise for their salvation in Jesus Christ.

There are also memories of the first reading from the Book of Daniel and the prophet Zechariah. The one who came on the clouds of heaven, like a son of man (Dan 7:13), is now the new, renewed humanity revealed in Jesus Christ. He is the pierced one whose identity was not clear in Zechariah 12:10, but has been revealed as the pierced and glorified one (John 19:34), and all those who recognize him will lament for the suffering of Jesus. With compunction, with the piercing of their hearts and mourning over their sinfulness, will come conversion of the enemies of Jesus Christ to which the Seer says his fervent "Amen."

Behind Christ is the God who reveals himself in Christ, the "I AM" who is the Alpha and the Omega, the Beginning and the End, the Almighty, who is not the cozy God but the dynamic, transforming, and cosmic God, the only one whose mystery is big enough to show us a new way into the experience of the holy and large truth when we are disenchanted by unholy minutiae and legalisms. Young people, especially, are often reaching out to traditions other than the Christian to make contact with some mystical roots. As we come to the close of this liturgical year, perhaps we might reflect on these words of Pierre Teilhard de Chardin with their loud echoes of the Book of Revelation and the glory of the Christ whom we are celebrating:

> Glorious Lord Jesus . . . power as implacable as the world and as warm as life; you whose forehead is of the whiteness of snow, whose eyes are of fire, and whose feet are brighter than molten gold; you whose hands imprison the stars; you who are the first and the last, and the living and the dead and the risen again; you who gather into your exuberant unity every beauty, every affinity, every energy, every mode of existence; it is you to whom my being cries out with a desire as vast as the universe. "In truth, you are my Lord and my God."[39]

Notes

1. William Shakespeare, *The Tragedy of* Macbeth, Act 5, scene V, line 19, in *The Complete Works*, ed. John Jowlett and others, 2nd ed. (Oxford: Clarendon Press, 2005) 991.

2. Timothy Radcliffe, *Just One Year: Prayer and Worship through the Christian Year* (London: Darton, Longman and Todd Ltd./CAFOD/Christian Aid, 2006) 79.

3. Pontifical Biblical Commission, *The Jewish People and Their Sacred Scriptures in the Christian Bible*, 2002, art. 1.

4. Ronald Rolheiser, "Finding God in Community," Column Archive, *Canadian Western Times*, 2001-06-10.

5. John Donne, "Holy Sonnet XIV," in *Seven Centuries of Poetry in English* (South Melbourne: Oxford University Press Australia and New Zealand, 5th edition, 2006) 492.

6. Donald Senior, C.P., *The Passion of Jesus in the Gospel of Mark* (Wilmington, DE: Michael Glazier, Inc., 1984) 61.

7. Ernst Käsemann, *New Testament Questions of Today* (Philadelphia: Fortress Press, 1969) 13.

8. Matthew Arnold, "The Buried Life," in *Seven Centuries of Poetry in English*, 248.

9. The terminology of Joel Marcus in *Mark 1–8*, The Anchor Bible, Vol. 27 (New York: Doubleday, 2005) 177.

10. For example, see J. Frank Henderson, *Liturgies of Lamentation* (Chicago: Liturgy Training Publications, 1994).

11. Francis J. Moloney, *The Gospel of Mark: A Commentary* (Peabody, MA: Hendrickson Publishers, Inc., 2002) 59.

12. Vatican II, Decree on the Missionary Activity of the Church (*Ad Gentes*), art. 11.

13. Vatican II, Pastoral Constitution on the Church in the Modern World (*Gaudium et Spes*), art. 92.

14. Ruth Padel, *The Poem and the Journey: And Sixty Poems to Read Along the Way* (London: Chatto & Windus, 2007) 34.

15. Fred B. Craddock and others, *Preaching Through the Christian Year* (Harrisburg, PA: Trinity Press International, 1993) 117.

16. Abraham Joshua Heschel, *The Sabbath: Its Meaning for Modern Man* (New York: The Noonday Press, Farrar, Straus and Giroux, 1981) 99.

17. Vatican II, Pastoral Constitution on the Church in the Modern World, art. 13.

18. For example, see Richard Dawkins, *The God Delusion* (London: Houghton Mifflin, 2007).

19. John R. Donahue, S.J., *The Gospel in Parable: Metaphor, Narrative, and Theology in the Synoptic Gospels* (New York: Fortress Press, 1988) 2.

20. Michael Casey, O.C.S.O., *Fully Human, Fully Divine: An Interactive Christology* (Mulgrave, Victoria: John Garratt Publishing, 2004) 118.

21. Viktor E. Frankl, *Man's Search for Meaning*, trans. Ilse Lasch (New York: Simon and Schuster, 1962) 114–115.

22. Maria Boulding, O.S.B., *Gateway to Hope: An Exploration of Failure* (London: Collins, 1985) 9.

23. Shakespeare, *The Tragedy of King Lear*, Act 5, scene I, lines 14–15.

24. See Raymond E. Brown, *An Introduction to the New Testament* (New York: Doubleday, The Anchor Bible Reference Library, 1997) 620.

25. See Robert Frost, "Mending Wall," in *Robert Frost: Selected Poems* (New York: Gramercy Books, 1992) 87–88.

26. For example, see *Didache* 9.3-4; *1 Clement* 34.7; Ignatius, *Letter to Polycarp* 4.2.

27. Walter Brueggemann, "Exodus," in *The New Interpreter's Bible*, Vol. 1 (Nashville: Abingdon Press, 1994) 814.

28. See Raymond E. Brown, *The Gospel According to John I–XII* (New York: Doubleday & Company, Inc., The Anchor Bible, 1977) 272–273.

29. St. Augustine, *Sermons*, 272.

30. Margaret Y. MacDonald, *Colossians and Ephesians*, Sacra Pagina Series 17 (Collegeville, MN: Liturgical Press, 2000) 341.

31. Eugene LaVerdiere, *The Beginning of the Gospel: Introducing the Gospel According to Mark*, Volume 1: Mark 1–8:21 (Collegeville, MN: Liturgical Press, 1999) 184.

32. Etty Hilesum, *Etty: A Diary 1941–1943* (London: Triad Grafton Books, 1985) 45–46.

33. A term used by Pheme Perkins in "The Gospel of Mark," *The New Interpreter's Bible*, Vol. VIII (Nashville: Abingdon Press, 1995) 625.

34. Terence E. Fretheim, "Genesis," in *The New Interpreter's Bible*, Vol. 1 (Nashville: Abingdon Press, 1994) 35.

35. Pontifical Biblical Commission, *The Jewish People and Their Sacred Scriptures in the Christian Bible*, 2002, art. 84.

36. Frankl, *Man's Search for Meaning*, 114–115.

37. Craddock and others, *Preaching Through the Christian Year: Year B*, 459.

38. Timothy Radcliffe, o.p., *What is the Point of Being a Christian?* (London: Burns & Oates, 2005) 113, 117.

39. Pierre Teilhard de Chardin, "The Mass on the World," in *Hymn of the Universe* (London: William Collins Sons & Co. Ltd., 1970) 33.

6

"With the Gospel as our guide"

Short conversations between the Sunday Lectionary for Year B and the Rule of Benedict[1]

At the beginning of his Rule, St. Benedict encourages his followers to "set out on this way with the Gospel as our guide" (RB Prol 21), and in the last chapter he expresses his conviction that "what page or even word of the divinely inspired Old and New Testaments is not a completely reliable guidepost for human life?" (RB 73.3). The placement of these two significant references to the importance of Scripture, the Good News or "Gospel" of both Testaments, make them the bookends that hold the Rule in place as a particular interpretation of Christian discipleship.

The first Prologue reference to the Gospel is in the context of "faith and the performance of good works," the practical living out of the biblical Good News applicable to all the people of God, not only those who follow the monastic way of life. In his last chapter, with the reference to Scripture as the guidepost for *human* life, Benedict again universalizes the relevance of his Rule.

The following reflections are, therefore, offered as a kind of liturgical and biblical "chat room" into which those who are interested can enter for a conversation between themselves, the Lectionary readings, and the Rule of Benedict. As if he wants to place all his words under obedience to the Word of God, Benedict often introduces a chapter by a quotation from Scripture that guides and governs the whole chapter; for example, RB 7.1; 16.1; 19.1; 27.1; 40.1. At other times he places the biblical word in the context of a direct and personal address to the monk: "Scripture urges us on when it says . . ." (RB 7.45), as a healing word (RB 28.3), a wise and practical word (RB 2.13; 39.8-9). As we listen to the Sunday readings, or reflect on them before or after the liturgy as our *lectio divina*, it is hoped that inviting Benedict to join us will add another dimension to our personal, practical, and human responses to the Word of God, no matter what our life situations. Like our everyday conversations, there will be variations in length and intensity. There will be no attempt to talk with Benedict about the three readings, but the focus will usually be on one or two points. Inevitably, over the fifty-two weeks of the year there will be some repeated conversations, just as with friends we often return to memories and issues that are more important than others, but these will be in different contexts and can serve to emphasize what Benedict considers most significant.

Benedict was convinced that the biblical word cannot be locked in the past. In his own fifth- through sixth-century life, he hears it speaking to his concerns for a new vision of community at the heart of a decadent society and in the midst of great social change. In such times there can be a temptation either to withdraw nostalgically behind the barriers of the past, or storm ahead into the future. Benedict was seduced by neither option. He chose a middle way, a lifestyle in which he tried to hold in dynamic balance both respect for individual differences and commitment to community, prayer and work, nature and grace.

Originally written for men and for the monastic life in the Roman church, its wisdom has also been inclusive of women who for centuries have lived and adapted the Rule to the feminine. As Columba Stewart comments, interpretations, modifications, supplementations have happened to the Rule ever since Benedict laid down his pen, and the cultural and contemporary set of situations have been considered. This is especially true with regard to women who follow the Rule.[2] Beyond the monastery, this Rule that comes from the time of the undivided church has proved to have an ecumenical appeal for those longing for an often undefined, but strongly felt "something more" that could be shared among those of different Christian traditions. In the mixing of cultures in our times there is also mutually enriching conversations between the basic values of the Rule of Benedict and the various forms of monastic life that exist outside Christianity.[3]

It is hoped, therefore, that there will be no gender, lifestyle, or faith barriers that prevent anyone's entry into this biblical, liturgical, and Benedictine "chat room." Given its original genesis, and out of respect for this, references to and direct quotations from the Rule are left in the masculine.

First Sunday of Advent

Not wanting to seek God can be a great Advent temptation, hidden as God may be by our frenetic and too early Christmas celebrations. Benedict reminds us that God takes the initiative in seeking for workers in the midst of the crowds (RB Prol 14-17), inviting us to set out vigorously with the Gospel as our guide (RB Prol 21) as we seek God.

At the very beginning of and throughout his Rule, Benedict reminds us of our need to wake up out of our comatose discipleship, because "inertia" or slothful lack of obedient effort can result in our settling down as comfortable dilettantes who consequently drift away from our commitment to Christ (RB Prol 2; RB 48.1, 23; 73.7). Our response to our seeker God should rather be that of long-distance runners heading purposefully for the finishing line of the kingdom (RB Prol 49-50). In all this is an echo of the Advent shout, "Keep awake!"

Second Sunday of Advent

Benedict's chapter on "The Daily Manual Labor" (RB 48) is a surprising one. Eight times in twenty-five verses he mentions freedom from manual work so that the monks may have space and time to be "free for" (*vacare*) the work of holy reading (*lectio divina*). This will contribute greatly to a flexible, realistic, and balanced lifestyle. These weeks are probably the busiest of the year, and to be "free for" the sacred reading of, for example, the beautiful Lectionary readings outside the Sunday liturgy requires a great effort of discipleship. Our schedules may not be those of a Benedictine monastery, but this freedom may mean deliberately turning off the TV, the transistor radio, or the mobile phone so that we can enter into the "wilderness" moments, moments where, like John the Baptist, we can grow stronger in spirit (cf. Luke 1:80). In such few moments of Advent space we can enter a bigger world than the crowded shops and our own pressing schedules, and reflect on those hopes that are as large as "the new heavens and the new earth, the place where righteousness is at home" (2 Peter 3:13).

As with all beginnings, something usually needs to be cleared away to enable a new start. The season of Advent should be the beginning of all in us that is not Christ, for: "Nothing is to be preferred to Christ" (RB 4.21).

Third Sunday of Advent

In the Prologue, Benedict speaks of the light that comes from God as a gift that demands openness, not drowsiness (RB Prol 9-10), and vigorous pursuit, not loitering in the darkness of sin. John the Baptist is the witness that the true light shines forth in Jesus, the Word made flesh, and before this light John is joyfully content that his own light grows dim and is eventually extinguished (John 3:29-30). In the Baptist's repeated "I am not . . ." is a wonderful example of someone who lives the biblical way of humility that Benedict refers to in the first verse of chapter 7, "On Humility." In John there is nothing of self-promotion; it is Jesus himself who praises his precursor (e.g., Matt 11:7-11).

Benedict wanted his communities to have the greatest respect for the fragile dreams of the poor in the spirit of the first reading from Isaiah. Special care for the poor should be the tool that every monk uses to build a compassionate household (RB 4.14-19). The poor guest is to be welcomed by the porter with "Thanks be to God!" for his or her presence, and "Bless me!" is asked of the *guest*. The community's hospitality to the poor and pilgrims is especially important, for in them is a special advent of Christ (RB 53.15). Clothes are to be kept for distribution to the poor (RB 55.9). In the consumerist atmosphere of these pre-Christmas weeks we would do well to take time to share Isaiah's and Benedict's dreams—and then wake up to some practical action transplanted into our own situations.

Fourth Sunday of Advent

At the center of today's Liturgy of the Word is Mary. Benedict says nothing explicitly in his Rule about her—perhaps because he believed that the primacy of her obedience to the word of God and her discipleship of her Son was so obvious? Assured by the angel that she should not be afraid, in Mary's obedience there is no cringing, slowness, or halfheartedness, no murmuring, but only the obedient love that offers the swiftest, intimate, and extraordinary hospitality to the Word made flesh in her womb (cf. RB 5.8, 14). Mary's humble "Yes!" can surely lead us into progress on the way of obedience to Christ whom, with her, we are to hold "more precious than all else" (RB 5.1-2).

Christmas Day

Mass during the Day

The first voice that we hear in today's readings is that of the Isaian messenger who is a herald of peace, and peace is almost a mantra, repeated in heaven and on earth, for this season of Christmas. Benedict urges his followers to "seek peace and pursue it" (RB Prol 17; Ps 34:14), and the double imperative is a warning that no individual or community ambles mindlessly into peace. Faced with the threat or reality of terrorism, with domestic and global violence, we may feel powerless and fearful, but Benedict knows there is nothing in the world that is not first in the human heart, and he offers some practical ways of seeking and pursuing peace, no matter what our way of life, that could well be our Christmas offering to the Child of Peace.

In our Christmas gatherings, we can keep our tongues from vicious or deceitful talk (RB Prol 17) and refrain from the insincere greeting of peace (RB 4.25) that is at best thoughtlessness and at worst mockery. In RB 64.16, Benedict lists tendencies that the abbot should try to control if he is to be at peace. Certainly few of us will be called to this role, but for anyone who wishes to live in peace—with himself or herself as well as with other people—this listing makes a valuable examination of conscience. How restless, troubled, extreme, headstrong, jealous, or oversuspicious am I? And can I make an effort to become more thoughtful, moderate, and discerning in my relationships (cf. RB 64.17)?

Feast of the Holy Family

Luke places two aged people, a man and a woman, in prophetic encounter with the forty-day-old Jesus and with his parents in today's gospel. It is a beautiful cameo of what is so often missing for many of today's families: intergenerational relationships that are mutually nurturing and enriching. Benedict also believed in the importance of such relationships, encouraging his monks to "Respect the elders and love the young" (RB 4.70. *RB 1980* trans.), even though his communities are not to be seen as families of children and parents, but as communities of adults. Both young and old have precious gifts to offer one another.

Octave of Christmas

Solemnity of the Blessed Virgin Mary, Mother of God

In her pondering and remembering, Mary is a model for our *lectio divina*, our reading of the Word of God, and our conversation between that Word and the events of our own lives. Present to that Word, we try to be progressively immersed in its mystery as this speaks to the hopes and fears, the joys and sorrows, the contradictions and affirmations of our lives. The Word that came to Mary and was made flesh in her womb, the Word to which she gave birth for the world, was the mystery into which she moved deeper and deeper, and surely often unknowing, throughout her life. Commitment to *lectio divina* is central to Benedictine life and spirituality. Eleven times in RB 48, "The Daily Manual Work," Benedict mentions *lectio* (vv. 1, 4, 5, 10, 13, 14, 15, 17, 18, 22, 23), a witness to the balance that he considered so important between work and the reading, predominantly of Scripture, that strives for a contemplative openness to God: "holy leisure, time spent only for God and with God."[4] Although the several hours a day of *lectio* envisaged by Benedict cannot today be the schedule of most people either inside or outside the monastery, to find a daily place and time for holy reading is still an essential aspect of Benedictine spirituality.

Epiphany of the Lord

As a day for seekers and stargazers and traveling strangers, today must have been very dear to Benedict. Whether someone who seeks entry into the monastery "really seeks God" (RB 58.7) is basic to the discernment of a monastic vocation. Such a search is, of course, a response to God's seeking and calling (RB Prol 14-15) without which no one's search, in any lifestyle, can begin. The search will last a lifetime and will be a journey of love that makes daily demands of fidelity (RB 7.27-29) until we come to that which we seek: a share in God's kingdom (RB Prol 49-50).

The mutual hospitality of the holy family and the Magi might make us stop and reflect on our readiness to welcome strange and unexpected guests in the spirit of Benedict's hospitality (RB 53.15), especially the contemporary "pilgrims" who bring their own gifts. These will not be the riches of gold, frankincense, and myrrh, but the wisdom of other nations and cultures, the longings of youth, the (often shaming) generosity of the poor, the many people who are searching for some guiding star and hope to find an open door and welcome in Benedictine households of God or in the Christian communities of home and parish.

The Baptism of the Lord

First Sunday in Ordinary Time

The baptism of Jesus is a humble event. Jesus lines up humbly, in solidarity with the sinners who are coming to the humble precursor for a baptism of repentance, and as he comes up from the Jordan waters there is no dramatic proclamation of his identity. It is Jesus only who hears himself named by his Father as "my Son, the Beloved; with you I am well pleased." Once again then, the central place that Benedict gives to humility is affirmed by the Gospel.

Michael Casey comments that:

> When Jesus came to John the Baptist, he was a long way from home. We may understand him as being on a journey of self-discovery—seeking means of putting into words his subliminal sense of God's presence and of solidarity

with all. In a typical gesture of humility, he embraces communion with sinners . . .[5]

Benedict concludes chapter 7, "On Humility," with verses suggesting that it is humility that entices us to come home to the perfect love of God that casts out fear, so that a monk who has climbed the twelve steps of the ladder of humility will now act "out of love of Christ, good habit itself and a love of virtue" (RB 7.67-70). Benedict suggests that this love is also the work of the Holy Spirit, and these verses are the only place in the Rule where he refers to the three Persons of the Trinity together, as does the gospel of the baptism of Jesus.

First Sunday of Lent

In RB 49, "On the Observance of Lent," Benedict says that "at all times the lifestyle of a monk should have a Lenten quality" (RB 49.1). But like the church, and with characteristic realism, he also recognizes that such consistent effort is difficult, and so the season of Lent is a privileged time of focus on fidelity. That Benedict's chapter is both directly and indirectly influenced by the Lenten sermons of Pope St. Leo (d. 461) to the laity of Rome indicates that the spiritual wisdom of this chapter is applicable beyond the monastery. Twice in this chapter, and nowhere else in the Rule, Benedict uses the word "joy." Lenten prayer and fasting are to be prompted by "the joy of the Holy Spirit" (RB 49.6), not by pious competitiveness or a negative and punitive spirituality. We are urged on "with joy" and renewed energy to the goal of Holy Easter through prayer that softens the heart and through sacred reading that jabs us out of our personal and social apathy and self-indulgence. In RB 48.14-16, Benedict stresses the importance of beginning Lent with extra effort at this *lectio divina* that is not just a revisiting of our favorite texts but is a persevering discipline of the continuous reading of a biblical book. The ancient tradition of fasting and decreasing somewhat the amount of food and drink should increase the hunger for God. Given the ecological dangers now confronting our planet, fasting may challenge us earthlings to more conscientious use of water and other far-from-inexhaustible natural resources in atonement for the many violations of nature in our lifestyles, and in compassionate and prayerful remembrance of our sisters and brothers for whom even our fasts would be feasts. Laura Swan also comments on another way of fasting in the Benedictine spirit that is possible for everyone:

> . . . fasting from *my* agenda, *my* opinions, *my* whatever. Then fasting moves us *toward* another person's worldview and life experience. This is Benedict's fast: no murmuring, grumbling, or complaining! It is the fast of speaking

gently and respectfully, straight from our heart. The fruit of the monastic fast is revealed in our deepened patience, empathy, and compassion.[6]

Benedict emphasizes both individual and community effort, since in or beyond the monastery it is difficult to "go it alone." This is a (perhaps unexpected) gentle chapter of the Rule, with Benedict only recommending "some" denial of food, drink, sleep, chatter, and joking (RB 49.7). Excessive or obsessive effort can end up the same as too little effort—in a collapse back into overeating, oversleeping, overtalking. So, tagged with the ashes as our pilgrim logo, warned and encouraged by the Word of God and monastic wisdom, we begin our Lenten journey to Easter glory not in doom and gloom, but in eager and joyful anticipation.

Second Sunday of Lent

Mark ends his description of the Transfiguration with the significant words about the disciples: " . . . when they looked around they saw no one with them any more, but only Jesus." For Benedict, everything is centered on "only Jesus." That the love of Christ must come before all else (RB 4.21) is the tool of good works that must shape the whole life of a follower of the Rule. And his words in RB 72.11 are even stronger, reinforced no doubt by long experience of the possibility of choosing either good zeal or evil and bitter zeal; the preference is to be for "absolutely nothing to Christ." Benedict is simply echoing the gospel call to listen to the Son who, because he is the Beloved Son of the Father, reveals this love to us and asks us to offer it to the world. It is Christ who will expand our hearts and give us the strength of a long-distance runner as we unswervingly head for the kingdom (cf. RB Prol 49-50). Lent is a season of special marathon training that builds up our endurance for such a race.

Like Jesus, we also need the support of friends and "ancestors" in the faith, those who have already climbed some way up mountains of difficulties and have enjoyed a glimpse of what awaits them in the kingdom. When the climb gets difficult, it is a blessing if there are other members of the community or family or friends who can help us carry our backpacks of burdens (RB 72.5) until we find eternal rest on the holy mountain of God (RB Prol 23; Ps 15.1).

Third Sunday of Lent

In his description of the oratory of the monastery (RB 52) Benedict supports a "mini-cleansing." He writes that the oratory "should be in fact what it is called," that is, a place of prayer, and not a storage room that might reflect the jumbled prayer life of those who tolerate such an environment. Spatially and liturgically, the oratory is to be a reminder of the desirable quality of monastic and all Christian prayer: uncluttered and free for service of God, especially at the Liturgy of the Hours. If someone wants to pray after the liturgy, this should be with heartfelt devotion and respect for others that guarantees one will not disturb the other.

There is such a thing as just anger, as Jesus shows us in the gospel. In the *Dialogues*[7] Gregory tells of the just anger of Benedict when, in a time of famine, the subdeacon Agapitus came to the monastery to beg for a little oil. Benedict had given away to the poor everything except one small flask of oil that he then commanded the cellarer to give to Agapitus. On discovering that the cellarer had disobeyed him, Benedict hurled the flask onto the rocks below to cleanse the monastery of something that was contrary to obedience and charity. Unbroken, the flask of oil was retrieved and the cellarer shamed before the community. Who today is "Agapitus"? and what should a monastic community or other Christian communities be ready and willing to give to those in need?

Fourth Sunday of Lent

Thomas Merton wrote that:

> The more perfect faith is, the darker it becomes. The closer we get to God, the less our faith is diluted with the half-light of created images and concepts. Our certainty increases with this obscurity, yet not without anguish . . . And it is in the deepest darkness that we most fully possess God on earth . . .[8]

Merton called himself "a solitary explorer" who "is bound to search the existential depths of faith in its silences, its ambiguities, and in those certainties that lie deeper than the bottom of anxiety. In these depths there are no easy answers, no pat solutions to anything."[9] Nicodemus, too, is such an explorer whose eyes are paradoxically opened "to the light that comes from God" (RB Prol 9) in the darkness of Golgotha when, with Joseph of Arimathea, he carries the dead body of Jesus in a royal cortege to a new garden tomb.

Fifth Sunday of Lent

Benedict's spirituality is a spirituality of the heart. For him, as in Scripture, the heart is the most intimate and personal core of a person, the depth (as Jeremiah tells us in today's first reading) to which God speaks and on which God inscribes the divine teaching to be constantly read and pondered. From the beginning of his Rule, Benedict encourages his followers to listen to God "with the ear of your heart," and then live practically according to what has been heard (RB Prol 1). The heart is the battleground for spiritual warfare that is Christ-centered (cf. RB Prol 28, 40-41) and, as one runs life's race with faith and love like a long-distance runner in training, our hearts are expanded and strengthened to make ever more room for the love of God and our sisters and brothers (RB Prol 49-50). No doubt Benedict is here speaking out of his heart—his personal experience.

The chapter in which Benedict refers most to the heart is "On Humility" (RB 7). Since the humble heart is the soil, the *humus*, for the Word of God, almost every verse of this challenging chapter is placed under obedience to the biblical Word. Like the Prologue, it also ends in love, the love of God in Christ and in the guiding presence of the Holy Spirit for those who struggle to be "down to earth" lovers who have come to disregard themselves as the holy center of their small universe (RB 7.67-70).

Palm Sunday of the Lord's Passion

Aquinata Böckmann sees RB 58 as an important chapter not only for those preparing for final profession, but also for all who have made their profession, perhaps decades ago, yet are still on the way to what was promised, still needing conversion to God and our sisters and brothers, still in a kind of novitiate after which we will make final profession at the hour of our death.[10] In that sense, perhaps there is no better time for reflection on the paschal dimension of religious profession than as we enter into the Great Week of the celebration of the paschal mystery.

As Benedict describes the monastic profession, after the newly professed has placed his or her vows on the altar, the *Suscipe*, "Receive me, Lord," is prayed three times and echoed by the community, with the addition of the "Glory be" after the third time. The newly professed then prostrates at the feet of each member of the community with whom he or she will seek God, and on whom monastic perseverance will depend so much (RB 58.21-23). The newly professed, having renounced all temporal possessions, is then stripped of former dress and clothed in the monastic habit (RB 58.24-28). Rather than speculate about the process of this, or the changes that have come into the ritual, it is more important to reflect on its symbolism against the backdrop of the Christ who, as Paul sings in the great hymn of Philippians, dispossessed himself of his divine privileges to become one with our humanity; who knew both the failure of his community of disciples and the support of a few friends; and whose confidence that his life and death would be acceptable to God was an agonizing but triumphant struggle to which God said "and you shall live" in his resurrection.

Easter Sunday

"To await Holy Easter with the joy of spiritual desire" (RB 49.7) is, for Benedict, the purpose of Lent, and he devotes a whole chapter (RB 15) to the Liturgy of the Hours for this season characterized by the joyful praise of God in the singing of "Alleluia." As Easter people, "Alleluia" ("Praise YAH") is truly our song.

Each Easter it pays us to reflect again on what Gregory recounts about one of Benedict's Easter Sundays when, as a young hermit at Subiaco and distanced from other Christians, he had lost track of the date of Easter. Our Lord appeared to a priest at a distance from that place and told him that, while he was preparing a fine Easter dinner for himself, Benedict was suffering from hunger. Hearing this, the priest set off with the food to search for Benedict with commendable obedience and commitment, since Gregory describes the journey as "among the mountain-tops and throughout the valley ravines and in the caves in the ground, and he found him hidden in his grotto." The two of them prayed together and talked about spiritual things. After this, the priest said to Benedict: "Rise up, brother, and let us dine, because today is the feast of Easter." Then came Benedict's charming response: "I know it is Easter because I have the honor of seeing you."[11] No matter what our judgment of Gregory's creativity or inventiveness, it was always to serve a pastoral and spiritual purpose. Given this instance, we might ask ourselves if part of our Easter joy lies in recognizing the mystery which easters in our brothers and sisters, in their companionship and conversation, and in their sharing of good things with us—and if they are able to enjoy the same experience with us?

Second Sunday of Easter

Benedict quotes three times (RB 33.6; 34.1; 55.20) from the chapter of the Acts of the Apostles that we hear today. As de Vogüé remarks, in the early Jerusalem church "common ownership of goods spells oneness of heart,"[12] and that ideal became an archetype for the early monastic approach to poverty to which Benedict subscribes. Having professed a radical renunciation of their own bodies and will (RB 33.4), the monks are to have no exclusive ownership of anything, but their needs are to be met by the abbot (RB 33.5)—graciously and respectfully, with full attention to individual differences (RB 34; 55.20-21). Although there is an individual ascetical dimension to Benedict's words, the communal concern of Acts is also and definitely present. In commenting on RB 33, Esther de Wahl writes of the relevance of Benedict's approach for those living beyond the monastery:

> Why this radical demand? What is it saying to me? Benedict is forcing me to see that it is not so much possessions in themselves that concern him, as the danger that they are, or can become, the vehicles for relations between people. They can either lead me to trust and to love, or they can lead me on to more and more acquisitiveness, and thus to greed, envy, resentment, competitiveness, bitterness. Rather than let any of this start to spread in my life, I should cut it out.[13]

After all, the idealized early Jerusalem community also had its Ananias and Sapphira, as Benedict remembers (RB 57.5)!

Third Sunday of Easter

A repeated Easter greeting of the risen Jesus is "Peace be with you!"—a gift so needed by the community of disciples in chaos after the death of Jesus and the death of their own hopes and illusions about themselves. Benedict knew only too well the tensions, the murmuring, the competitiveness that can so easily spring up in a community, be it a monastery or family, to destroy peace. For this reason, as a Gospel proclamation that God will forgive us as we forgive others, Benedict inserted the recitation of the Lord's Prayer into both Morning (Lauds) and Evening (Vespers) Prayer. "This is done because of the thorns of quarrelling that often spring up" (RB 13.12-14). In the morning the community pledges to try to forgive and be reconciled in the relationships of the coming day. The Lord's Prayer said in the evening may help individuals to reflect on the successes and failures in such forgiveness during the day and pray that they will not be led into the same temptations tomorrow. Kardong suggests that the odd instruction (now no longer observed) that the community listens to the superior recite the prayer (RB 13.12), responding aloud only with "Forgive us as we forgive," may have been influenced by Augustine's remark that some omit the prayer as an excuse for *not* being obliged to forgive![14] What you don't say, you don't have to do! Familiarity can breed contempt with this most privileged prayer, yet mindfully prayed in community or family, or as individual Christians, it is a call to us to be a people of peace, some small leaven in a world and church that, in so many aspects, needs to rise into the reconciliation that is the gift of the risen Christ. None of us ambles mindlessly into peace on our own. The nonviolent life demands that we "seek and pursue it" vigorously (RB Prol 17), with integrity (RB 4.25) and together, day in and day out (RB 4.73).

Fourth Sunday of Easter

Benedict sees that the special role of the abbot is to have concern for the members of the community who are wavering or failing in their commitment. The "penal code" chapters of the Rule (RB 23–30) are not the most attractive aspects of the Rule for contemporary Christians, and not interpreted nor practiced literally today; yet in the middle of this section we find the chapter on "The Abbot's Preoccupation with the Excommunicated" (RB 27), and this preoccupation is not punitive, but concerned and loving. Benedictine authority is to be truly Gospel shepherding that neither tosses aside the weak nor dominates the strong (RB 27.6; 64.12-13, 19). The bold, direct strokes of the prophet Ezekiel and the more gentle lines of the Johannine "good" shepherd are used to draw the portrait of the abbot (Ezek 34:3-4; RB 27.7-8) in this chapter. The abbot is to be humble enough to seek the help of other wise and discerning members of the community who may confidentially approach the one who is failing, and so avoid any misconception on his part of an authoritarian attitude. And because the reconciliation and reintegration of the brother into the community is a concern of the whole community, the abbot is to encourage all to pray for the one experiencing difficulties.

"A brother who had sinned was turned out of the church by the priest; Abba Bessarion got up and went with him, saying, 'I, too, am a sinner.'"[15] True pastoral concern does not aim to condemn or exclude, but to love, to heal, and to absorb the other's hurt—even to the extent of laying down one's life (not necessarily physically) in service for them, as did the Good Shepherd. Such pastoral qualities can be expanded beyond the monastic context to offer wisdom to all who are in positions of authority in family or church, in caring ministries, or in relationships in the world of work.

Fifth Sunday of Easter

The Benedictine concept of stability has been described as "sticking with it," of remaining grafted onto the members of your religious community, husband or wife, family or friends or church—even if it seems that they change and become more disagreeable or dull, less beautiful or healthy. It is quite likely that at times they might feel much the same about us! Stability is not a matter of gritting one's teeth to obligations but of pruning one's heart and abiding patiently, perseveringly, and faithfully in a dynamic relationship that grows by abiding in the love of God. Stability requires pruning for such growth, especially in our mobile world of disposable relationships, communications, careers, and travel.

For some men and women the vow of stability may mean commitment to lifelong physical stability in one monastery, but whatever the external expression of this first of the Benedictine vows (RB 58.9), the most important aspect of the promise of stability is always the deeper, covenantal stability of heart, the commitment to a continuing search for God in a particular way of Gospel life, and a readiness to stand firmly together with God and one another in the concrete realities of daily life. A husband and father writes of stability in this way:

> . . . stability prevents daydreaming about "what if. . ." and inserts us totally into what we are doing, causing us to live with a new intensity. It breathes new life into commitment and reawakens the awesome gift of fidelity, revealing a new kind of truth revealed only to those who are brave enough to stay in one place long enough.
>
> Marriage, work, our spiritual journey—all take on a new dimension. We are present, fully present to the people around us, the tasks at hand, the inspirations that used to pass unnoticed before our eyes, because before our focus was ever *there* and never *here*.[16]

Sixth Sunday of Easter

In his Rule, Benedict sees growth in love as the indicator of continuing progress in spiritual maturity. With a heart expanded by love of God (RB Prol 49), by the end of his Rule Benedict can speak of the members of the community offering to one another "the warmest love," which is both respectful and realistic about "weaknesses of both body and character" (RB 72.3-5). As Michael Casey writes:

> True monks are great lovers. This is why the monastic tradition gladly appropriated the classical theme of friendship and baptized it, seeing in spiritual friendship a primary source of encouragement, guidance and correction in personal and religious development.[17]

Above all, to remain a friend demands loyalty, as the twelfth-century Cistercian St. Aelred of Rievaulx wrote in *On Spiritual Friendship*: ". . . the most important quality of all is loyalty, which is friendship's nurse and guardian. In good or ill fortune, in joy or sorrow, in happy times or bitter, loyalty shows itself as steadfast and unchanging."[18] For Aelred, spiritual friendship has its beginning and end in the love of God and, as today's gospel proclaims, this abiding and most "loyal" love is shown to us in Jesus who lays down his life for his friends.

Seventh Sunday of Easter

Feast of the Ascension

The desire for eternal life, for our homecoming to heaven, is the focus of this feast. It is this desire, says Benedict, that should urge us to "run and accomplish now what will profit us for eternity" (RB Prol 44). The author of the *Cloud of Unknowing* tackles the "space travel" problem of this feast: "For in the realm of the spirit, heaven is as much up as it is down, behind as before. . . . The high road there, which is the shortest road there, is run in terms of desire and not of paces of feet."[19] Benedict encloses his Rule with notes of urgency, with running and hastening to the heavenly homeland (RB Prol 49; 73.8). Even for long-livers, time is short, and so there is a need to "run while you have the light" (RB Prol 13) and head purposefully to the kingdom along the track of good deeds (RB Prol 22). A strong heart, expanded by love, will enable the runner to keep going until the finishing line is crossed in death and the prize of eternal life is won (RB Prol 49-50). In his last chapter, Benedict continues to encourage his monks to hurry eagerly along the way of obedience and "with Christ's assistance carry out this modest Rule for beginners" (RB 73.8). If the grace of Christ is necessary to begin on this way of life, it is all the more necessary for finishing it. Along the way Benedict notes some of the "good deeds" to which one hurries: the rising from sleep for the Work of God (RB 22.6); the eager speed with which the guests are welcomed (RB 53.3); the response expected of the porter who, though he may be aged and slowing down physically, is to be quick with a greeting and blessing to the one who knocks or the poor man who calls out to him (RB 66.1, 3-4).

Pentecost Sunday

This feast that brings the Easter season to a close is a day of fire and wind and shaking into the ardent love of the Holy Spirit so that we may be forged into new women and men, the kind of people that Benedict describes as full of good zeal. Aquinata Böckmann describes such zeal as "a radical passion in people. It is exclusive, permeates everything, and knows no half measures. It is a dynamic reality, the direct opposite of weak, tired, timid, or hesitant movement."[20]

To be such people is always a challenge, as the Desert Fathers tell us in, for example, the conversations between Abba Joseph and Abba Lot:

Abba Joseph said to the Abba Lot, "You cannot be a monk unless you become like a consuming fire."

Abba Lot went to see Abba Joseph and said to him, "Abba, as far as I can I say my little office, I fast a little, I pray and meditate, I live in peace as far as I can, I purify my thoughts. What else can I do?" Then the old man stood up and stretched his hands towards heaven. His fingers became like ten lamps of fire and he said to him, "If you will, you can become all flame."[21]

The Most Holy Trinity

During the Liturgy of the Hours, Benedict wants his communities to be mindful of the Triune God in whose presence they pray. He details when the "Glory be . . ." should be said, accompanied by the physical gestures of bowing their bodies, or at least by inclining their heads, and sometimes by standing (RB 9.2, 6-7; 11.3; 13.9; 17.2; 18.1). Our bodies as well as our voices are involved in "respect and reverence for the Holy Trinity" (RB 9.7), because liturgical prayer is not just a matter of talking heads! The other significant occasion when the doxology is prayed is at the monastic profession. After the newly professed sings the *Suscipe* ("Receive me") three times, and the community echoes this prayer, the "Glory be . . ." is added (RB 58.22). With this praise of the Trinity, the foundation of all community, ringing in his ears, the newly professed prostrates at the feet of each member of the community, for there is the mutual responsibility of showing forth the love of God—Father, Son and Holy Spirit.

The Most Holy Body and Blood of Christ

Benedict does not elaborate on the sacramental life of his communities, and we may be surprised, or even mildly scandalized at this omission. In the chapter dealing with "The Weekly Reader," who begins his service on Sunday, reference is made to the reader asking the prayers of the community to protect him from pride in his intelligence and (probably) hard-earned gifts that were not universal in the community. He does this "After Mass and Communion" (RB 38.2), and also receives some diluted wine to help him endure the fast (RB 38.10). There is no suggestion that there was Mass or a Communion service every day, and de Vogüé comments that "at most it is possible that a conventual Mass was celebrated in St. Benedict's monastery on Sundays and feast days. But perhaps Mass was celebrated less often, even without fixed regularity."[22]

As someone who told his community to listen to what the Spirit is saying to the churches (RB Prol 11; Rev 2:7), we can be sure that Benedict would welcome the liturgical reforms and challenges in the eucharistic life of today's church.

One thing that was to be celebrated regularly was the communion of love for one another (cf. RB 72). Without this, no matter how often the Eucharist is celebrated it is only an empty ritual that dishonors the loving sacrifice of Christ for us. Paul says it strongly: ". . . all who eat and drink without discerning the body, eat and drink judgment against themselves" (1 Cor 11:29), for with our sisters and brothers we are the Body of Christ.

Second Sunday in Ordinary Time

(The First Sunday in Ordinary Time is the Baptism of the Lord, which also completes the Christmas cycle. See pp. 25–28.)

At the beginning of his Rule, Benedict tells his followers to do exactly what the aged Eli tells Samuel to do: to listen as servants of the Lord. Aquinata Böckmann comments that:

> If we want to find out an author's purpose, we usually look at the introduction and the closing of a book. The introduction will indicate the content as a whole, state the purpose and significance of the writing and invite us to read.
> It is no different for the Rule of Benedict.[23]

"*Obsculta*," "Listen," (RB Prol 1) is Benedict's first word, and his last is "*pervenies*," "you will arrive" (RB 73.9), an indication of Benedict's conviction that listening, and then acting as a servant of God as was Christ, is the way to reach our heavenly home. As we begin our journey through Ordinary Time such listening is also a call to us to be personally present and attentive to the way in which the Lord is speaking to us: to receive the word of God not only at our Sunday Eucharist, but also in our *lectio divina*, in the people we meet, and in the events of our times. Then we hope that, like Samuel, the Lord will be always with us and grant us, in turn, to speak fruitful words to our sisters and brothers.

Third Sunday in Ordinary Time

As Mark announces in today's gospel, all Christian discipleship involves some dispossession. Benedict knew that if we are to "prefer nothing to the love of Christ" (RB 4.21), "absolutely nothing" (RB 72.11), much would have to be left behind that might be good in itself. It is just a fact that to make one significant life choice excludes another, be it for marriage rather than the single life, for religious or priestly life rather than other ways of being one of Christ's faithful. Calling, leaving, and following is the dynamic of a disciple's call. If he has material possessions, Benedict says that at his profession the monk gives all these either to the poor or to the community. Symbolically, he is stripped of his own clothes and puts on the habit of the monastery (RB 58.24-26). When writing about Benedictine poverty, Augustine Roberts makes a comment that has far wider application than to the monastic when he says: "In practice this means going against the overwhelming value that society puts on wealth, money, worldly success, comforts, power, and a superficial freedom of choice. This type of society is at war with the poor Christ."[24]

Fourth Sunday in Ordinary Time

Benedict makes the refrain to today's responsorial Psalm 95 (94) a prayer for "astonished ears" (RB Prol 9) that are open to the voice of God spoken daily—and often surprisingly—in our holy reading of Scripture, in the signs of the times, and in the words and actions of our sisters and brothers: "Today, if you hear his voice, do not harden your hearts" (RB Prol 10). Psalm 95 (94) is one of the invitatory psalms of the Liturgy of the Hours (cf. RB 9.3), inviting us in the first prayer of the day to have a supple, receptive "heart"—a biblical metaphor for the deep intimate core of a person—to the call of God throughout the day. Such a refrain is a simple yet profound mantra that can help us to be attentive, always ready for and rejoicing in the "new teaching— with authority," that Jesus still speaks to us.

Fifth Sunday in Ordinary Time

In the gospel we see Jesus not sparing himself in his healing ministry, but then going in the early morning to seek in prayer the God who works in him and through him. To live a balanced life, a life of prayer and work, is a Gospel and a Benedictine ideal, and is expressed in the frequently used Latin motto of Benedictine communities: "Ora et labora." Benedict has no time for pseudo-contemplatives who are so busy finding God in esoteric "experiences" that they miss God in the everyday; nor does he want worka- holics in the monastery! For our consolation, Benedict says that "everything should be arranged in moderation because of the fainthearted" (RB 48.9) when he speaks about work, and chapter 48 is a wonderful statement of the integration of work and prayer (*lectio*). For those who are nourished by the word of God, there is no place for fasting, bingeing, or fastidious nibbling in personal and communal prayer.

Sixth Sunday in Ordinary Time

Only once does Benedict use the word *humanitas* (kindness), and that is in the context of the welcome of the guest who is to be shown "every sort of kindness" (RB 53.9); but a humane spirit that respects the grandeur and the fragility of our humanity permeates the Rule. Just as Jesus reached out with compassion to the leper, one treated most unkindly in the socioreligious culture of his time, so Benedict calls his communities to reach out to those who need kindness and compassion in a negligent society. Within the community, the sick "are to be cared for before and above all else, for it is really Christ who is served in them" (RB 36.1), and it is not hard to imagine that there would also have been many sick among the poor who came to the monastery. Schooled in this kindness, the porter was to greet them as a blessing (RB 66.3-4).

Paul encouraged his Corinthians to do all for the glory of God, even the necessary and mundane actions of eating and drinking, and to look down the index of the chapters of Benedict's Rule and see the range of his concerns is to realize that he had a similar vision. Even the most insignificant aspect of a monk's life has great significance when lived for the glory of God.

Seventh Sunday in Ordinary Time

We do not have to carry our paralyzed friends up onto the roof and let them down into the presence of Jesus the healer, but there is another kind of "carrying" that Benedict expects of his monks when he writes that "they should bear each other's weaknesses of both body and character with the utmost patience" (RB 72.5). Not to do this in a community, or a family, can so easily contribute to the spiritual "paralysis" of a neglected or alienated individual and so infect the health of the whole group. The abbot, especially, is to have concern for those who are physically sick or weak in the moral sense (RB 28.5), but Benedict recognizes that everyone has his or her own weaknesses or idiosyncrasies, and each one depends on the other for patient acceptance and mutual understanding. To read slowly and reflectively "What are the Tools of Good Works?" (RB 4) should leave us in no doubt about such weaknesses. To support one another, to walk the way of the Gospel together, is a sign of warm love that is the good zeal of RB 72. It is a necessary way of saying our committed "Yes" to God in Christ that both Paul and Benedict expected of a disciple.

Eighth Sunday in Ordinary Time

For Paul, his committed Corinthians were his letters of recommendation of the success of his ministry. For fifteen hundred years, many men and women have sought to follow Christ by drawing wisdom from Benedict and his Rule, and how they do this surely makes them "letters of recommendation" for this way of life—or, sadly, when unfaithful, makes them an unacceptable reference, and a "source of embarrassment and shame" (RB 73.7). The "recommendation" of Benedict is today being eagerly seized by many lay men and women who are drawn to experience monastic life for a short day or a longer time. As Paul Wilkes writes of his time with the Cistercian community of Mepkin:

> Seeds blown to the winds are falling on fertile ground. Lines are blurring between the sacred and the secular to a degree that would make both Rahner and Merton—even Benedict and Bernard—smile. Lay people are entering the monastic world and carrying their experiences there into the outside world . . . During my Mepkin days it was not that I had discovered something so hidden or so new. Nor had I undergone some dramatic conversion. I would have welcomed either, or both; but neither occurred. Instead, what I had found beneath the brambles of my life was a simple path, monastic wisdom for everyday life.[25]

Not a bad "letter of reference."

Ninth Sunday in Ordinary Time

Benedict pays special attention to the Sunday celebration of the Liturgy of the Hours (*Opus Dei*). This was to be a day, a "first," on which in the midst of the everyday, his community was to remember that their lives are inserted into the life of the risen and Sunday One who transfigures our ordinary existence with extraordinary possibilities. No one, even in the monastery, would now follow Benedict's prescriptions exactly as in RB 11 and 12, but the longer and more solemn details indicate his underlying intention: that Sunday is to be kept as a special day of celebration and thanksgiving in which we try to find ways of being conscious of "the face of God shining upon us" (Ps 66/67:1; RB 12.1). How can we return that contemplative gaze, aware of the mutual presence of God and all creation to one another as "very good"?

Tenth Sunday in Ordinary Time

Like Paul, Benedict always has his vision fixed on the dwelling prepared for us in heaven. This is the "tent" that awaits us when our earthly life, our tent of flesh, has been folded up in death. But to find a place in which to pitch our tent in heaven demands that we live justly, truthfully, practically for the Lord on earth (RB Prol 22-27). Patiently but eagerly, our nomadic life will become a joyful running toward sharing in the kingdom where we will tent forever with God (RB Prol 39-44; 50).

Eleventh Sunday in Ordinary Time

The image of a large shrub that grows from a small seed can be a wonderful image of a religious community. John Bede Polding, o.s.b., was originally a monk of Downside Abbey in the south of England, and came to Australia as the vicar apostolic of New Holland in 1835. In 1842 he became the first archbishop of Sydney—but with the whole of Australia as his "diocese," an area equal to that of the United States minus Alaska! In 1857 he founded the first religious women's congregation to begin in Australia, the Sisters of the Good Samaritan of the Order of St. Benedict, and twenty-three years later he wrote of its growth in terms that could be applied to many religious communities:

> This little plant has become a noble tree, and it has so grown, not by human effort and contrivance, but under the unmarked breathing of God's grace— and thus as ever there is no room for us to boast, but a loud, loud, call for thankfulness, and such future co-operation by gift and prayer as we shall have the grace to offer. "*Magnificat Dominus facere nobiscum facti sumus laetantes.*" "The Lord hath done great things for us: we are become very joyful."[26]

As all true sons and daughters of Benedict know, we need to "pray the Lord to command the help of his grace to aid us in that which we cannot accomplish by nature" (RB Prol 41).

Twelfth Sunday in Ordinary Time

For the disciples, the gospel crossing on the Sea of Galilee became an early experience of transformation from fear to faith. Benedict wanted his monks to be overwhelmed by the waves of the love of Christ (RB 4.21; 72.11) that would help them make this same spiritual crossing. At the end of his chapter "On Humility" he writes that because of humble love of God in Christ that drives out fear, the monk "can now begin to accomplish effortlessly, as if spontaneously, everything that he previously did out of fear" (RB 7.68-69).

Storm-tossed, "turbulent" or excitable individuals can make others in a community or family driven and disturbed. Benedict is explicit about this when describing as necessarily "nonturbulent" the abbot and the cellarer, two significant leaders in the community who were responsible in different ways for the peace and good order of the monastery (RB 31.1; 64.16). "Turbulence" is catching and can scuttle the community!

Thirteenth Sunday in Ordinary Time

Christopher Jamison, abbot of Worth Abbey, comments that death is inherently frightening, and that the contemporary marginalization of death adds to our fear of it.[27] In contrast to this attitude, Benedict wants the monastery to be a place where monks should keep an eye on death every day, not for any morbid reason, but because of a yearning for eternal life (RB 4.46-47). Mindfulness of our mortality gives a sense of urgency to "run while you have the light of life, that the darkness not overtake you" (RB Prol 13; John 12:35).

Thomas Merton saw death as the last free and perfect act of love by which we surrender ourselves into the hands of God, the final seal that our freedom sets upon our efforts to live for God in love and trust. Death is, he says:

> . . . a critical point of growth, or transition to a new mode of being, to *maturity* and fruitfulness that I do not know (they are in Christ and His Kingdom). The child in the womb does not know what will come after birth. He must be born in order to live. I am here to learn how to face death as my birth.[28]

At Monte Cassino is a sculpture of *Dying Benedict*. Benedict is standing, but is so weak that he can no longer lift his arms in prayerful praise of God, and so on either side one of his brother monks supports his arms. Dying and living both need the help of our sisters and brothers.

Fourteenth Sunday in Ordinary Time

Just as the Nazareth people were critical of Jesus because he seemed to be too "ordinary" for them to believe in, so Benedictine monastic life may seem "scandalously ordinary," insofar as it is usually undramatic, and anyone looking for great external excitement and status should look elsewhere. The great adventure is one of faith, of setting out to follow Christ, clothed "with the Gospel as our guide" on the way to the kingdom (RB Prol 21). Yet this is a journey where reason and justice are to accompany any strictness (RB Prol 46-48). In concerns as different as, for example, the measured actions of the abbot who tempers his response to suit the weak and the strong (RB 64.19), the sufficient food provided (RB 39.3), the restraint in communication with guests in the time of the great silence after Compline (RB 42.11), the measured evenhandedness in disciplining young people (RB 70.4-5), there is "ordinary" wisdom to be recognized in faith. It is this spiritual accessibility that seems to be one of the great contemporary attractions for many of Christ's faithful, married or single, who are seeking nourishment for their faith by some contacts with Benedictine communities and spirituality.

Fifteenth Sunday in Ordinary Time

On their first mission the disciples are to be content with the hospitality they are offered, only moving on if their presence seems counterproductive to their ministry of the word. There are certain discontented kinds of monks, too, that Benedict describes as "gyrovagues" (RB 1.10-12). These are the ones who spend most of their time gyrating from place to place, shopping around for better accommodation or a more congenial community companionship. They end up, says Benedict, as "wretched," aimless drifters who abuse both the hospitality offered to them and their own Gospel commitment. He is not condemning travel for legitimate reasons of community business, and those who are sent on a journey are commended to the prayers and support of the community, with appropriate rituals for their departure and return (RB 67). In this context, travel that is necessary today for study, lecturing, or other business is certainly not "gyrovaging"—and should not be criticized as such—but even in this regard, it is not unreasonable to expect that Benedict would want balance and moderation.

Sixteenth Sunday in Ordinary Time

Benedict's abbot is imaged as the shepherd to whom the "flock" of the community is entrusted, but not in a proprietary way, as he must always be answerable to God, the true Shepherd of the sheep (RB 2.7). Just as Jeremiah voiced God's displeasure and distress because of the failure of the religious and civil leaders of Israel, so also Benedict warns the abbot that he will bear the blame for the community that is failing in its commitment because of his poor pastoral care. If, on the other hand, members of the community are willfully uncooperative, the responsibility will not be attributed to him (RB 2.8-10). In his shepherding the abbot must be aware of the individual differences and needs of the members of the community so that his ministry is not only one of maintenance but also of joyful growth (RB 2.31-32). While caring for others, he must never forget to scrutinize his own behavior and be answerable to the Shepherd of all our souls for his own actions and his own spiritual health or sickness (RB 2.37-40). There is much wisdom here in Benedict's experience and expectations that has relevance beyond the monastery, especially for people in positions of middle management and social and ecclesial leadership.

Seventeenth Sunday in Ordinary Time

In the Rule of Benedict there are many echoes of the reading from the Letter to the Ephesians that we hear today. Throughout his Rule, Benedict speaks of all kinds of people that made up his sixth-century communities: free men and former slaves (RB 2.18), old and young (RB 37), craftsmen (RB 57) and laborers (RB 48.8), literate and illiterate (RB 58.20), the restless and the obedient, the negligent and the committed (RB 2.25), and all the "in between" vagaries of human personalities. All these are to love one another "with ardent zeal," "vie with each other in mutual respect," "bear one another's burdens of both body and character with the utmost patience," and practice mutual obedience toward one another (RB 72.3-6). Whether in the Christian communities of first-century Ephesus, the Benedictine communities of sixth-century Italy, or twenty-first-century religious communities, the same range of personalities and the same challenges to loving unity exist, with the same challenge to witness the possibility of such love.

Eighteenth Sunday in Ordinary Time

Benedict detested grumbling, well aware of its pervasive and destructive effect on community life. It may be manifest in the everyday routines of kitchen service, in dissatisfaction with the amount of wine served, or the quality of the goods distributed (RB 34.6; 35.13; 40.8). In RB 4, "What Are the Tools of Good Works?" there is an interesting sequence of three verses (RB 4.38-40) in which loafing, grumbling, and running down the reputation of others seem to be related in some kind of cause and effect. Grumbling can even be a link in the chain of persistent negativity that drags a monk toward excommunication (RB 23.1). We surely find it easy to realize, in any way of life, the truth that "God loves a cheerful giver" (RB 5.16; 2 Cor 9:7), and that God found it as taxing to put up with the Exodus generation as Benedict and ourselves do with contemporary grumblers!

Nineteenth Sunday in Ordinary Time

Once again the importance of community relationships is emphasized in the reading from the Letter to the Ephesians. Both its author and Benedict are very aware of the destructive power and the healing potential of speech in our relationships. Truth in both our hearts and mouths is a significant "tool" with which to shape loving community life (RB 4.28). Out of the heart the tongue can speak to offer an insincere greeting of peace (RB 4.25) or a blessing, even to those who hurt us (RB 4.32); we can bluster (RB 7.56-58) or we can be patient (RB 7.42). Speech that is perverse, conversations that are long-winded, mindless babbling that is psychically exhausting, and banter and jokes that are hurtful, are all condemned by Benedict (RB 4.51-54; 6.1, 8). This does not mean that he wanted his communities to be places of dour gloom

in which frosty silence chills the warmth of love, but rather that it is the kind
and friendly word that "is better than the best gift" (RB 31.14; Sir 18:17).

Twentieth Sunday in Ordinary Time

The Rule of Benedict has often been described as Wisdom literature. In
that tradition, as in the biblical books of Wisdom, spirituality is grounded
in the encounter between God and humanity in the experiences of ordinary
human life, in the harmony to be desired between the individual and the
community, in the wonder of the cosmos. At the center of biblical Wisdom
literature stands the beautiful image of the Wisdom Woman or Sophia who,
as in this Sunday's first reading, sets the table with life-giving nourishment
and invites those who are willing, who know they are not self-sufficient, to
enter and partake of the feast of God's abundant gifts of wisdom.

Benedict saw his monastery as "a school" (RB Prol 45), but lest this image
conjures up harsh memories he hastens to add "for the Lord's service," a
foundation in which there will be "nothing harsh, nothing burdensome" (RB
Prol 46) unless there is sometimes a reasonable need for a little strictness in
order to preserve love in the community (RB Prol 47). The monastery, therefore, is to be a place of learning in this spirit of love, an acquiring of wisdom
that will never be completed until death. Benedict quotes more from the
biblical Wisdom books of the Psalms, Proverbs, and Sirach (Ecclesiasticus)
than from any other Old Testament books, and for significant members of
the community wisdom is a gift of God that is necessary for their service.
"Merit of life and wisdom of teaching" (RB 64.2) create the desired balance
for which a community should look when electing an abbot, even if he is
last to have entered the monastery. The care of guests and the guesthouse
require wise monks (RB 53.22), and the person of important initial contact
with the monastery, the porter, needs to be "a wise old monk," experienced
and discerning in dealing with the variety of people who present themselves
(RB 66.1). Likewise, the cellarer is to be chosen for his wisdom and maturity
in dealing with the delicate matters of material goods—and needs as opposed
to wants (RB 31.1). Given the feminine image of Wisdom, women may find
it delightful that it is she who is present in and presiding over these aspects
of community life and, indeed, Benedict's wise formulation of his Rule.

Twenty-first Sunday in Ordinary Time

Even though the reading from the Letter to the Ephesians is mainly concerned with relationships between husbands and wives, the first verse has

relevance to all lifestyles. Benedict's call to mutual obedience (RB 71) echoes Paul's concern expressed here: that all the Ephesians should be "subject to one another out of reverence for Christ." Benedict names such obedience, such attentive listening to one another, as "a blessing" (RB 71.1), a sharing in the love of Christ that shows no partiality (cf. RB 2.22). Ever the realist, Benedict acknowledges that there can be aggressive and querulous behavior in a community, and the delicate art of fraternal correction is a necessary companion of mutual obedience. Although the external way of practicing this today would not be as Benedict describes it, the internal spirit is still necessary, and the "how to" an ongoing challenge in most communities. It is the younger members of the community to whom most attention is paid in RB 71, but this needs to be balanced by the mutuality of respect and obedience of RB 63.10-12 and 70.6-7. Obstinate and irreconcilable violation of mutual obedience indicates a hostility that may indicate unsuitability for the community life of monastics.

Twenty-second Sunday in Ordinary Time

For Benedict as a disciple of Jesus, the "heart" is what matters in a person, because this is the deepest, essential core of our loving and thinking, and so the source of all our external behavior. Especially at the beginning of his Rule, Benedict stresses that relationships with God, listening, willing obedience, truthfulness, the energy and strength with which one runs toward the kingdom, are matters of the heart (RB Prol 1, 10, 26, 28, 40). "The unspeakable sweetness of love" (RB Prol 49) expands the heart and enables the monk to maturely accept difficult things so that they become easier (RB 50) as we journey toward eternal life. As Kallistos Ware writes: "We are on a journey through the inward spaces of the heart, a journey not measured by the hours of our watch or the days of the calendar, for it is a journey out of time into eternity."[29] It is a journey to be made with such humility of heart that gradually this internal disposition manifests itself externally also, in the whole personal presence of the monk (RB 7.51, 62, 65) to his God and other people.

Just as Jesus enumerates the evil that can come from the heart, so Benedict recognizes that the shriveled heart bears the undesirable fruits of contentious self-centeredness and defiance of authority (RB 3.8-9), and grumbling and grudging obedience (RB 5.17–19).

Twenty-third Sunday in Ordinary Time

To have open, unplugged ears enables us to hear physically; the open "ear of your heart" allows us to listen to the call of God in the depths of our being (RB Prol 1). It is under the obedience of listening that Benedict places his whole Rule and the relationships of his followers with God (RB Prol 9, 16-20), with one another's counsel (RB 3), with the Spirit who moves in the churches (RB Prol 11; Rev 2:7), and with the reading of the Scriptures (RB 4.55). Given the cacophony of contemporary life with its transistors, Walkmans, iPods, mobile phones, and ubiquitous "white noise" background bombarding our physical hearing externally, it can be difficult to listen to any internal voices. Perhaps we may be afraid of what we might hear in our hearts—about God, our sisters and brothers, or ourselves. People who come to a monastery often find the environment of silence the most difficult challenge. In 2005, the Worth Abbey community and five very modern young men accepted the mutual challenge of living together for forty days and having a documentary entitled "The Monastery" filmed by the BBC for its TV audiences. About this experience, the first comment that Abbot Christopher Jamison makes is:

> Yet the five men were not only accepted; they were also challenged. They were asked to listen continuously and deeply to themselves, to other people and to God. Forty days later, this profound listening had reshaped their hearts and minds as it has reshaped the hearts and minds of many generations of monks and nuns. These men left 'The Monastery' more in touch with life than when they had arrived.[30]

All Christ's faithful are challenged to find the way of listening appropriate for their own way of life.

Twenty-fourth Sunday in Ordinary Time

One of the tools of good works that Benedict hands us is honed by the sharp words of Jesus in today's gospel: "Deny yourself in order to follow Christ" (RB 4.10). Renunciation is necessary if the persevering and peaceful seeking of God is not to be blunted by preference for the easier way of self-gratification. Packed next to the tool of self-denial are those against with which the monk is to work: overindulgence in and excessive seeking of physical pleasure, with fasting specially mentioned, probably in the tradition of sharpening one's hunger for God (RB 4.11-13). But as the spiritual monastic "toolbox" must also be well equipped with loving service of others, the next tools that Benedict mentions in this section of chapter 4 are the outreach of the monks to the poor, the sick, the dead, the naked, the sorrowful, and all who are in any kind of trouble. Throughout this chapter, asceticism and practical charity are packed closely together (RB 4.10-19).

Jesus died because of the way he lived, in selfless and loving service of humanity. Those who take the Gospel as their guide (RB Prol 21), who want to be a follower of Jesus, are called to put the love of Christ before all else (RB 4.21) as *absolutely* their first preference (RB 72.11). They have no other option.

Twenty-fifth Sunday in Ordinary Time

The leadership that Benedict expected in his communities was to be that of an authority of service by which the abbot recognizes "that his goal must be for the profit of the monks, not preeminence for himself" (RB 64.8 *RB 1980* trans.). The latter is always an occupational hazard for those in authority, be it Jesus' first disciples or contemporary ecclesial leaders. This was recognized by Benedict especially in regard to his priors, about whose role and necessity he has serious reservations, as seen by the defensive and hesitant tone of RB 65. It seems reasonable to conjecture that Benedict had personal experience of power struggles that had made him wary of this position of leadership, although other theories about the reason for the different tone of this chapter have been advanced.[31]

Just as Jesus embraced the child, the symbol of all "little ones" whom the disciples were to serve, so Benedict names and makes central to the concern of his monastery those who have no special status. Even though "human nature itself is indulgent" to the aged and to children (perhaps debatable in some contemporary societies), Benedict wants to add to this compassionate inclination the authority of the Rule (RB 37). Likewise the guests, especially those who are poor or strangers, are to be welcomed as Christ (RB 53.1, 15) and recognized as a blessing to the monastery (RB 66.3). The sick (RB 36.1-3) and the needy are to be embraced with special kindness and hospitality (RB 4.14-19).

Twenty-sixth Sunday in Ordinary Time

James is fierce in his condemnation of the rich who abuse the poor; Benedict also uses strong language when he speaks about the "vice" of private ownership that "must be torn up by the roots" (RB 33.1). A particular expression of Benedictine life is the communion of goods. Possessiveness that discourages this is to be condemned, but appropriate tools, clothing, and goods are to be provided for the members of the community, with mutual respect for their individual differences and needs (RB 32; 34). The cellarer is to handle the material possessions of the monastery "as if they were the holy bowls of the altar," and be a model of waste prevention (RB 31.10-11).

Benedict senses what is becoming more and more obvious on our planet earth: that the willingness to exploit or abuse physical resources is often an indicator of a similar and unfortunate attitude toward other human beings. For this reason, the responsible and pastoral role of the cellarer is to be exercised by a monk who shares many personal qualities with the abbot with whom he is to be a close and trusted collaborator. Wastefulness and extravagance, a temptation when dealing with material resources both in and beyond the monastery, is condemned (RB 31.12).

Whenever the work of the monastery's artisans are sold, the evil of avarice must also be avoided, so the price asked should be less than that set by people outside the monastery. "And in all things God may be glorified," adds Benedict (RB 57.7-9; 1 Pet 4:11).

Monastic history witnesses to the sad truth that some of its darkest and most disintegrating moments came from disregard of these aspects of the Rule, with monastics acting much like the rich people whom James condemns in his Letter.

Twenty-seventh Sunday in Ordinary Time

Benedict saw patience as a most significant way of participating in the sufferings of Christ. Just as the author of the Letter to the Hebrews speaks of Christ as crowned with glory because of his suffering unto death, Benedict ends his Prologue with the great encouragement that "we will participate in the passion (suffering) of Christ through patience so as to deserve to be companions in his kingdom" (RB Prol 50) as his brothers and sisters. Benedict asks for patience that is not dramatic or stoical, but practical and persevering. It suffers the wrongs that others do to us (RB 4.30), a tool of good works that is packed demandingly among those concerned with love of enemies, tools sharpened painfully by blessings rather than curses, and the bearing of persecutions for the sake of healing relationships (cf. RB 4.29-33). The suffering caused by difficult obedience is to be embraced patiently (RB 7.35, 42). The community is to show patience with what can sometimes be the querulous demands of the sick, and the sick, on their part, are not to make excessive demands on those who care for them (RB 36.4-5). Patience and perseverance are a test of the spirit of the one who comes seeking entry into the community (RB 58.3), and during initial formation in the novitiate (RB 58.11) continue to be an important aspect of the community's discernment in the context of the candidate's readiness to share the sufferings of Christ, not some artificially concocted tests. All this leads to and forms a community worthy of Benedict's superlative expression of "the utmost patience" with which the members bear with one another's "weaknesses of both body and character" out of the warmth of zealous love (RB 72.5).

Twenty-eighth Sunday in Ordinary Time

Benedict was convinced that the biblical word is so "alive and active," as the Letter to the Hebrews proclaims, that it is the great animating presence in the prayer life of his communities. What we now call the Liturgy of the Hours (Benedict's Work of God or *Opus Dei*) and *lectio divina* weave the biblical word throughout the monastic day. Benedict devotes twelve chapters to the recitation of the Liturgy of the Hours (RB 8–19). In the cosmos and in our own bodies there are the rhythms of the seasons, of night and day, sleeping and waking, birthing and dying. So seven times a day Benedict called his community to the recitation of the psalms, to the singing of biblical canticles, and listening to holy reading in this public prayer of the church. His delightful humanity is shown in his concern for adequate time for sleep, digestion, and provision for toileting mixed in with his first chapter on the celebration of the Work of God in RB 8! And near the end of his detailed writing about what psalms are to be said and when, he humbly concedes that he may not have the perfect arrangement. He wants to make it clear that "if this distribution of the psalms displeases anyone, they should arrange them as they see fit" (RB 18.22)—but without omitting any of the 150 psalms. Following the liturgical reforms of Vatican II, many monasteries have developed different schemas of psalmody.

The frequent mention of *lectio divina* in RB 48 has already been remarked. It is not reading for information but for formation and transformation by the word of God that always has priority in *lectio* as "a completely reliable guide for *human* life" (RB 73.3; italics mine). The biblical word prayed and sown throughout the Rule should become so ingrained in the heart that it pulses, alive and active, throughout the monk's whole day.

Twenty-ninth Sunday in Ordinary Time

For Benedict, those who hold authority in the community are to exercise it in a spirit of service of others, and with humility. Unlike James and John and their illusions of grandeur and self-confidence, the abbot "should realize that he must profit others rather than precede them" (RB 64.8), and distrust his own frailty (RB 64.13). The physically weak (RB 36.6) and the spiritually fragile (RB 64.12) are to be the special concern of the abbot, and nowhere in the Rule is this more compassionately described than in the extraordinary chapter on

"The Abbot's Preoccupation with the Excommunicated" (RB 27). The abbot is to serve the failing monks like Christ, the healing physician, and like the Good Shepherd who carries the lost sheep back to the fold of the community. Because the excommunicated monk is out of sight of the community, at least temporarily, and particularly at the table and in the oratory, the abbot must also ensure that he is kept in the mind of the community who are to pray earnestly for him. When the cellarer is dealing with material things and concerns, these are an aspect of his spiritual service, to be handled as reverently as the vessels of the altar and, even more important, is his "handling" of the people who come to him for their needs. To them he is to relate humbly and gently (RB 31.13-16).

Thirtieth Sunday in Ordinary Time

Even though not speaking about prayer in the dusty roadside, Benedict would approve of the blind Bartimaeus's prayer: short, urgent, reverent, and humble, laying petitions before the Lord God of the universe who calls us, like the poor beggars that we all are (cf. RB 20). In faith, Bartimaeus leapt up at the call of Jesus, came to him, was healed, and followed Jesus along his way. It is with such faith that Benedict expects the same energetic following, the continuing "race along the way of God's commandments," whose finishing line is only crossed in death (RB Prol 49-50).

Thirty-first Sunday in Ordinary Time

Benedict quotes the love commandment that we hear in today's gospel at the beginning of his chapter on "What are the Tools of Good Works?" (RB 4.1-2) for this Word of God is to guide and govern the whole chapter. There is very little that is specifically monastic about this chapter except the last verse, and it may be based on catechetical instructions such as those contained in the second-century *Didache*. This association underlined the fact that baptism is the foundation of the monastic life, and it is an ecclesial life of listening to what the Spirit is saying to the churches (RB Prol 11; Rev 2:7). It could also suggest the need for basic catechetical instruction for many of those entering the monastery in Benedict's day and, as present-day religious life formators would agree, this need is still very real for many candidates who may indeed be professionally and intellectually able, but theologically "illiterate" to varying degrees. That God seeks and calls unexpected men and women in a multitude of unexpected places, and that they respond with their "I do," is a continuing cause of holy wonder and hope. Initial and ongoing formation is to be a work of love of God and neighbor, a faithful and hard work, until we receive the reward that God has promised (RB 4.75-78) when the toolbox is closed by death.

Thirty-second Sunday in Ordinary Time

In *Wisdom Distilled from the Daily: Living the Rule of Benedict Today*, Joan Chittister writes that:

> We can practice the power of the powerless to show us all how little it really takes to love, how rich life is without riches, how strong are those who cannot be owned, how clear is the gospel about the rights of the poor. We can be the voice of those who are not heard and the hand of those who have no bread and the families of those who are alone and the strength of those who are weak. We can be the sign of human community.[32]

We can be, Benedict would agree (RB 4.14-19), but are we? Early in the Rule, Benedict reminds us that if we want to draw near to God we must act justly in our relationships, not selfishly or untruthfully (RB Prol 24-26). In contemporary and affluent societies, justice will often make economic demands for the sharing or redistribution of something of our livelihood although not, like the poor widow, all we have to live on. The abbot's authority and teaching are to permeate the community "like the leaven of divine justice" to transform what, without this influence, would be flat and distasteful (RB 2.5). It is not easy to be just; not only a matter of listening, but also a way of acting that may bring its own persecution (RB 4.33; Matt 5:10), the bearing of which Terrence Kardong describes as "nonviolent resistance."[33]

Thirty-third Sunday in Ordinary Time

As we come near to the end of this liturgical year, a verse from today's responsorial psalm (Ps 16:10) that Benedict uses in the twentieth verse of his Prologue offers us encouragement to continue to answer God's call. Benedict reminds us that it is God's steadfast love for us to which we should respond with committed love because: "Look, the Lord in his devotion shows us the way to life." That way has the Gospel as our guide (RB Prol 21).

Thirty-fourth Sunday in Ordinary Time
The Solemnity of Our Lord Jesus Christ, Universal King

To "take up the powerful and shining weapons of obedience to fight for the Lord Christ, the true King" (RB Prol 3) is the urgent call at the beginning of Benedict's Rule and repeated in RB Prol 40. We do not find militaristic or royal terminology or symbolism much to our taste today, and so we may need to remember the emphasis on the inner warfare so explicit in a text such as Ephesus 6:10-17 and familiar in the baptismal catechesis of the early church, with monastic life recognized as a particular expression of baptism. Holzherr uses the secondary meaning of "to fight," namely, "to serve," commenting that the war to be waged is on the inner front, against the enemy that is in our own hearts, especially self-will and self-centeredness.[34] The reigning presence of God over all creation is fully established in Christ the King, but for the members of Christ's Body, guided by the Gospel, acting in love, and speaking out for truth and justice (RB Prol 23-27), there is the lifetime challenge to serve not a "cozy" Christ, but the cosmic Christ whom this solemnity celebrates. And our service continues until the day when, hopefully, we "deserve to be companions in his kingdom. Amen" (RB Prol 50).

Notes

1. Unless otherwise indicated, quotations from the Rule of Benedict (RB) are from Terrence G. Kardong, o.s.b., *Benedict's Rule: A Translation and Commentary* (Collegeville, MN: Liturgical Press, 1996). Occasionally the reference is to Timothy Fry, o.s.b., ed., *RB 1980: The Rule of St. Benedict in English* (Collegeville, MN: Liturgical Press, 1982). References to the Rule are abbreviated RB or RB Prol for the Prologue.

2. Columba Stewart, o.s.b., *Prayer and Community: The Benedictine Tradition* (London: Darton, Longman and Todd Ltd., 1998) 80.

3. See, for example, Mayeul de Dreuille, *The Rule of St. Benedict and the Ascetic Traditions from Asia to the West*, trans. from the French with the collaboration of Mark Hargreaves, o.s.b. (Leominster, Herefordshire: Gracewing, 2000).

4. Kardong, *Benedict's Rule*, 401.

5. Michael Casey o.c.s.o., *Fully Human, Fully Divine: An Interactive Christology* (Mulgrave, Victoria: John Garratt Publishing, 2004) 34.

6. Laura Swan, *Engaging Benedict: What the Rule Can Teach Us Today*, Christian Classics (Notre Dame, IN: Ave Maria Press, 2005) 110.

7. Gregory the Great, *The Life of Saint Benedict*, commentary by Adalbert de Vogüé, trans. Hilary Costello and Eoin de Bhaldraithe (Petersham, MA: St. Bede's Publications, 1993) 126.

8. Thomas Merton, *New Seeds of Contemplation* (London: Burns & Oates, 1961) 105.

9. Thomas Merton, *Faith and Violence* (Notre Dame, IN: University of Notre Dame, 1968) 213.

10. Aquinata Böckmann, o.s.b., *Perspectives on the Rule of St. Benedict: Expanding Our Hearts in Christ*, trans. Matilda Handl, o.s.b., and Marianne Burkhard, o.s.b. (Collegeville, MN: Liturgical Press, 2005) 103.

11. Gregory the Great, *The Life of Benedict*, 10–11.

12. Adalbert de Vogüé, *Reading Saint Benedict: Reflections on the Rule*, Cistercian Studies Series 151 (Kalamazoo, MI: Cistercian Publications, 1994) 186.

13. Esther de Waal, *A Life-Giving Way: A Commentary on the Rule of St. Benedict* (London: Geoffrey Chapman, 1995) 111.

14. Kardong, *Benedict's Rule*, 187.

15. *The Sayings of the Desert Fathers: The Alphabetical Collection*, trans. Benedicta Ward, s.l.g., Cistercian Studies Series 59 (Kalamazoo, MI: Cistercian Publications Inc., 1984) 42.

16. Paul Wilkes, *Beyond the Walls: Monastic Wisdom for Everyday Life* (New York: Doubleday, 1999) 72.

17. Michael Casey o.c.s.o., *An Unexciting Life: Reflections on Benedictine Spirituality* (Petersham, MA: St. Bede's Publications, 2005) 109.

18. In *The Cistercian World: Monastic Writings of the Twelfth Century*, trans. and edited by Pauline Matarasso (London: Penguin Books, 1993) 183.

19. Anonymous, *The Cloud of Unknowing and the Book of Privy Counselling* (New York: Doubleday, 1973) 113.

20. Böckmann, *Perspectives on the Rule of St. Benedict*, 55.

21. *The Sayings of the Desert Fathers*, 103.

22. Adalbert de Vogüé, "Problems of the Conventual Mass," *Downside Review* 87 (1969) 328.

23. Böckmann, *Perspectives on the Rule of St. Benedict*, 13.

24. Augustine Roberts, o.c.s.o., *Centered on Christ: A Guide to Monastic Profession*, Monastic Wisdom Series, Number 5 (Kalamazoo, MI: Cistercian Publications Inc., 2005) 145.

25. Wilkes, *Beyond the Walls*, 231–232.

26. Gregory Haines and others, eds., *The Eye of Faith: The Pastoral Letters of John Bede Polding* (Kilmore, Victoria: Lowden Publishing Co., 1978) 335.

27. Christopher Jamison, *Finding Sanctuary: Monastic Steps for Everyday Life* (London: Wiedenfeld & Nicholson, 2006) 158.

28. Quoted in William A. Shannon and others, eds., *The Thomas Merton Encyclopedia* (Maryknoll, NY: Orbis Books, 2002) 107.

29. Kallistos Ware, *The Orthodox Way* (Crestwood, NY: St. Vladimir's Seminary Press, 1986) 7.

30. Jamison, *Finding Sanctuary*, 1.

31. See Kardong, *Benedict's Rule*, 553–555.

32. Joan Chittister, o.s.b., *Wisdom Distilled from the Daily: Living the Rule of St. Benedict Today* (San Francisco: Harper & Row, 1990) 200–201.

33. Kardong, *Benedict's Rule*, 87.

34. George Holzherr, *The Rule of Benedict: A Guide to Christian Living*, trans. Monks of Glenstal Abbey (Dublin: Four Courts Press, 1994) 21, 28.

Scripture Index

61:1-2a, 10-11	Advent 3	4:26-34	Ordinary 11
63:16b-17, 19b;	Advent 1	4:35-41	Ordinary 12
64:2-7		5:21-43	Ordinary 13
		6:1-6	Ordinary 14
Jeremiah		6:7-13	Ordinary 15
23:1-6	Ordinary 16	6:30-34	Ordinary 16
31:7-9	Ordinary 30	7:1-8, 14-15, 21-23	Ordinary 22
31:31-34	Lent 5	7:31-37	Ordinary 23
		8:27-35	Ordinary 24
Baruch		9:2-10	Lent 2
3:9-15, 32–4:4	Easter Vigil	9:30-37	Ordinary 25
		9:38-43, 45, 47-48	Ordinary 26
Ezekiel		10:2-16	Ordinary 27
2:2-5	Ordinary 14	10:17-30	Ordinary 28
17:22-24	Ordinary 11	10:35-45	Ordinary 29
36:16-28	Easter Vigil	10:46-52	Ordinary 30
		11:1-10	Passion Sunday—
Daniel			Procession with
7:13-14	Ordinary 34—		Palms
	Christ the King	12:28b-34	Ordinary 31
12:1-3	Ordinary 33	12:38-44	Ordinary 32
		13:24-32	Ordinary 33
Hosea		13:33-37	Advent 1
2:16b, 17b, 21-22	Ordinary 8	14:1–15:47	Passion Sunday
			in Palms
Amos		14:12-16, 22-26	Most Holy Body
7:12-15	Ordinary 15		and Blood
		16:1-7	Easter Vigil
Jonah		16:15-20	Easter 7/
3:1-5, 10	Ordinary 3		Ascension
Matthew		**Luke**	
2:1-12	Epiphany	1:26-38	Advent 4
28:16-20	Most Holy Trinity	1:46-50, 53-54	Advent 3
		2:16-21	Solemnity of
Mark			the BVM—Jan 1
1:7-11	Baptism of	2:22-40	Holy Family
	the Lord	24:35-48	Easter 3
1:1-8	Advent 2		
1:12-15	Lent 1	**John**	
1:14-20	Ordinary 3	1:1-18	Christmas—
1:21-28	Ordinary 4		Day Mass
1:29-39	Ordinary 5	1:6-8, 19-28	Advent 3
1:40-45	Ordinary 6	1:35-42	Ordinary 2
2:1-12	Ordinary 7	2:13-25	Lent 3
2:18-22	Ordinary 8	3:14-21	Lent 4
2:23-28	Ordinary 9	6:1-15	Ordinary 17
3:20-35	Ordinary 10		

3:16–4:3	Ordinary 25	3:1-2	Easter 4
5:1-6	Ordinary 26	3:18-24	Easter 5
		4:7-10	Easter 6
1 Peter		5:1-6	Easter 2
3:18-22	Lent 1	5:1-9	Baptism of
			the Lord
2 Peter			
3:8-14	Advent 2	**Revelation (Apocalypse)**	
1 John		1:5-8	Ordinary 34/
2:1-5a	Easter 3		Christ the King